Public Masks
and
Private Faces

Previous books by the author include:

Life in Cambridge
Germany After the War
St Andrews
Newmarket
Swing to Better Golf
Journey Through Cornwall
Grand Prix World Championship
The Beauty of Woman
The London Season
The Old Inns of London
Collecting Staffordshire Pottery

Louis Stanley in Chicago with Adlai Stevenson, who might have been one of the great Presidents of the United States

Public Masks
and
Private Faces

Louis T. Stanley

Quartet Books
London   New York

First Published by Quartet Books Limited 1986
A member of the Namara Group
27/29 Goodge Street, London W1P 1FD

British Library Cataloguing in Publication Data
Stanley, Louis T.
    Public masks and private faces.
    1. Great Britain —— Biography
    I. Title
    920'.041   CT774

ISBN 0 7043 2601 9

Phototypeset by AKM Associates (UK) Ltd
Ajmal House, Hayes Road, Southall, London
Printed and bound in Great Britain

Contents

Preface

It has been my good fortune to have come into contact with several of the great ones of our time, sometimes as a colleague, occasionally as a friend. Usually the experience was stimulating, though it could be depressing when the dictum of the philosopher applied: 'The difference between great men and ordinary men is the difference in length between angle worms.' Recognizing genius is not always easy. So many factors have to be considered. The temper of the hour can determine public estimation. In times of peace Winston Churchill might have been only an eminent, not a transcendant personality. Some would name figures like T. S. Eliot, Stanley Spencer and John Masefield as instances when assessments were influenced by current tastes. Such a list is bound to be personal. Mine would be no exception, but I would single out Walter de la Mare, a man born with a love of words. He created his own world. It may have been a bubble world, but it held together. I think it was because of his dream world that he never lost the intensity of enchanted loveliness. He discovered beauty in the darkness as a man might find a rose in the night. Few have been able to gather so fine a vintage from life's varied vineyard as this man of genius.

Robert Graves

A gritty, austere, tempestuous poet, who resented authority and enjoyed controversy. That was the public image of Robert Graves. But what sort of a man was this writer who turned down numerous D. Litts, and refused the CBE? Few English poets of the twentieth century aroused as much interest as Graves, none stimulated so much discussion as this flamboyant, pugnacious eccentric. That in itself was unusual. Englishmen do not habitually oppose poets. They ignore them. Graves refused to be ignored. But it was not controversy alone that made his name known to many who had never heard of any other contemporary poet. His work was such that it provoked definite reaction. There is an enormous amount of confused thinking about poetry, and Graves suffered the criticism of many incompetent judges. Poetry seems to attract vague, inconclusive writing by pretentious critics who obscure the subject and frighten genuine enthusiasts with endless technical jargon. But Graves drove a wedge into the literary world. He was a poet in the complete sense of the word.

As a man, Graves ran counter to the accepted pattern. He displayed none of the traditional characteristics of the romantic-type poet – willowy, hypersensitive, long-haired, sandal-wearing, delicate in frame, fascinated but terrified by women. The type is common enough. There was a hint in the picture that Graves gave of himself in his early autobiographical work *Goodbye to All That* published in 1929, but no suggestion in the later years. On meeting Graves you were confronted by a rugged hulk. He looked like a prize-fighter, an impression accentuated by a broken nose acquired at Charterhouse. He had the rare gift of being accepted by the people of another generation, for he treated everyone without condescension or conscious posing as was so clearly demonstrated at his home in Majorca where his extrovert boyish charm found easy expression. In many ways primitive in his naïve enjoyment of life, the Mediterranean island made a perfect backcloth with its amiable Spanish locals, its pretentious colony of poets and artists, the sea and the lovely mountain village of Deya on the unfashionable northern coast; but it was not all studied Mediterranean informality. Graves had a very fine collection of Georgian silver and hated eating off anything else.

Married twice, Graves had eight children, countless grand-children and presided over a delightfully unconventional court at Deya. It was particularly enjoyable for the grandchildren who, however young, were always given a little wine to drink. 'Wine in moderation', said Graves, 'does not harm babies.' Despite his large family, Graves was self-sufficient. His outlook was best summed up in his own words, 'My main theme was always the practical impossibility, transcended only by a belief in miracle, of absolute love continuing between man and woman.' Always a studied extrovert, he was conscious of his own ego. This asserted itself when we met in St John's College, a stone's throw from the room where as a student he developed his friendship with T. E. Lawrence.

Lunch-time in Oxford was too conventional for Graves. He knotted a colourful silk scarf round his neck, donned a floppy Mexican-type hat, collected a string-bag and shovelled an untidy mass of notepaper, liberally covered with firm classic handwriting, into a brown-paper parcel. That was how one of his books was sent to the publisher. For each page written there were pages of rejects. Not for nothing did he say, 'My best friend is still the waste-paper basket.' A shopping expedition in the Oxford market soon resembled a bazaar outing, before we retired for food.

Graves added colour to the Oxford scene, but did not fit. His lectures when Professor of Poetry were an enormous success, but too discordant and biting. He was not a natural academic. His spell as first Professor of English at Cairo University, with the sponsorship of men like Arnold Bennett, T. E. Lawrence and John Buchan, only lasted a year before he escaped. The Oxford chair was a three-year appointment, but, just as Maugham belonged to Cap Ferrat, Beerbohm to Rapallo and Browning to Florence, so this vigorous man with a noble head was more at home on the hot dusty road from Palma to Deya.

His output was prolific, about 125 books, all written in longhand as he scorned the typewriter. Though highly professional in his approach, the standard fluctuated. Graves had certain limitations, but throughout his work one dateless quality persisted. It was fervour. Hardly a poem is unmarked by it. When Graves gave of his best and reached the peaks of inspiration, he found the

Robert Graves resented authority and enjoyed controversy

Dame Barbara Hepworth's inspiration was fired by the enthusiasm of others

Gloria Swanson was a challenge to any man who thought he could tame her

Augustus John was one of the most remarkable of English artists

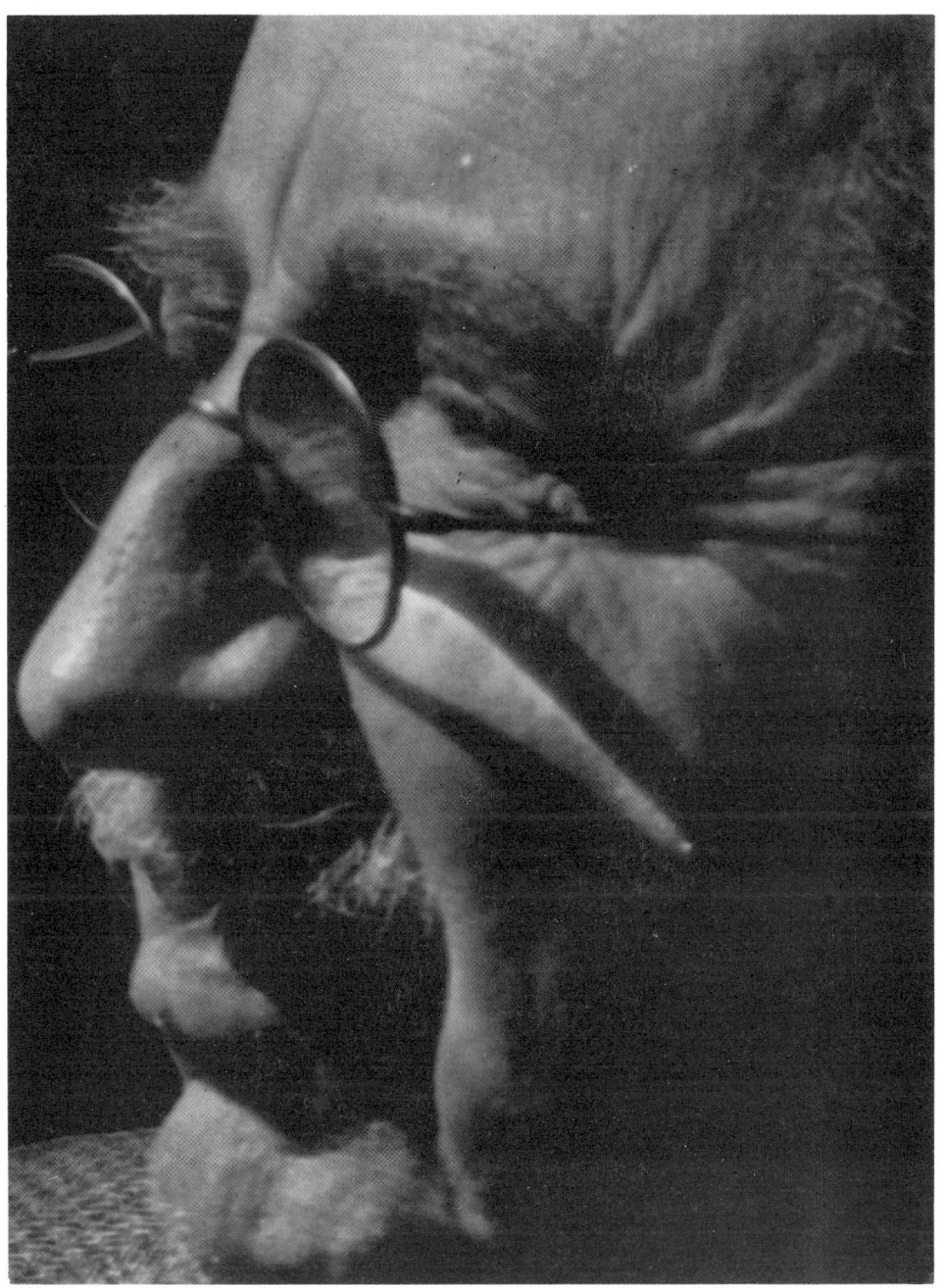

E.M. Forster was the embodiment of a comfortable, liberal nineteenth-century way of life

T.S. Eliot's influence was purely aesthetic

Robert Frost's vitality belied his years

Stanley Spencer was an enigma and a rebel

Richard Burton rehearsing Hamlet

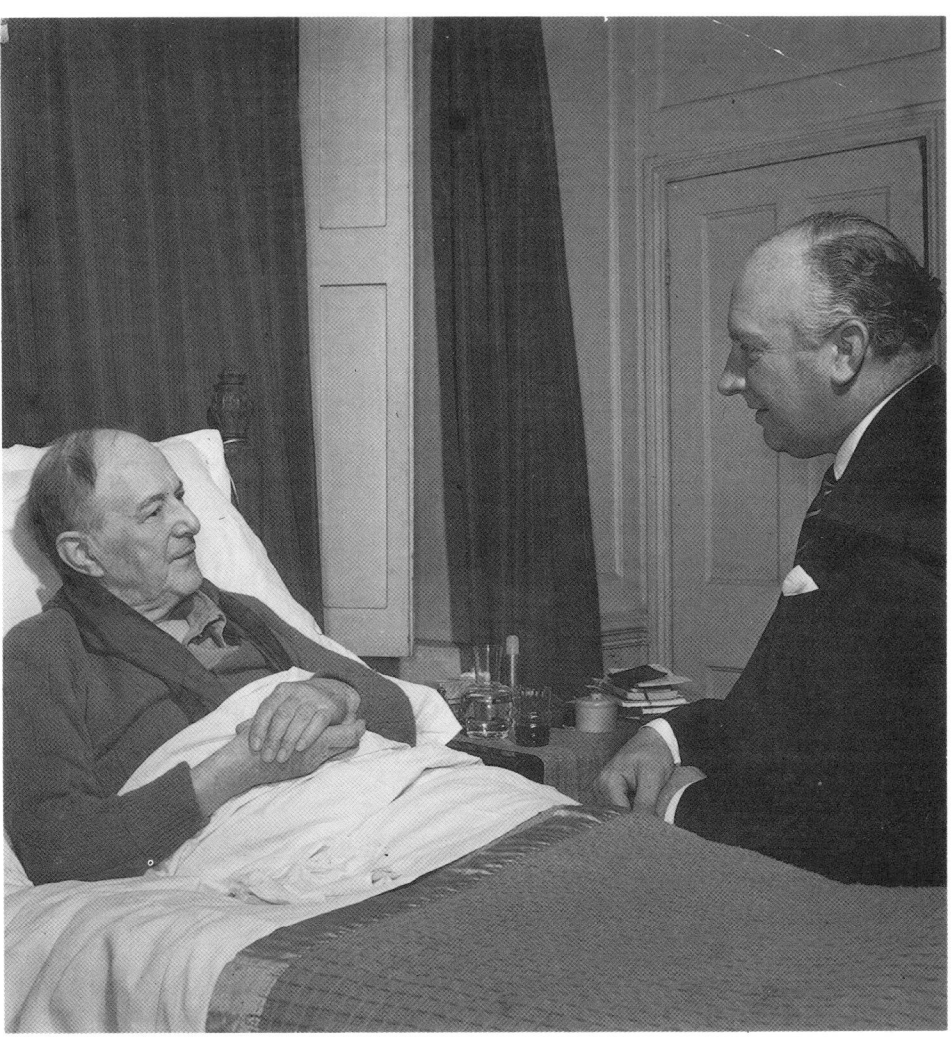

Walter de la Mare's life was an individual dream

mainspring of his writing to be his love of life and compassion for all around him. Graves once said that poetry, especially his own, is a form of autobiography. If style and content are literary fingerprints which reveal the man, the edition of Graves's poems which first appeared in 1926 and has been revised several times, does just that.

The reason for choosing this volume is that with each new edition Graves amended or eliminated poems which he considered did not ring true. This volume conformed to Graves's own exacting standards. In that sense it reflects the man himself. The words used are easy and diffuse, not tightly knit. Graceful and vivid, their power and charm lie in the ease with which they express spontaneous emotion. The appeal of the poetry is direct, its images have an immediate impact on the senses. Graves's work is full of delicately observed situations. He analysed his impressions, going into them not only far but, as they say in Norse sagas, 'far and farther than far'. But there were times when Graves was the most masculine of our poets, when his style and rhythms laid stress on the English language itself. Occasionally one can pick out lines suggestive of the crisp but coarse style of Hardy, whose poetry Graves admired.

Graves was a great poet, but his widest public was gained through the two books on Clandius, which gave new life to the historical novel, and the original presentation of Greek mythology in *The Greek Myths*. He brought to these and other historical works not only the lyrical beauty of poetry, but a highly developed sense of duty as a historian. His treatment of subjects confirmed G. M. Trevelyan's view that the present takes us by surprise only because we do not sufficiently know and consider the past. Poetry, scholarship, observation; these were the constituents of Graves's varied writings. Despite all his other works, Graves remained first of all a poet. This is certainly how he saw himself. He once wrote, 'A true poet writes because he must, not because he hopes to get a living from his poems.' Graves himself made a good living from his historical and other works, but as he also said of himself, 'There's no money in poetry, but then there's no poetry in money either.'

Alas, Robert Graves is no more. At the age of ninety, he died in the village of Deya. The final tributes were simple. Dressed with a neckerchief and the familiar flat-brimmed Cordova hat by his folded hands, the body was carried on the same day into Deya church. The plain coffin was borne by three of his children,

William, Thomas and John, and three personal friends. The funeral service was Anglican. Early on the Sunday morning, the same pallbearers carried the simple coffin to the graveyard. The grave is marked, in accordance with his wishes, by a plain cement slab that bears the words:

Robert Graves, Poet – Wimbledon 1895, Deya 1985.

So passed from our midst the greatest love poet in English since Donne.

Stanley Spencer

Stanley Spencer's art grew out of the very life of the community in which he lived. This thought was reaffimed when the artist showed me an exhibition of his work in Cookham Church. It highlighted his capacity for wonder at ordinary things, his ability to see the familiar for the first time and the divine in the familiar. It was like listening to his paintings. Artistically, they resembled more a voluntary on a powerful organ, intended to show its compass, rather than a musician's constructed masterpiece. All the Spencer stops were pulled out, one after another. The familiar scene of the Biblical Passion, almost mystically imaginative, with a subtle, sensual undercurrent, is tinctured perhaps with melodrama, but never a drop of genuine sentiment. Spencer's figures seem to fall together through the crust of ordinary experience into a bloodless world of stark reality. To look at them induces a sensation of revulsion. They are nasty, earthy creatures, goblinesque, ghoulish. And yet, these paintings show that Spencer was a splendid colourist, a genius of composition, and an accomplished draughtsman with complete mastery over his materials.

As to the man himself, Spencer was an enigma. There were so many masks, each one different, each one true. In his time he was called a rebel, a village idiot, and a genius. He was a recluse yet an egotist who couldn't stop talking, obsessed by religion and eroticism, and plagued with the complexities of emotional involvement with women plus marital problems. Mix that together in a diminutive frame and you have Stanley Spencer. No wonder he became enigmatic. Controversy followed him everywhere. He hit the headlines in 1935 after resigning from the Royal Academy. When elected an Associate three years earlier, the Secretary sent him a copy of the rules which clearly stated that, while members could exercise their right to exhibit six paintings in the annual May Exhibition, these had first to be approved by the hanging committee. Spencer objected in principle. No committee was going to pass judgement on his work. In 1935 two of his pictures were declined, *Lovers* and *St Francis and the Birds*. The artist was insulted and resigned.

He hated criticism but encouraged it by his actions. I recall being on Newmarket Heath with Sir Alfred Munnings to see the start of the Cesarewitch, the long-distance race on the Rowley Mile Course, which the then PRA described as 'hanging about in Suffolk to see a race that is run in Cambridgeshire'. It was on such occasions that, free from public interference, many of his familiar studies were made. As the horses were circling, I happened to mention that I had spent the previous day with Spencer at Cookham. Immediately the race was forgotten. Indignantly Munnings took his wallet and fished out a number of photographs. 'Here is that hypocritical charlatan who imagines himself to be the outstanding ecclesiastical painter of the decade. He produces canvases like the controversial *Resurrection* and *Christ Preaching at Cookham Regatta* and then paints pornographic filth like these.' He handed them over for inspection.

There was no doubt about the erotica. A self-portrait of the artist, naked and clearly in a roused state, was not only over-exposed but hardly undeveloped, in fact, somewhat self-flattering. Such was Munnings's spleen, that we suddenly realized the Cesarewitch had started and the horses were well on their way.

Munnings's reaction to Spencer was always vitriolic. He couldn't stand the man and never missed a chance to attack him. There was the occasion when he noticed in a dealer's gallery a Spencer painting that he felt was obscene. He checked how the dealer had acquired it. It took him to Zwemmer, who had purchased it with a number of Spencer's drawings. Munnings next took the paintings and some of the improper drawings on approval, had them photographed and handed them to the police for them to prosecute under the obscenity laws. Enquiries were made, then the Director of Public Prosecutions was asked to sanction a prosecution. The news reached the press and was released with sensational flavour. Sir Gerald Kelly, who had succeeded Munnings in the presidency of the Royal Academy, arrived back from America. On hearing the facts, he saw the DPP and convinced him the case should be dropped.

This particular incident worried Spencer far more than usual. Normally he was indifferent to critics, but this bit deep. All he wanted was to be left alone so he could get on with his work, preferably in a small room with the bare essentials of life. Even then, he was a troubled man, haunted by inner fears and worries.

He tried to justify his actions. At the outset he found an explanation for life in the Bible, but the fervour died and he looked elsewhere for inspiration. He told me that he had found the answer in sex. The only way to realize true love and peace was through sexual indulgence. The Church might preach the efficacy of prayer and meditation, but in his mind nothing could equal the spiritual renewal that came with the physical act of love. He believed that erotic pictures captured something of the mysteries of life.

With that in mind, Spencer painted a series of canvases, *The Beatitudes of Love*, thirteen in all. The first was *Adoration of Girls*, in which he imagined he was married to each of the village girls. They formed his harem. The second was *Adoration of Old Men*. Here a group of wenches stood around in rapturous attitudes before ten foolish-looking old men. The third was *Sunflower and Dog Worship* that supposedly inferred preoccupation with a sexual activity. *Promenade of Women* and *Village in Heaven* had Cookham village featured. Others were *Contemplation*, *Desire*, *Worship* and *Nearness*. Spencer's theme throughout was consistent, but he questioned whether the public would understand the underlying message behind the sex pictures. Many felt it was too basic to require explaining or justify serious interpretation. Spencer's idea was to house them in a building which he thought should be known as the church-house, where sacred and profane could meet. When asked, he denied there was any hint of self-identification, though in *The Beatitudes* it is always a small man who is dominated by fearsome, almost grotesque women, with more than a hint of a masochistic relationship.

There is nothing like controversy to attract a type of fame, but in Spencer's case, it was unnecessary. To many people he was a significant influence. The genuine artist has his individual speech. Genius is always an enigma. Stanley Spencer qualified in part for both.

E. M. Forster OM

Edward Morgan Forster was rooted in Cambridge. He was the embodiment of a comfortable, liberal, nineteenth-century way of life. Talking to him in his rooms at King's College was like entering an atmosphere where a few hours earlier conversation might have touched on the evils of child labour, the problems of evangelical work, the 'world mountain' symbolism of Hindu temples, or the state of the West Indian slave market. Edwardian taste in a Victorian setting was everywhere. High-ceilinged, spacious, sun-lit rooms, armchairs carelessly draped with Indian shawls, books galore, gilt-framed period portraits, selective pieces of porcelain, and a piano. It was a time-capsule of personal memorabilia presided over by the gentle, scholarly figure of Forster.

He used to say that it felt as if he had never been away from Cambridge. India, Greece, Italy and the East seemed like exploratory interludes. Such experiences had to be gained, but his roots were in Cambridge. He always returned, though there were times when he felt an imposter. At the Founder's Feast of 1952 he confessed, 'I have to tell you that I do not belong here at all. I do nothing here whatsoever. I hold no College office. I attend no committee. I sit on no body, however solid, not even on the Annual Congregation. I co-opt not, neither am I co-opted. I teach not, neither do I think.' Good stuff, true in part, but it ignored the fact that to many people he was part of the King's tradition.

Forster never ceased to appreciate King's, nor the reaction on going through the impressive gateway from King's Parade of the pinnacles and cupola flanked by the screen-wall and window tracery, the immaculate lawn of the Great Court, the fountain and bronze figure of the founder Henry VI, and the lines of the Chapel, the glory of Cambridge architecture. As Forster remarked, its deeper significance may be lost on an agnostic, but no one can ignore its sheer beauty. Commenting on his room, he pointed out that the piano was not just ornamental – no one could disagree – it was there if he wanted and the mood was right, so he could play

8

from his strictly limited repertoire. The effect on others was probably not soothing as he played badly, but music was always a great comfort, particularly Beethoven and Verdi. He was a thwarted musician, which possibly accounted for the immense pleasure he had in assisting Eric Crozier by writing the libretto for Benjamin Britten's opera *Billy Budd.*

Forster acknowledged the formative influences of Cambridge that were perhaps even greater than he realized, some far from good. Freudian understones could be traced to an unhappy, female-dominated childhood. His father, Edward Morgan, an architect, died when he was a child, and his upbringing became the responsibility of his mother, and two maiden aunts, Emily and Laura, who condemned the youngster to the purgatory of school life at Tonbridge, which he recorded in *The Longest Journey* by depicting the snobbish venality of the masters at Sawston, a school based on Tonbridge. The experience was responsible for Forster's detestation of the public school system and its product.

As a classical exhibitioner to King's College, he was introduced to what by comparison was the paradise of Cambridge. Everything about the milieu was bliss, a rarified atmosphere that unfortunately wakened a latent homosexuality. Through Lowes Dickinson, a Fellow of King's, he became a member of the conceited secret intellectual club known as the Apostles. He became part of an élitism that repudiated personal liability to obey general rules, developed a contempt for the intellect, at least of women, and accepted homosexuality under the guise of the Higher Sodomy which in those days had to be secret, but was not entirely confined to members of the élite. In such a hothouse atmosphere, Forster made friends with those who later became the Bloomsbury set, names like Vanessa and Clive Bell, Lytton Strachey, Roger Fry, John Maynard Keynes, Virginia and Leonard Woolf. This early obsession with a sexual mystique tinged the tone of his writings.

It was regrettable that after *A Passage to India* Forster wrote no more novels. Not that it affected his standing for he used to say that his reputation as a novelist grew with every book he didn't write. Actually there was a sixth novel, but he would not allow it to be published as long as he was alive. It had a homosexual theme, was begun in 1913, but did not appear until 1971. The response to *Maurice*, as it was called, would have disappointed the author. Time had softened the impact to shock. Homosexuality was no longer anathema to society, while only a few were able to relate to the background of the First World War. Forster once hinted of another novel on the same subject, but it has never surfaced.

A Passage to India was probably Forster's most satisfying novel. It was translated into twenty-one languages and won the Femina Vie-Heureuse and James Tait Black prizes. Begun in 1913, it was not completed until 1924. At times he admitted there were doubts whether it would ever be finished. In 1912 he went to India with Lowes Dickinson, then returned after the war and felt that the novel as written was inaccurate. Drastic alterations revised the passages dealing with Anglo-Indian relations and dealt more fully with the failure of understanding between East and West. He stressed that the novel was not political, but it nevertheless gave plenty of scope for argument between Imperialists and anti-Imperialists. At the outset there was a feeling among British officials and merchants that Forster was too biased against the British sahibs and memsahibs by portraying them as so many caricatures. In the sense that Forster was out of sympathy with English public school behaviour and treated it in satirical fashion, it would be true to say that his approach tended to be slightly jaundiced, but he captured accurately the speech and mannerisms of the Indian characters. The narrative is a true reflection of the oriental mind. He handled the thorny question of Anglo-Indian relations with sympathy and gained approval from both Hindu and Muslims.

The crux of *A Passage to India* rests on the brilliant passages describing the visit to the Marabar caves where a young woman believes herself to have been assaulted by a Muslim doctor, and levels charges against him which could have ruined his life. He is clearly innocent, and the young woman retracts her charge when in the witness-box. We are not told what did happen, whether the young woman had a hallucination or whether she was in fact assaulted. We should like to know, but Forster never told us. He would have been interested in Sir David Lean's filming of the novel which attempted to find the answer. It was Lean's first picture for fifteen years and by comparison with previous films like *Dr Zhivago* and *Ryan's Daughter*, relatively short. He proved the ideal director with a rare pictorial sense and a gift for narrative. The story unfolds with an inevitable sense of logic up to the mysterious Marabar caves when Adela Quested may or may not have been raped by Dr Aziz and shows her inability to come to terms with the totality of life. The adaptation of the novel came from David Lean. Such was its success that the film had eleven

Oscar nominations. Some critics were not so impressed, but Forster would not have been of their number.

Forster was conscious of the break in the flow of his writing. He would have liked to have done more, but never succeeded. It was not due to pressure of other commitments for he had all the time in the world to develop a theme. For some reason after *A Passage to India*, inspiration died. Not that he was forgotten. When his mother died, he was invited to return to King's as an Honorary Fellow. He refused a knighthood offered by Clement Attlee. In 1953 he became CH. His eightieth birthday was celebrated by a lunch-party in the college hall attended by ageing literary friends of the former Bloomsbury days, figures like Leonard Woolf, Clive and Vanessa Bell, Duncan Grant, David Garnett, and the Greek poet George Seferis. The following year was marked by the conferring of an honorary degree by Cambridge University. Then his ninetieth birthday was marked by a concert in the Chapel for which he selected the music and the ultimate honour of being admitted to the Order of Merit.

But it is not the closing years of Forster's life that should be remembered. There are times when old age can be cruel. The run-up to death was anything but kind to Forster. I prefer not to think of that pathetic geriatric with failing eyesight, shuffling about like a lost soul in shabby raincoat and cheap cloth cap before finally dying in the Coventry home of a young policeman with whom he had been friendly for many years. Instead I like to remember Forster as a brilliant writer, shy and retiring in manner, but with the spirit of a rebel and a touch of conceit. His own act of faith is worth repeating: 'The people I respect must behave as if they were immortal and as if society were eternal. Both assumptions are false: both of them must be accepted as true if we are to go on working and eating and loving, and are to keep open a few breathing-holes for the human spirit.'

Molotov

The setting was California, some thirty miles from San Francisco: a private house transformed into a citadel of suspicion with strong-arm men forming a protective cloak reinforced by a network of security measures. Questions galore and credentials checked before being ushered into the presence of Vyacheslav Mihailovitch Scriabin, nephew of the composer, who had come to symbolize oppression. As a revolutionary young bourgeois, Scriabin became a Bolshevik at the age of seventeen instead of entering the Civil Service as intended by his father. He took a *nom de guerre* that translated means 'The Hammer', but became known to us as Molotov.

This trafficker in misery and suffering had come to epitomize Soviet power, holding a sequence of high offices as Prime Minister, Chairman of the Council of People's Commissars, and Commissar for Foreign Affairs. He had been a key factor in Trotsky's impetuous career; knew the Litvinov era; the period when Kamenev and Stalin returned from Siberian exile after the March Revolution; the preparation years for Lenin; and the clash between Stalin and Trotsky ending with Trotsky's banishment and death in Mexico by ice-axe wielded by Stalin's agent.

Molotov survived the turbulent purges and was chief instigator of the horrors associated with the early five-year plan to transform Russia from an agricultural nation into an industrial one by collectivizing the farms to recruit labour for industry. Molotov acted with such ruthless efficiency that some 10,000,000 died from beatings, imprisonment, torture and murder. Molotov was the hard man who carried out the Party programme and always escaped retribution. All his comrades were removed from the scene, even the Secret Police did not escape. Mussolini hung by his heels outside a garage in Milan, mutilated by an Italian mob. Hitler committed suicide in the Berlin bunker. Only Stalin and Molotov survived. Between them the world became a chess-board.

Such was the man I met. He did not match the reputation. The

Soviet spokesman for Foreign Affairs who was attending the United Nations Conference in San Francisco, could easily have been mistaken for a retired suburban grocer. Small, pallid, with ill-fitting suit, gun-metal watch on his wrist and wearing old-fashioned rimless glasses, it was difficult to reconcile the mild demeanour with revolutionary adherence to Stalinism.

In conversation the impression changed. Glacial in manner, his words had a sense of cold detachment. Opinions were non-commital and cautious. Only once did the iron curtain lower a fraction. He allowed himself to speak somewhat disparagingly about Lenin, whom he felt always retained traces of his family nobility with the hint of a bureaucrat. In one sense Lenin was some-what insignificant, with limited ability, an impression that was mis-leading. He pointed out that the world failed completely to discern the inherent qualities in both Mussolini and Hitler which enabled them later to shake the world. Lenin was a similar example. Molotov questioned whether the German High Command realized when they sent Lenin across Europe in a sealed train in 1917 that they were sending a political atom-bomb into Russia.

Only once could I get Molotov to comment on personal disappointments. He admitted he could never forget the day when Hitler broke the Molotov–Ribbentrop Pact of 1939 and advanced his armies into the suburbs of Moscow, an act of betrayal that marked the beginning of Russia's contribution to the Allied victory in the Second World War.

An earlier meeting with Molotov had been in Vienna at the signing of the Treaty of Independence. The ceremony took place in the Belvedere Palace, once the Château of Prince Eugene and later the residence of Archduke Francis Ferdinand of Habsburg. After seventeen years of Anschluss, war and occupation, agree-ment had finally been reached after innumerable meetings of the Big Four, when everyone, most of all the Austrians, had lost faith in it. When Herr Figl, the Austrian Minister for Foreign Affairs, appeared on the balcony and had Molotov, Pinay, Macmillan and Dulles join hands in a symbolic gesture, the bells of Austria pealed and thousands cheered in the vast gardens. During drinks afterwards, Molotov put his glass down and went on the balcony to be greeted by tumultuous cheers led by Communist cheer-leaders. Dulles hearing the outburst, looked round, saw Molotov holding court, and not to be outdone, went on the next balcony vigorously waving his handkerchief. Unfortunately there were no American cheer-leaders.

13

At the official banquet that night in the Imperial Schönbrunn Palace, decorations, uniforms and dazzling gowns were worn. The Austrian National Ballet performed in the flood-lit grounds with cascading fountains as a background. Kurt Bohm conducted the Vienna Philharmonic Orchestra and never had the Radetzky March been played with such abandon. Molotov had accepted the invitation on behalf of the Soviet delegation. Theoretically they appeared. Entering at one end of the Great Gallery, they marched in wedge-formation with Molotov in the centre, elbowed guests aside and exited at the other end. As Molotov said afterwards, they were present – in Soviet fashion.

All things come to an end. Stalin fell from grace. His body was removed from display with that of Lenin and reinterred at the foot of the Kremlin Wall. Khrushchev, once fulsome in praise, denounced him as a sadist and mass-murderer. Stalin's daughter, Svetlana, after defecting to the United States, concurred in her *Memoirs*. Finally, Molotov lost favour and was exiled to Siberia. Then the wheel turned once again. Stalin was re-established, and Svetlana, who had settled in Cambridge and was always bitter about her father, was forgiven by the Soviet regime and returned to Moscow, accompanied by an unwilling schoolgirl daughter who later was allowed to return to England and complete her school education at Saffron Walden. Molotov, now a very old man of over ninety, justs waits for the gates of death to open. This time there will be no escape for the watch-dog of the Revolution.

Richard Burton

Richard Burton was a man of real power, unafraid of the big gesture, and endowed with rare charm that tended to become lecherously flamboyant when he was drunk. He was a man's man. If you didn't like him, you knew what you could do about it. Women loved him and were not discouraged. He was married five times. Some of the weddings were bizarre, but the brides always looked lovely. Suzy, former wife of James Hunt, I knew from motor-racing days. She succeeded in bringing him back to self-respecting health after a wearisome spell of trying to solve a drink-problem. It was never fully cured. His last wife, Sally Hay, whom he met on the set of *Wagner* in Austria and married in Las Vegas, was twenty-two years younger, but the age-gap seemed not to matter. The marriage worked. A week before he died, I found him leaner, fitter and alert. Some years earlier Richard had accepted my invitation to act as a patron on the Jim Clark Foundation and always wanted to know of the Foundation Research projects. It became a routine discussion whenever he was in this country.

His last marriage was different, for Sally was unlike his usual type. Clearly they were very happy. She was good for him. His sudden death was a terrible shock, but she responded to his whimsical humour up to the very end. He won a bet made with his old friends, Peter O'Toole and Stanley Baker, who predeceased him, by saying that no one would see him without at least one item of clothing that was red. Sally chose a jacket, polo-necked sweater and trousers all red, so in death he had the last laugh.

Without in any way detracting from his obvious love for Sally, there was never anyone like Elizabeth Taylor, the Cleopatra to his Antony. They had differences and violent rows, the relationship was volatile, almost volcanic, anything could happen and often did, like the time when I gave a dinner party at the Dorchester Hotel in London to celebrate winning the Formula One World Championship. Guests, including the Burtons, were a cross-section of industry, sport and the arts. Late in the afternoon the floor-manager came to the suite to tell us that the table-plan might have to be altered, the Burtons were having a violent disagreement. I asked if he would let me have a progress report. Half an hour later I learnt that Elizabeth had locked herself in the bathroom. The next bulletin was to the effect that her dinner had to be served in the bathroom. That was that. The plan was altered. Duke Ellington was put in her place. The next day Richard said that a migraine had been the trouble. I suggested he changed his scriptwriter.

At times Richard's repartee about Elizabeth was lusty, particularly on the size of her 'rump'. Once over drinks with a group that included Alaistair McLeod someone recalled how the artist who painted Helen of Troy used five young women as models to produce a synthetic ideal of beauty by taking the arms of one model, the shoulders of another, the breasts of a third, and so on. Richard applied a similar synthetic model of his wife with relevant parts recalled by memory but ended by saying he preferred the statue of Venus Kallipygem better known as the Venus of the Beautiful Buttocks.

Billy Graham

Judging by church attendance, Britain is one of the most irreligious countries in the world. On that score alone the effect of Billy Graham is remarkable. In 1954 he attracted the astonishing total of nearly 1,500,000 people to Harringay. Twelve years after this sensational début, a repeat campaign drew 18,000 people every night to Earl's Court. The eighties brought a concentrated mission to the Universities of Oxford and Cambridge, again with remarkable response, followed up with yet a further campaign in the country. The impact is sensational, though clerical response has been lukewarm. It is argued that after the warmth, friendliness and theatricality of these meetings, potential converts find the austerity of chapels and empty churches something of an anti-climax. It is more likely that these unsuccessful pastors are affected by sour grapes.

Such criticism is double-edged. The indisputable fact remains that Graham claims the ear of the people. They come in their thousands to listen. Maybe personality plays a part, for this tall, good-looking, square-jawed, wavy-haired evangelist from North Carolina knows its value. His voice is strong with an accent neither flat nor Middle Western. His rhetoric is skilful. He is an extrovert. An opinion poll makes him the fourth most admired man in America, though for a time his allegiance to Nixon caused uneasiness among some people.

Billy Graham is a wholesaler. Using the medium of established churches, he claims to reach more than 80,000,000 consumers. It is ecclesiastical big business. He is president of a communications empire. The Billy Graham Evangelistic Association owns a city block in Minneapolis, has an annual budget of some twelve million dollars, deals with eighty million items of mail every year, including four million copies of the monthly magazine *Decision* for the United States and Canada. There is a Spanish edition for Latin America, with editions for Great Britain, Germany, France, Japan and Australia printed abroad. It is claimed that it has the largest circulation of any religious magazine. Other activities include the World Wide Pictures of Burbank, California, described as the world's largest producer and distributor of religious films. The radio programme, *House of Decision*, goes out to over one thousand stations and claims an audience of twenty million. Television specials of edited tapes of personal crusades are shown on 250 stations without commercials. In Minneapolis a team of clergymen do nothing else but answer letters from people with problems or in distress.

The very range is staggering, motivated by a man who greets you with wide-eyed simplicity. The disarming approach is perhaps misleading. On an early visit to England, Graham joined me for dinner at the Dorchester Hotel, London, with his personal assistant, Gerry Beavan, and a supporter from Texas. I was curious to know why he was booked in at the Ritz Hotel. Somehow it seemed out of character. If there was a Second Coming, I imagine Christ might stay at a Salvation Army hostel rather than a five-star hotel. Graham agreed, but added the choice was influenced by the fact he found work easier in such surroundings. So be it. I also enquired why he favoured a somewhat expensive car only to be told that as it was the make used by the Queen, there couldn't be much wrong with it. The point seemed to have been missed.

After dinner we left for Euston to catch the night train to Glasgow. We arrived early so Beavan asked us to stay in the car while times and platform were checked. He returned accompanied by a group of women. Graham adjusted the angle of his hat, straightened the tie, stepped out and spoke to a woman who was not in the group. He took her newspaper, autographed it, and returned it to the bemused female who had no idea who he was or what it was all about. Somehow that particular picture found its way into a newspaper with the caption that the prayerful woman was wishing the evangelist well at the start of the campaign. Even without her support, there was no doubt about the eventual impact on Scotland. Some publicity gimmicks are bound to fail. Another incident occurred at Gleneagles Hotel. Returning from a round of golf, I noticed Graham by the window making gesticulations and facial contortions. I mentioned to the duty manager in the hall that perhaps Graham was unwell. It was a false alarm. He was practising mannerisms and facial expressions in front of the bedroom mirror. Nothing is left to chance. Everything is superbly stage-managed. Skilful blending of mood music, mingling of colour effects, volume of sound and choral support, with strategically placed supporters who lead the way in their conversion-walk to the platform, slightly hesitant so as to encourage others. Spontaneity is there, but it is helped. The overall effect is superb.

Orthodox clerics with conservative outlook eye these evangelistic jamborees with suspicion. The fact remains, it works. The flavour cannot be to every taste, but it shows how the communications media can be used. Maybe Billy Graham's personal success is due to the fact that he is a good man, the Mark McCormack of evangelism, and just as effective.

Gloria Swanson

Motor-racing has a fascination for film stars, past and present. It is only necessary to see them parading in the pit area and hotel lounges of Monte Carlo to realize how ingrained is their urge to be noticed, a trait shared by would-be stars of all kinds, the hip and the square, the dug-in and the far-out, while the traffic between categories is thick. Occasionally the real headliners are rewarding. One of Hollywood's legends, Gloria Swanson, whose career spanned thirty years of the twentieth-century cinema, made considerable impact. For three generations she epitomized romantic fantasy, while her own life was as torrid as the film roles that so often scandalized people. An artist of consummate skill, she rivalled such stars as Pola Negri, Mary Pickford and Lilian Gish, had Rudolph Valentino as a leading man, became Hollywood's first million-dollar-a-year artist, lived in that style and introduced a new dimension to the screen.

Arrogant and wilful, Gloria Swanson was a challenge to any man who thought he could tame her. When sound came to movies, her image changed. Publicity gimmicks switched from her black marble bathroom with solid gold bathtub to the human side of her life and there was no shortage of material. Innumerable romantic attachments and six marriages, beginning with Wallace Beery, provided copy for journalists who focused on her affair with Joe Kennedy, patriarch of the Kennedy political dynasty, when even private intervention by Cardinal O'Connell of Boston failed to end the four years' liaison in which Rose Kennedy outwitted the actress. Years later Gloria said she could never decide whether Rose was a fool, a saint, or just a better actress than she was. Her sixty-third film, *Sunset Boulevard*, touched the peak and won an Oscar. In 1975 she was asked to play an old drunken movie star in the second *Airport* film, disliked the role and turned it down. She would play herself or not at all. She had her own way.

Gloria Swanson was the movie aristocrat with credentials to justify the claim. In Monte Carlo for the Monaco Grand Prix, she was in her favourite suite in the Hotel de Paris overlooking the Casino, the sitting-room balcony giving a clear view of the cars as they streamed into the square and snaked down the hill. Living up to her reputation for exotic clothes, she was in a dress trimmed with ostrich feathers. The strong voice that made her one of the few silent stars to transfer successfully to the talkies was just as pronounced.

Looking at the crowded square, she remarked that the build-up to the race reminded her of a bullfight. All the ingredients were there. The *aficionados* arrive in their thousands, pay pesetas for a seat in the shade and wait for the ceremonial slaughter of an animal with all the attendant, bloodthirsty formalities – a nauseating contradiction for Spaniards are not cruel to animals. They are a nation of horse-lovers, yet they condone horses being disemboweled, bulls slaughtered and men gored for an afternoon's entertainment. In many ways a Grand Prix could be just as cruel though doubtless those who watched would disagree. I pointed out that while motor-racing was dangerous, the emphasis was on safety. Everything possible was done to make it as safe as possible for spectator and driver with medical facilities available should an accident occur. Again I was told the similarity was there. The differences were minimal. The bullring has a special infirmary with an operating theatre up to hospital standard for gored matadors, though there was an extra touch of hypocrisy: at the end of the infirmary is a little chapel with a statue of Our Lady smiling innocently on the proceedings.

I admitted that in the Grand Prix Mobile Hospital we did not bother the Blessed Virgin, but I was puzzled by what, if she felt so keenly, induced her to watch either event.

The answer was candid.

'I don't want anyone hurt, let alone killed, yet deep down, as at a bullfight, is a subconscious wish for something like that to happen. I am ashamed of the emotion, but in my heart I am intrigued by the mystery of death. It has nothing to do with my age, though with so many friends passing away, I am beginning to think of myself as a last survivor, but here in Monte Carlo I might see that moment happen in front of my eyes.'

'Such thoughts are morbid. Have you tried to analyse why you have them. Could it be that in some way you are afraid of dying?'

'Not at all. Naturally I want to live as long as I enjoy all my faculties and as you can see they are sharp enough now, but, when it comes to what the *aficionados* call the "moment of truth", it is instinctive to draw back and yet it fascinates me. In any case, death itself is complex. After a death certificate is signed, hair still grows. Does that mean the hair cells are still charged with life? The heart can be removed and kept in a jar still beating. Blood can be drained and, if quickly restored, life can be resumed. I wonder what happens to consciousness in these intervals. For that matter, what happens to individuality when consciousness is stayed during sleep. No one knows. These are thoughts that bother me, particularly in the early hours of the morning when life is at its lowest ebb.'

No one was killed and there were no serious accidents in the Monaco Grand Prix that our car, the BRM, won for the fifth time. Later that night we met again for a few minutes.

'Did you enjoy the race in spite of there being no crashes in the square?'

Eyes that were so provocative on the screen flashed irritably.

'Stop being flippant. You don't enjoy a race. I am sure you didn't even though you won. No one can. It is an experience. In my case I would describe it as an exciting nightmare without a pay-off line. I think I shall sleep well tonight.'

In the end Gloria Swanson had what probably was her wish. Death came to her in New York as she slept peacefully.

The time was 4.45 a.m.

Augustus John OM

Fryern Court, the Hampshire home of Augustus John, was expressive of the artist himself. The garden was wild yet tended, with overgrown box-hedges and mossy paths. On one side·the house looked over meadows: only the rooks, strutting and fluttering, suggested life; everything else was as idle as a plough at the furrow's end. Beyond a tall Elizabethan wall, with its swelling bays, lay an orchard planted for the eye's delight each spring. In fact, everything about the house was there to please the eye, and through the eye to rouse a pensive wonder. Everything was designed by someone who knew that Time is an artist, and knew the secret of creating beauty: choose well, then let alone.

In the library, over a bottle of choice Burgundy, Augustus John indulged himself in the luxury of nostalgic memories. He was an astonishing figure. He had the kind of manners which improved those of a guest beyond recognition. His eyes were fierce and accusatory, but their fire was mitigated by deep lines of character. The length of his head from chin to crown impressed, and this was accentuated by the beard, which a backward carriage of his head on broad shoulders projected forwards. Beetling eyebrows, prominent nose and hunched shoulders gave him a hawk-like look. He talked about his sister, Gwen John, who died in 1939, and of her friendship with Rodin. 'He was very fond of her, made a lot of sculptures of her, in fact he told me she had a beautiful body. That was true. I once found a particularly fine figure of Gwen in the Musée Rodin. It was meant for the London memorial to Whistler, but one of the arms was not quite finished and the fellow they sent to see it, reported it was unsuitable, so they used the Burghers of Calais instead. Bloody stupid. It was a misfit.'

The Gwen train of thought continued – how she became infatuated with France. 'At one time she wanted me to buy a castle in Brittany. Marvellous idea, but I was short of money. Galway would have been better. Ideal in every way, but Gwen's tastes included odd quirks. She was something of a recluse. Liked to cut herself off, in fact she once lived in a place underground. Like me, she was a mixture of extremes. Just because her pictures were often sad, did not mean she had no sense of humour. On the contrary, she could be full of fun.' John recalled how he almost bought a house in Galway. It belonged to some nuns, but the local priest thought he would be painting naked women there, so the deal was off. He stubbed out his umpteenth cigarette. 'Gwen would have reacted better by returning to grass roots in Wales, but I'm no one to talk. I'm always going to polish up my Welsh, but I never do. Perhaps one day.'

In the dining-room we were joined by his wife, Dorelia, the subject of scores of paintings and drawings over a period of forty years. She was still beautiful and serene with a hint of the Romany days. Over the fireplace was a vigorous portrait of a youth. 'That was one of my sons – Caspar', John explained. Talk focused on artists he had known in his youth, names like Conder, Derain, Sickert and Modigliani . . . legends given flesh and frailty. Later we walked through the orchard to the studio. It was then that Augustus John the artist came into his own. Originality of mind in an individual counted little for him if unaccompanied by an aesthetic sense. He was a man who disliked and distrusted introspection, the type who was more or less happy when being praised, not particularly bothered when being abused, but had moments of uneasiness when being explained. It was not that he feared to be unveiled, but he knew what clever misconceptions could be hailed as discoveries. As in the case of all men of subtle intellect, John's feelings were probably a great deal simpler than was believed.

He was one of the most remarkable of all English artists. The unrestrained originality of his conceptions, the gusto of execution, and the variety of production made him an artist who could not be ignored even by those whom he did not attract. Few artists have so delighted and disquieted their contemporaries. No man con-quered and bewildered them so completely by his rugged charm. His work was not the result of an intellectual absorption from outside, but the spontaneous expression of his personality. It was the tremendous gusto with which John experienced life that made his art so vigorously healthy.

On the other hand, honesty compels the admission that Augustus John's work is not to every taste. In the Royal Academy Exhibition of his work that filled the four rooms of an upper floor once known as the Gibson and Diploma Galleries, I overheard in the North Gallery a critic dismissing a canvas as hideous because it lacked the specific beauty and the form of resemblance to life to which he was accustomed. The bias ignored the fact that John did not paint like other artists. In his portraits, he was the artist first and only secondly the portraitist. Whatever the subject that came under his brush, the significant thing was the painting of it. It was not important aesthetically that the likeness should express the sitter, but that the painting expressed Augustus John.

It is interesting to assess the formative influences of John's Slade days. While he was there he met Wilson Steer, Ambrose McEvoy, William Orpen, and Ida Nettleton – the lady who was later to become his first wife. It is difficult today to picture the pre-war conditions in which he studied at the Slade. It must have been an interesting time, yet the age was essentially dull. Feelings and interest were abnormal in aesthetic, intellectual and social matters, yet everyone was enveloped in a pall of stagnation. Change was regarded with horror, yet all felt something was coming. Women had discovered the strength of their sexual appeal yet it could not be realized that they were approximately half the population of the world. The internal combustion engine had not yet changed the face of the earth, though it was apparent it was about to shrink it. The Channel had been crossed by air, yet the sea still kept this country in a state of isolation and dreadnoughts were the only political thoughts. And in this silence before the storm could be heard the vague rumblings of guns. In this lull after so many summer days, the nerves of a placid people were really taut. This consciousness, vaguely felt by all, of an impending disaster, accounted for the abnormal opposition shown to any form of experiment, and accounted for the Slade students' adoption of a priggish attitude of superiority towards all affairs and conditions that affected their lives. Of works of art, every nerve was strained, not only by criticism, but by the public in general, to make a *bon mot*, displaying not the wit of the nineties, but a blathering buffoonery.

The Slade students in those days had divorced themselves from all contemporary thought and fashion: largely through the leadership of Augustus John, they had adopted a form of bohemianism, a pose which at the same time was a protection and prevented diversion of thought from the study of drawing and painting, which was pursued with an earnestness and sincerity unknown in any of the other art schools of London and Paris. Draughtsmanship and craftsmanship were rightly placed by the students as the first essentials of good art. Post-Impressionism had not yet upset the ideals of representational painting, and the Impressionists had brought back the study of nature; the New English Art Club was stealing the prestige of the Royal Academy.

It was this background that helped John to gain such a mastery over his materials, and gave scope for his luxuriant invention. People submitted themselves to John, but he never submitted himself to them. He stood out as one of the most talented draughtsmen of all times, a brilliant colourist, a master of composition, and an etcher of fine achievement. Largely because of his impeccable accuracy, he was able to take liberties with his subjects. At times he was divided between truth to his subjects and truth to himself. Here comes the distinction between stylism and distortion, the former being a variation dictated by the artist's temperament, the latter a deliberate alteration prompted by the requirements of an abstract design. Augustus John came under the first heading and could be classified with Greco, Rubens, Cranach, Cosimo Tura and Gauguin.

John was continually trying to say something which cannot be expressed in words. Indeed, he not only said something to us, but did something to us. The iridescent colours he put on the canvas, as elusive as that of oil spilt in a puddle, vibrated along our nerves, creating a sensation of pleasure in our minds. He did not merely record what the camera could record of a person – his imagination pierced the veneer of appearances and bared the inner structure of what the eye sees. With his keen senses he felt what we call the personality of a human being, and these immaterial qualities he incorporated in the form and colour of his work. The work of Augustus John is the only key to his artistic personality.

Talk about art ended when John lit up a short clay pipe. 'I would like to get away from all this,' embracing the studio with a sweep of his arm. 'Easter Island is the place. Only one post a year when a Brazilian man-of-war brings it. In the meantime risk your money on a shove-ha'penny match before dinner.' A chancy business. John invariably won.

Sir Malcolm Sargent

Stravinsky once said that great conductors like great actors were too often unable to play anything but themselves and that every member of an orchestra knew that a conductor could be less well equipped for his work than the least of his players. No one could say that about Sir Malcolm Sargent. He was always the same – articulate, a natural musician with dazzling stick technique, immense energy, and nimble footwork. He had a highly developed sense of occasion. His personality was anticipated before he stepped on the platform, reaching almost a hysterical crescendo among promenaders on the last night of the Proms.

To many Sargent is linked with Handel's *Messiah*. He used to say that though he had loved, rehearsed and performed the three-part oratorio for over forty years, the results had never been worthy of this masterpiece that the German-born composer had created in twenty-four days. Others will recall the fierce but sensitive tension in his interpretation of Walton's first symphony. He is remembered with affection and admiration by thousands of choristers, for no one knew better than Sargent how to control large choirs and inspire them, an ability maybe gained when he was a Melton Mowbray organist-choirmaster. Those early days were full of promise. He studied the piano under Benno Moiseivitsch, became the youngest Doctor of Music when he qualified at Durham University in 1914, and quickly matured into an international maestro.

In some respects Malcolm Sargent was two people. In public he projected an exhilarating sense of companionship and was a man of extraordinary vitality. He was a great champion of British music, although at times uneasy with a contemporary work. When that happened he would give that part of the concert to a younger conductor who could tackle it with more sympathy. In private he could be just as delightful, but there were occasional bouts of depression. Loneliness was his greatest fear, loneliness and the thought of old age, which he deliberately countered by adopting an ageless pose to become the Peter Pan of music. His flat next to the Albert Hall mirrored its owner. Everything about it was fastidious and meticulous, like his personal appearance. A *Voyage de ma chambre* – the stand-by of every French writer gravelled for a theme – was rewarded by a display of signed photographs of the Royal Family with favourite musicians added for light-weight. The keynote was elegance. Everything well manicured with exquisite taste. It matched his appearance, even to the inevitable carnation. Sargent accepted with good humour the nickname of Flash Harry, but emphasized it did not refer to his choice of clothes which he regarded as a tribute to the skills of tailoring. It originated from a remark made by Sir Thomas Beecham, who, being told that Sargent was conducting in the Far East, drily remarked that it would only be a flash in Japan.

There was no doubting Sargent's love of animals. He took very seriously his duties on the Council of the Zoo and the Presidency of the RSPCA. Pride and joy was Hughie III, a budgerigar who had the freedom of the flat, flying from picture to picture before settling on a friendly shoulder. There were times when the bird was even more adventurous. A favourite Sargent rendezvous for tea in London was the classic lounge of the Ritz Hotel and the corner table by the pillar. Hughie, perfectly well mannered, would sit on Sargent's shoulder patiently waiting for a tiny morsel, completely indifferent to waiters or the public. Sargent used to say that the bird was sufficiently intelligent to imitate a stock phrase whenever the telephone rang, 'Of course, I remember you.' I never heard the utterance, but at least it was apt.

Sargent was pernickety about food. In that respect he was a dead loser as a guest. The menu would be studied with relish. Care was taken over the choice. The impression was that of a pending gourmet's delight.

The pleasure was in anticipation. The courses were merely picked over. On the other hand, he never stopped talking. It was swings and roundabouts with listeners reaping the benefit with quips and witticisms.

The mention of Sir Henry Wood would invariably bring a reaction. Sargent felt he was Wood's successor in the Promenade Concert tradition. He spoke of the coincidence that 1895 not only marked his birth in Bath Villas in Ashford, Kent, but was the year when Henry Wood took his stand at the conductor's desk of London's new Queen's Hall and raised his baton for the opening of the first of the annual concerts that became the Promenade

Concerts. Sargent envied that moment, not only because it was the beginning of an historic musical chapter, but also because he would have preferred to have enjoyed life at that particular time. He almost savoured the atmosphere and could recapture the mood and spirit of that period. London then was at a much slower tempo. It was smaller. Even with the suburbs, it went little beyond a six-mile radius. No giant blocks of white concrete. Regent Street was still the street designed by Nash. Portland Place and Park Lane held the town houses of the great. Dickens could have recognized the Strand. Leicester Square the nightly rendezvous of Inverness capes and opera-hats. Sargent felt the women then must have been delicious creatures, with twelve-inch waists, leg-of-mutton sleeves, trailing skirts and monstrously absurd sailor hats. Musicians did not try to look like bank managers. You could travel to any part of Europe, except Russia, without a passport; buy what you wanted at almost any hour. Income tax was a shilling in the pound, château-bottled Bordeaux fifty shillings a dozen, whisky four shillings a bottle, cigarettes sixpence for twenty, and there were nine evening papers – five at a penny, four at a halfpenny. These were moods of nostalgia, even when loved only by hearsay. As Sargent said, the gold of that time was perhaps never more than gilt, but its brief life was full of glitter.

At times Malcolm Sargent's life was saddened by bereavement and illness, but he left behind a standard of conducting that would have been applauded by his idol. The courage shown during those last few months when he knew the worst was an inspiration. No one will ever forget that memorable Last Night when, though he could not conduct, Sargent walked on to the platform to a shattering welcome, acclamation and love for a man who had given so much. Sensitiveness always prevented him from talking of a personal faith, but this great lover of life accepted death, not morbidly, but with a quality of belief that under-girded his final weeks.

Adlai Stevenson

A question that can never be answered is whether Adlai Stevenson would have been one of the great Presidents of the United States. We shall never know, though his supporters had no doubts. Few American politicians have had more devoted followers. The fact that he twice met defeat as the Democratic candidate for the Presidency failed to depress his admirers who wanted him nominated again. They argued that he lost in 1952 and 1956 to President Eisenhower because the General was an extraordinarily popular candidate with an extraordinarily popular appeal as a great war figure. Although Stevenson insisted he was not a candidate in 1960, there were many who endorsed him for standard-bearer a third time. Everywhere he went before the Democratic National Convention that year there was evidence of strong support, but in the end Senator John F. Kennedy was the overwhelming choice of the delegates.

Adlai Stevenson was probably the most famous loser of all time. At times he seemed marked for failure and almost carried within himself a realization that fate would deny him its ultimate rewards. He had, in the words of Stephen Benet, 'all things except success', yet knew 'such glamour as shall wear sheer triumph out'. Maybe it spared him the ultimate test of character for while the responsibilities of the White House office can call forth un-suspected powers and virtues, they can also reveal unsuspected flaws.

Stevenson was aloof and it was this that made it difficult to get to know him. Over a period of time I saw something of the man behind the public mask, moments when he was neither cold nor austere. In a relaxed mood, Stevenson's wit, like John Kennedy's, could be irrepressible. It bubbled up at the most unlikely moments, never malicious but sophisticated and wry, directed more often than not to his own predicament. At such times he would talk about disappointments, set-backs, his beliefs and attitude to life. He was a fervent advocate of the United Nations and often said that had it not existed, it would have been invented. He felt it was essential for the preservation of world peace. His attitude was understandable, for Stevenson was a key figure at the 1945 San Francisco Conference when the United Nations Charter was drafted. He was also present at the London meeting of the Preparatory Commission when the structure of the world organization was forged. In one sense Stevenson was fortunate. He was spared disillusionment about the real influence of the United Nations. Instead he never ceased to take a hopeful view of the human condition and allowed himself to indulge in optimism for the future of mankind, even for the chances of peace. I remember him saying that the Republicans were always afraid of tomorrow. Stevenson, too, like all sensible men, was afraid of tomorrow, but he knew it would come and prepared a welcome for it.

A deep disappointment was that both President John Kennedy and President Johnson passed him over as Secretary of State, a post he wanted above all others. When I asked why he had been ignored, the answer was surprisingly frank. He believed they thought he was not enough a man of action, that he did not understand the use of power. It was a hypothetical judgement. He was never given the chance to prove or disprove the inference that effectively ruined his influence in that field. Instead he accepted the post of Ambassador to the United Nations in the hope that it would give him a significant voice in the making of foreign policy. The fact that under the Kennedy and Johnson Administrations he also held Cabinet rank unquestionably gave more authority to his words, which were more closely listened to than most of the other nations' envoys.

I once asked whether he had been involved in international negotiations not strictly connected with his United Nations post. Stevenson admitted that he helped to maintain communications between the United States and Russia at the time of the Cuban missile crisis. He was also active in the negotiations that finally brought about the nuclear test-ban treaty in 1963, which he described as the logical culmination of his proposals in the 1956 presidential campaign. He always stated that progress in dialogue, be it at domestic or international level, only came about by compromise, and with a wry smile added that he had had an early grounding. He was born in Los Angeles of a well-to-do family. His mother was a Republican and a Presbyterian, his father a Democrat and a Presbyterian. He ended up in his father's party and his mother's Church. His grandfather, after whom he was named, was Vice-President of the United States under President Grover Cleveland from 1893 to 1897. The background was invaluable for whatever we are told or whatever we read, America is a country where a self-perpetuating aristocracy counts.

In Stevenson's case, he was not only an intellectual, but an aristocrat who was ill at ease in the *brouhaha* of American elections. At times he was inadequate on the hustings, yet in spite of this the results for the Governorship of Illinois, when he was elected as the Democratic candidate, showed a record margin of 572,000 votes. He was at his best on the academic podium. In one sense John Kennedy came to power in the wake of Stevenson's popularity. The Kennedys were not members of the Stevenson-style aristocracy by stud standards, but they made it politically, eventually becoming a self-perpetuating aristocracy, though the Kennedy clan was suspect in some eyes on several counts. They were Irish, Catholic and lived in exquisite houses surrounded by Early American furniture, sound English chairs and the best of French porcelain. They were resented by the professionals because they appeared to break the rules like an intermixture of the later soap-box sagas of *Dynasty* and *Dallas*. Historically, Americans prefer their Presidents to be born in log cabins and when they are not they invent the trappings for them. The combination of Kennedy and Stevenson was a new and exhilarating mixture that appealed.

Stevenson was not just a theoretical academic. He was essentially practical. He carried out far-reaching reforms in Illinois by plain talk, hard work and prairie horse-sense. Every month he broadcast by radio a report on the progress that had been made. He never pulled a punch.

Kennedy came in for criticism for not having the guts to speak out against McCarthy instead of skirting the issue by being discreet. Stevenson never hid his belief that McCarthyism was evil, driving the point home during the presidential election, and shrugging-off counter-attacks as gutter-inspired. But not everything was so cut-and-dried. He defended the Bay of Pigs failure at the Security Council and the American role in Vietnam, but was half-hearted in his support of these policies. As a result his eloquence in the United Nations lacked resonance. In retrospect Stevenson denounced the Administration's erratic and vacillating handling of the Suez Canal crisis. He admitted that at times he contemplated resigning from the taxing United Nations post, but could not bring himself to do it.

Of his more personal experiences, Stevenson pin-pointed his world tour in 1953 when he visited thirty countries in six months and broadened his education by talking with everyone 'from cobblers to kings'. He recalled – possibly exaggerated – the occasion in East Berlin when he and his party were held up by the Russians and told that if they moved they would be shot. Then over the Malayan jungle his helicopter caught fire but landed safely. After a visit to Russia he wrote a book about the trip, arguing that Americans had to learn to live with the Communists on a fairly long-term basis instead of dealing with each crisis as it arose. He thought the biggest headache for America in the future would be China rather than Russia, but he was under no illusions about Russian aims and clashed regularly with Soviet delegates. Their feelings were reflected when he died. The news was reported in a one-sentence dispatch by Tass News Agency.

Making a retrospective assessment of Adlai Stevenson is not easy. He never held national office so in that sense could not claim credit for concrete achievements. Of all his services, perhaps the greatest was the most intangible. He raised decisively the whole standard of debate in America on domestic as well as foreign issues. It was in the tradition of Lincoln – and Stevenson was a lifelong student of Lincoln – who made no concession to the vulgar taste in his debates with Douglas or his Cooper Union address. It was in the tradition of Woodrow Wilson who scorned talking down to the American electorate. Alone of his generation of politicians, Stevenson had something of the Wilson literary elegance without the Victorian rhetoric. He added wit, charm and lightness of touch more rare in American than in British politics.

In public and in private Stevenson mirrored an elementary honesty. It was a form of pride, a pride that would not let him stoop to intellectual trickery and would not permit his country to assume that power was a substitute for justice. He took to heart Justice Holmes's admonition that the first step in wisdom is to recognize that you are not God. The name Adlai comes from the Bible. It means 'the just', an appropriate epitaph to the life of this gentle, kind man who personified the pathos, all the poetry of a Greek tragedy.

Epilogue

Pining to live, I was constrained to die,
     Here, then, am I
Love is my meed, fountain of its bliss.
     Now, only this.
The image of thoughts & feeling that I was!
Of all earth's marvels the blest looking-glass!
The all-desired; the little brought to pass!
     Alas!" ...

For Louis Stanley from Walter de la Mare
Monday, May 3, 1954

Walter de la Mare OM

In the car on my last visit to Walter de la Mare, I turned over the pages of *The Traveller*, a long metaphysical poem in which a traveller and his horse journey across a strange land towards death, and come to death at last – a spiritual and a physical journey. Their world is quite literally a dream world: it has no local habitation. We reached the house in a secluded Georgian terrace with a heavy entrance gate, large plane tree and tall windows. The study was small. The centre pane of the window had these words engraved on it:

> Look thy last on all things lovely,
> Every hour. Let no night
> Seal thy sense in deathly slumber
> > Till to delight
> Thou have paid thy utmost blessing;
> Since that all things thou wouldst praise
> Beauty took from those who loved them
> > In other days.

'Laurence Whistler inscribed that!' It was the housekeeper who led me to the poet's room. He was in bed. The curtains were partly drawn across the windows, but the shafts of light panelled the low, narrow bed with its deep cleft in the swelling pillow. Outside a dazzling sun had long ago drunk up the freshness of the morning. His face, beneath a flurry of thinning grey hair, had a ravaged handsomeness. I guessed him to be one of those men who seem bigger seated than when on their legs. The keen look in profile, as of an upward-pointing arrow, was still there. The vitality which had inspired many a page still vibrated in his voice, and told in his grave but shy greeting. There was no hint of misty churchyards and lingering twilight in those features.

He had just completed that morning a manuscript on Thomas Hardy. It was tempting to compare the two men, for at first sight Hardy was so superficially different. Walter de la Mare, like

Hardy, belonged to, and was the greatest living representative of that specifically English tradition, which is neither Celtic nor Symbolist, but something as autochthonous as the fools and fairies of Shakespeare. The latter, like many leading modern poets, was a regionalist: his work came from a specific soil. But I defy anyone to tell from de la Mare's work tht he was a Kentish man. His world was unreal. It could not be localized. Some critics regarded this as a failing. Politically I follow their arguments as to regionalism, devolution and the parish pump, but I think it is a civilized virtue to think and write universally. For this does not automatically imply a lack of that most essential poetic quality, precision. Walter de la Mare had more precision, both of image and expression, than Hardy. He had refinements and nuances beyond the ken of Hardy's crisp but coarse homespun. Hardy never wrote anything so delicate as the *Epitaph* nor was he capable of the genuine ballad emotion which we derive from *The Listeners*. Walter de la Mare can be likened to William Blake, though he was not in any strict sense a mystic, for both men affirmed the values of the visionary innocence of childhood and the timeless reality of dreams.

During our conversation Walter de la Mare talked of his early childhood. He used that fascinating trick of asking odd questions, which gave the imagination a lift. When he asked one of his odd questions, he really waited for an answer. He launched a discussion as to what was my earliest recollection. His own contribution had all the elfin loveliness that I associated with his mind – on a par with his earlier recollection of a faraway Christmas morning. Whether the air was frostbound, whether snowflakes were slowly drifting across the window, he could not remember. But he could very easily descry – in a vague spectral fashion could even again have become – the small boy of six or seven as he then was. He was sitting up in bed, his wits still fringed with dream, and in the folds of his counterpane lay an orange, a red-cheeked apple, a threepenny-bit, and a limp stocking that had well served Santa Claus's purpose. It was not, however, the orange or the apple or the threepenny-bit that made the occasion so memorable, but a book; a limp, broad picture-book, printed in bold type, with half a dozen or so full-page plates in the primary colours – Gulliver, pinned down by lank strands of his hair and being dragged along by a team of cart-horses, fifty strong, on a vast shallow dray with wheels like reels of cotton. *Gulliver's Travels*, then, was that small boy's first rememberable book.

It was part of this poet's innate humour to analyse and hearken to the world with the delighted wonder of a child; a child who was entranced by things minute and delicate: song, stone, flower, sound, grass, beast and bird, even though he portrayed that wonder, that delight, with the lingering melancholy and touch of sadness that comes to a man. His uncanny word magic, his gaze, his ear enriched our minds – the clashing plough-team, the inky rook, the nettles sour and lush, the snow-pulped kernel of the palm-nut, the knife-winged birds, the raven's stagnant eyes, the clank of the chaffinch. And how we stirred from our thoughts when the 'trumps fee-faugh defiance' and 'the storm cock bugles his *qui vive*'. Of all poets Walter de la Mare held us with a word.

It is inevitable in discussing de la Mare to speak of his technique, because it is the first thing that impinges on the reader's attention. His life was a very individual dream composed of diverse and incongruous elements. There was no wantonness in his poetry, cleanly or otherwise; his work was almost completely devoid of eroticism. Even when he touched an erotic theme at second-hand, as in his poems on Ophelia and Imogen, the heart was sterilized, the image cold and glassy. There is no living poet in English or any other language, with whom he could be compared. His work was unique. It leads the reader like will-o'-the-wisp until he reaches the silent silver lights and darks undreamed of which pervade his poetry; the two worlds, one actual, the other spun of dream, in both of which de la Mare lived and moved as a native; and the third world of childhood so reminiscent of Alice's Wonderland garden.

Oliver Elton once wrote of Herrick: 'A stormy age is incomplete without at least one artist who sits by himself and cares only for his craft.' It is a thought we reserved for Walter de la Mare. As a poet he ripened to flowering summer, and deepest autumn, yet even in the fading sunset the roses were still rich. Not once in thirty volumes of poetry and grace, matchless since earlier generations, did he lose the intensity of enchanted loveliness:

> What lovely things
> Thy hand hath made . . .

Sir John Sheppard

King's Parade – of all the elegant streets in the world, none is so enigmatic as this proud thoroughfare of beauty, culture and quality. Compare it with the international streets of fashion. New York has Fifth Avenue, London has Bond Street, Rome the Via Condotti, Paris the Rue de la Paix, Oxford the High. Each symbolizes wealth and luxury, vanity and leisure, but none possesses the austere vitality and stately snobbishness of King's Parade. It is utterly unselfconscious. Residents take it for granted. Visitors gravitate towards this thoroughfare and take it to heart. In their eyes King's Parade is the crystallized expression of Cambridge. The very magnificence of King's College is breath-taking. The gateway under the octagonal dome and pinnacles of the porter's lodge leads into a court with a fountain in the centre. On a pedestal is a bronze figure of the gentle founder, King Henry VI. The first stone was laid on 2 April 1441. Along the whole north side of the court, dwarfing all else, is the fabric of King's Chapel, the brightest jewel of late Gothic in Europe. Presiding over these noble buildings is the Provost, always an academic of rare distinction.

One such was Sir John Sheppard, a scholar of fastidious taste and many idiosyncrasies for in that domain a Provost can indulge in personal quirks and fads. In appearance Sheppard was almost a caricature of the traditional don. Silver-haired, he always walked slowly with the aid of a stick expecting everyone to give him unimpeded progress. He played the part of the old man for so long that when the years finally caught up he didn't like it. Only once did I see the bluff called. Cambridge railway station has the longest platform in the country and the morning train to London is always at the farthest end. I went through the barrier with a couple of minutes to spare, followed by the Provost leaning heavily on his stick. He had a difficult decision. His usual dignified slow pace meant missing the train. There was no alternative. A sprint did the trick and destroyed the legend.

John Sheppard was a superb play-actor, on the look-out for an effect. He loved ceremonial occasions with all the trappings. The Festival of Nine Carols broadcast live from King's Chapel on Christmas Eve appealed to his sense of the dramatic. The moment he savoured was when the last touches of colour were fading in the massive stone windows and candles flickered as the strains of *in dulci jubile* soared to the vaulted roof hidden by an enveloping gloom. The last Lesson had been reached. The vast congregation stood as the dignified figure of the Provost made his way slowly to the lectern. In the silence we listened to the opening words of the Gospel of St John – always read in measured fashion and timing – the unfolding by the Evangelist of the great mystery of the Incarnation. He would linger over the closing words,

> And the Word was made flesh
> And dwelt among us.

The congregation joined the choir in singing 'O Come all ye Faithful', then the Collect for Christmas Day, the Benediction, and the Recessional hymn. A double line of scarlet-and-white figures filed out of the choir stalls and passed out of sight, their trained voices rising above the greater volume of the congregation. That was Sheppard's annual emotional orgasm. It appealed to all his senses. The public liked it. Those who listened approved the traditional format and the cadence of his voice, but in one sense it was a façade.

The other side of John Sheppard was quite different. It was linked with that intellectual secret society known as the Cambridge Apostles which attracted such men as Anthony Blunt and Guy Burgess. During its 165 years the Apostles had changed with each generation, but an undercurrent of homosexuality persisted, becoming almost a hot-house creed at the beginning of the century. The trend declined after the First World War, but revived in the 1920s and 1930s. Sheppard was elected to the Society in 1902, the same year as Lytton Strachey, and became the main recruiter of promising young Apostles between the two wars, adopting mannerisms and affected phraseology that invited comment. Another close friend was Leonard Woolf, who married Virginia Stephen. Between them they formed an inner circle with Maynard Keynes, James Strachey, Desmond MacCarthy, Henry Norton and Roger Fry, becoming known as the Bloomsbury Group, but their sexual preferences were constant. The core of their belief was that the love of man for man outweighed that of man for woman. Virginia Woolf had no illusions, summing up in succinct fashion their activities as a group of clever, arrogant men who preferred to be apart from women.

My last contact with John Sheppard was in an unexpected setting – Monte Carlo an hour before the start of the Grand Prix of Monaco. Thousands were pouring into the Principality as we walked across the Casino Square to a chemist's shop in the main street. Outside on the pavement, slumped on an upright wooden chair, was a vagrant who had seen better days, yet there was something familiar about the head. On the way out I stopped, stooped down and recognized the Provost of King's. I listened to a sorry story. He had motored with friends from Menton and had been left in the chemist's. Nobody had realized that all roads into Monte Carlo were to be closed for the duration of the race. Sheppard was stranded without money, daren't move; in any case he had difficulty in walking. He looked awful, unshaven, dirty shirt, frayed cuffs and shabby suit.

It was a difficult situation as I was due in the pits by the harbour. Back at the Hotel de Paris I arranged for a porter to bring him back to the hotel in a wheeled invalid chair, seat him on the balcony with adequate refreshment and I would look after him when the race ended. Events made it impossible because our car, the BRM, won the Grand Prix. When we eventually returned, Sheppard had gone, presumably collected, for there was no message.

I never learnt how this fastidious scholar, the pride and joy of the Cambridge Apostles, could have become an aged tramp. Shortly afterwards his death was announced in the papers.

Gilbert Murray OM

It is always difficult to convey to others the personality of an individual. Very often it is hard to know what feature to isolate. For instance, we seldom realize how vital, yet how incommunicable, an element in any individual is the quality of the voice. How regrettable it is that those who have known the outstanding figures of the past failed to realize that almost a third part of any individuality is bound up with the tone or inflection of their speaking voices. Even Boswell, who sketched a vivid physical pen-portrait of his companion, failed to hand down to future generations a convincing sound-picture of the way he spoke. We know that Dr Johnson thundered and wheezed and panted. We know that Napoleon spoke in a low voice, and that only when roused by anger did the Corsican accent assert itself. We know that the voice of Shelley was shrill and that of Byron soft. We know that the resonant tones of Tennyson's voice were blended with the broad vowels of the Lincolnshire Wolds. We know that Gladstone's tones were deep and rounded, while Bismarck could only summon the accents of a child. Yet, only when we compare these fragmentary allusions with the effect made upon us by contemporary figures from Winston Churchill onwards can we realize that posterity with such recordings will inherit far more complete sound-pictures of the personalities of the great than was possible to earlier generations.

I remember Gilbert Murray, the scholar, teacher, poet, dramatist and crusader for peace, not by his frail figure or noble head, but for the quiet cadence of his voice – a voice in which was mingled the grace of a scholar and the delicacy of a man of taste. I sat with him over a period of months in a House of Commons committee-room, where his quiet voice epitomized the keynote of his philosophy. In the sphere of international politics, Murray was an influential figure in the effort to banish war and to establish a rational control of the social economy and the working of its ethical machine. Throughout all the sessions, Murray's calm voice concealed a strength that nothing could defeat. His philosophy explained it. '*Sophrosyne*', he said, 'however we try to translate it – temperance, gentleness, the spirit that in any trouble thinks and is patient, that saves and not destroys – is the right spirit.'

This quality was evident in so many ways, but nowhere more so than in his home at Boar's Hill in Oxford, where he could withdraw from the world whenever the world threatened his peace of mind and be with his family, neighbours who included Bridges, Masefield and Robert Graves, and a wide range of friends. The hospitality at Yatscombe was well known. Guests were plentiful, ranging from undergraduates, poets, politicians, scholars and invariably eminent visitors from other countries, all made to feel at home by the tireless Lady Mary Murray.

The house itself was not particularly attractive, but it had about it an air of friendliness. On a sunny day the rooms were flooded with light. More important they were lived in, had become a family background rich with memories. One mantelpiece used to have the photographs of the innumerable young friends who had died in the First World War, among them being a particularly sensitive likeness of Rupert Brooke. The garden, with its magnificent azaleas, had an impressive, almost impenetrable, bamboo thicket, the centre of which had become a small clearing as a result of a heavy snowstorm. It was a place of mystery for the children, grandchildren and all impressionable youngsters, who were fascinated by the legend of the elusive boar. It always appeared after they had gone. Somehow Gilbert Murray was the only one to see it, but he vouched for its friendliness towards children.

Murray had likes and dislikes. A phase that lasted for some time was a rash enthusiasm for a motor-bicycle, which he rode with scant regard and only escaped injury by the skills of other road-users. Tennis was another pastime that lasted well into his eighties. What he lacked in stamina was compensated for by guile. He had touches of gamesmanship that would have done justice to Stephen Potter. Dislikes were few, but heartfelt. Somewhat surprisingly they included music and Shakespeare. Teetotaller and vegetarian, though there were occasions when self-imposed food restrictions were waived so as not to embarrass an unknowing hostess.

Particularly rewarding were Murray's occasional reminiscences of people and events. During one visit to Yatscombe this took an unexpected turn. He asked if I would mind if the wireless were turned on. The request was surprising until across the room came the sound of his own voice. It was a talk that had been recorded in the room where we sat. In the same way that the Emperor Aurelius began his book *Meditations* with a list of people who had special influence on him and taught him how to live, so Murray spoke of colleagues and individuals who in various ways had given shape to his life. It was interesting to listen to opinions on the radio and then hear amplified comments immediately afterwards. There were glimpses of Murray's association with Cambridge: his stay with Professor A. W. Verrall, then leading Euripides scholar, in a house full of courtesy, hospitality and wit; his talks with Mrs Verrall about psychical research, in which she was an expert critic; his meeting with Jane Harrison, in whose magnificent *Prologomena to Greek Religion*, and its sequel, *Themis*, he co-operated; his friendship with Bertrand Russell, Cornford, later Professor of Ancient Philosophy, George Trevelyan, A. B. Cook, and a brilliant poet like Rupert Brooke. He recalled a rehearsal of Milton's *Comus* in which Cornford was the evil enchanter and Rupert Brooke a most spirit-like spirit. He related an endearing experience when, unable to make Professor Chadwick, the Professor of Anglo-Saxon, aware of their presence because of a broken doorbell at the garden gate, he was shown by Bertha Phillpotts, the Icelandic scholar and Mistress of Girton, how to enter the house by climbing through a small window into a boot-hole.

He recalled some of his experiences as Charles Eliot Norton Professor of Poetry at Harvard when he met such people as President Wilson and Theodore Roosevelt. He described how Edison, a tireless genius, would fall asleep in his laboratory so he could resume work the moment he woke. General Smuts impressed him as a man of extraordinary gifts. Not only was he a considerable lawyer, but when forced by events to be a soldier, proved himself a great military man. He was also a scientific botanist of high repute and author of an original and important book on philosophy. Murray afterwards told of breakfasts with the great Mme Curie, the discoverer of radium. Completely unpretentious and simple in tastes with no trace of make-up, he found she was totally disinterested in politics, but being a Pole, had the true Polish distrust of Russia. He recalled in detail her reaction when she received an invitation to receive the gift of one whole grain of radium from the women of America.

Einstein was another who impressed Murray by the simplicity and absence of egotism that comes more easily to a great scientist than to a great artist or writer. Apart from his mathematics and music, which were beyond his range, Murray's lasting recollection of Einstein was his gaiety and instinctive kindliness. In another field it was interesting to listen to Murray reliving his experiences in theatrical matters. He was a student of modern French plays, from Victor Hugo onwards, and was greatly stirred by Ibsen, who was just beginning to be recognized in England through William Archer's translations. He became involved in the verse translations of one or two plays by Euripides. Archer arranged with a private theatrical society to present *Hippolytus* at the Lyric Theatre for four nights with Edith Olive for Phaedra, Brydon for Theseus, and Granville Barker for the Messenger. It proved a collector's piece. On the fourth night a queue stretched a long way down Shaftesbury Avenue.

Murray described some memorable performances of the Euripides plays given by Barker and Lewis Casson. He also recalled suggesting to Bernard Shaw that he should write a sequel to *The Taming of the Shrew* in which Katharina, when married to Petruchio, should completely twist him round her finger by allowing him, from time to time, to give exhibitions of her ostentatious obedience. He described how Shaw replied that it was impossible as he was already doing a play called *Murray's Mother-in-Law*. The play was *Major Barbara*, in which Gilbert Murray and his wife were portrayed or caricatured.

Gilbert Murray made the Greek theatre an integral part of the English theatre. With a first-class brain, a natural gift for scholarship, a simple, fluent and resourceful style, and untiring energy, this Regius Professor of Greek at Oxford University became, more than any other writer, the link between the two worlds. The rhythmic flow of his verse translations, their simplicity and vigour, lifted these dramatists out of the ancient world into the modern. His work, with its unswerving aim, its faith in the greatness of the civilization which served as a commentary on his own activities, linked that classical past to the Greece of our day. He interpreted the essence of the genius of Greece. But his interests ranged far beyond the study and the lecture-rooms.

He was one of the principal initiators of the League of Nations at the end of the First World War. By the early 1930s, after years of painstaking preparation, the International Disarmament Conference, organized by the League was in session at Geneva. The so-called National Government was in office in this country. This period changed the main purpose of Murray's life. His hand had a part in the drafting of the Covenant. He was President of that forerunner of Unesco, the International Committee of Intellectual

Co-operation. He was Chairman of the League of Nations Union for fifteen years, later becoming joint President with Viscount Cecil. In 1946 he became joint President of the United Nations Association. He was an idealist, but realistic at the same time. This was made very clear when in later years he talked about the critical events that shaped policy.

He admitted that the Conference was lost in a maze of technical committees and sub-committees engaged in incessant discussions with no decisions. The United States had refused to join the League. It was represented at Geneva by observers, but contributed no driving-force. Japan had no intention of agreeing to anything effective, being preoccupied preparing for the conquest and occupation of China. Italy and Germany were already incubating their military dictatorship and all three soon withdrew from the League. When Britain and France surrendered to Italy's aggression in Abyssinia, the League collapsed. Hitler and Mussolini had a clear field. Then followed the pact between Russia and Germany with the Second World War as the immediate consequence. When the war ended, Murray looked to the United States to initiate some form of international control.

Murray's Hellenism and his practical idealism were not separated activities. Each alike was derived from his broad humanity, his faith in peace through justice and enlightenment. He expressed this admirably in a broadcast on his ninetieth birthday when he said, 'There has never been a day, I suppose, when I have failed to give thought, both to the work for peace and for Hellenism. The one is a matter of life and death for all of us, the other of maintaining amid all the dust of modern industrial life our love and appreciation for the eternal values.' If anyone were asked to give an example in our own time of what we mean when we speak of a truly civilized man, he could not do better than name Gilbert Murray. He was one of the outstanding figures of his generation. This fact was recognized after he crossed the threshold of old age when he was admitted to the Order of Merit, a distinction which he honoured as much as it honoured him.

There was perhaps one final sad note. When he died at the age of 91, he remained steadfast in his resistance to all forms of religious belief. There was no change of heart. He was convinced about the finality of death.

The Image of Women Golfers

Some time ago members of the Anti-Women's Society for Men's Rights, deploring that education of girls along masculine lines was having disastrous results, complained that 'strenuous, manly exercises for girls in schools was making them hairy-legged, that young women were losing womanly qualities and feminine attributes'. A misogynist might agree after watching young ladies play what it supposed to be football; trying to get a respectable grip in all-in wrestling; been intrigued by Russian women athletes after they had convinced medicos of their sex; while trading blows in a boxing-ring convinced bachelors of the wisdom of their choice. I have followed an event called the official Women's Boat Race between Oxford and Cambridge. Both crews rowed lustily with victory going to Cambridge by a comfortable margin. Official recognition of this sport was conceded with reluctance. An early rule of Newnham College reads: 'Any form of boating on the river is to be regarded as an expedition for which leave must be asked and a chaperon is required.' In 1893 a few students succeeded in getting permission to go on the river unchaperoned. The Newnham College Rowing Society was formed, from which sprang the Cambridge University Women's Boat Club. Problems of today are very different from those in 1911 when the girls wanted to wear shorts and socks instead of gym-tunics. The request was refused because the Press would immediately feature the girls with bare knees, and such publicity would prejudice the voting on degrees for women which was to take place at the end of that term.

Women have gate-crashed several sports traditionally regarded as masculine. Diehard critics at Lord's still regard women playing cricket as sacrilege. They argue that the majority of women cannot field a hard ball, throw, or know now to hold a bat, ignoring the historical fact that females have played cricket since 1754. Moreover they throw accurately and fast a ball that is the same as used at Lord's although half an ounce less in weight, while they hold the bat as convincingly as Botham or Gower. As regards technique, some women in style and stroke-play are as good as many county players. Only in muscular power are males superior. After all, we must be conceded some points.

The image of women in sport is all-important. Show-jumping and lawn tennis are obvious examples where appearances and performance match. Golf should be in the same category, only unfortunately the public image of women golfers is poor. They have themselves to blame because they refuse to co-operate. The curtain-raiser to the season is the Avia Watches International Foursomes at The Berkshire, Ascot, often played in conditions more suitable for winter sports. One of the organizers, Joan Rothschild, disappointed by the entrants' appearance, offered a special prize for the best-dressed player. Her comments were apt: 'I am frequently dismayed by the way golfers are turned out. Men dress badly, but women are even worse. Very few seem to bother how they look on the course. They turn up in old jeans or a crushed and tatty skirt that they keep only for golf. It is not good enough and doesn't happen in other sports. It does not cost a lot to dress nicely and if you are well turned out, it can boost your ego and help you to play better.' The following year Joan Rothschild went one better. She complained bitterly that the golfers still shambled round in shapeless clothes. There was no need to appear on the links 'looking like a sack of potatoes'. A judge awarded one entrant, who shall be nameless, half a point out of ten – and that was charity. A statistical survey revealed that only a quarter of the entry of over three hundred required larger sizes. Most measured 37–26–37 which meant that theoretically they were in good shape, though at times it was difficult to believe.

For some reason this trait is common. Women, well groomed and smart at home and on social occasions, walk the fairways like dowdy creatures, an appearance for many years seemingly condoned, if not encouraged, by the Ladies' Golf Union, whose attitude has been puritanical. Extremes in garb or mannerisms were bad taste. Players who attempted to create a popular personality image were frowned upon. If official advice was ignored at LGU events, trouble followed. This happened in a big way at Westward Ho during the 1933 English Championship. Gloria Minoprio shattered LGU equanimity by stepping on the first tee in immaculately cut black slacks, close-fitting black tunic up to the neck, black toque, and dead-white complexion caused by protective cream to prevent sunburn. From head to foot this tall, slender girl was in jet black. Had she appeared in the nude, officials could not have been more affected. Officials and competitors met in the clubhouse and formally expressed regret at the first appearance of slacks in a championship and deplored the departure from normal dress. Additional consternation was caused through Gloria using only one club, a cleek which was adapted for all emergencies. A caddie followed behind carrying a spare in case it broke. This was the first time a woman golfer had hit the headlines because of what she wore. It was also a classic example of psychological gamesmanship. Opponents panicked at the thought of their full armoury of clubs being beaten by a lone club.

When the English Championship was played at Hayling Island, I refereed the Minoprio match against a Miss James, a far superior shot-maker who played like a mesmerized rabbit and was beaten. Afterwards in the clubhouse a wager with Henry Longhurst was settled. In the clubhouse Gloria never sat down. I maintained that was because her slacks were so tight and narrow it would have been hazardous, if not impossible. I was right in part. Tight straps under the shoes ensured that her trousers were without creases, but the strain of sitting might have been too much.

The 1948 Curtis Cup match between Great Britain and America at Birkdale provided another example of LGU convention. For the duration of the event the clubhouse was taken over by the women. Before lunch on the first day I rushed into the changing-room to find that not only had it been commandeered, but the stalls had been hidden by draped flags to avoid embarrassing the females. It became necessary to lower the Union Jack to half-mast before nature could have its way. Today all that has changed with America taking the lead. Women's professional golf across the Atlantic is now big business. Players are sponsored and marketed like commercial commodities. Stake money is substantial, provided the projected image is spot-on with current trends. In this field British women professionals have still a lot to learn. Few of them can attract a gallery. Shot-making ability is lacking. Charisma is an unknown word. Rounds of 80 and 85, even 90s hardly inspire spectators, while appearances tend to match the scores. What are needed are strong, colourful characters before a shot is struck. In short, someone like Mildred 'Babe' Zaharias, who was one of the most remarkable sporting females America has produced.

Her record was outstanding. She covered the 80-metres Olympic hurdles in 11.3 seconds, hurled a javelin 143 ft 4 in, tossed a baseball 296 ft, high-jumped 5 ft 5¾ in, and threw the shot 39 ft ¾ in. With gold medals, 'Babe' Didrikson was acclaimed America's star girl athlete. Her début as a golfer was on a driving-range in Dallas. The first drive was over 250 yards. That was to be her attitude to the game. Competing against other women was like watching Jack Nicklaus playing in a boy's championship. Opponents were outdriven by fully a hundred yards. Her shots had the incisiveness and power of a professional. There was nothing pretty or dainty about her style. The ball was there to be hit. And hit she did with every ounce of strength. Few women have had such a powerful back or such strong leg muscles that belied her slender, graceful build and highly developed dress sense. Mildred was both feminine and feline. Her nickname 'Babe' derived from the famous Babe Ruth, the baseball player.

Completely extrovert, Mildred revelled in describing how she played and beat without the aid of strokes every member of the American men's Walker Cup team. During a round over the punishing championship links of Muirfield she had not wanted anything in excess of an eight for her second shots. I always regretted that the British Professional Golfers' Association declined to accept her entry for the Open Championship. Had she competed there was every chance of finishing in the first ten, which would have left quite a number of professionals with red faces. On the last day of the British Ladies' Championship at Gullane I saw her arrive in red-and-white check gingham shorts. Old ideas never seem to be forgotten. The lady captain of Gullane persuaded the American to return to the hotel and swap the offending garment for conventional blue corduroy slacks. She did so with good grace, then surprised the officials by vaulting over a six-foot railing in front of the first tee. After the Gullane success, Mildred turned professional and began a barn-storming tour of the States. In the process she accumulated a bevy of feminine talent, women golfers who had made their name as amateurs and decided that dollars were more useful than silver plate. She visited England with the circus known as Fred Corcoran's young ladies. The golf she produced would have beaten half the field in any men's tournament. The 'Babe', more than anyone else, put women's golf on the professional map by creating a vital public image matched by a rare skill. Tragically she became a victim of cancer at the age of forty-two. Of her private life, she used to refer to her romantic meeting with George Zaharias. It happened in January 1938 in the Los Angeles Open Tournament, a seventy-two-hole medal event, for which there was no qualifying test and nothing in the rules to prevent a woman entering. The officials put her down to play with the Reverend C. P. Erdman, a Presbyterian minister, and George Zaharias, a well-known professional wrestler. The threesome drew an enormous crowd. In the summer their engagement was announced, but Mildred laughingly used to claim that it took him a fortnight to throw her!

'Q'

During the Second World War, the Cambridge University Pitt Club had its building commandeered for the duration. Members had to look for alternative premises and eventually settled for rooms above the post office in Trinity Street. The removal was marked by a change of name to the Interim Club. In some ways the new site was an improvement on Jesus Lane. The windows overlooking the Great Gateway of Trinity College were a constant reminder of the proximity of history and the centuries-old traditions of the University. Above the Royal Arms in a niche over the entrance could be seen the statue of Henry VIII placed there by Thomas Neville, the Master of Trinity who had been appointed by Queen Elizabeth I.

A frequent visitor to the Club in the afternoons was an elderly man, heavily built, stooping, with an old-fashioned, high stiff white collar, starched cuffs and rimless glasses attached to a cord. Invariably he sat at the head of the long table. The routine then became predictable. He would refuse the offer by a club servant to pour out his tea, preferring instead to mix the brew himself. So far, so good, but unfortunately the teapot handle was always too hot to hold for more than a few seconds. The operation was painful and hazardous. This stubborn masochist was Sir Arthur Quiller-Couch, the King Edward VII Professor of English Literature, better known by the pseudonym 'Q'.

Today his name is almost forgotten, yet before the war 'Q' was widely read, with some sixty books, mostly romantic novels, to his credit. He was also editor of the *Oxford Book of English Verse* and author of several outstanding books of criticism with an enormous following from undergraduates who formed capacity audiences at his lectures. His abrupt fall from fashion was remarkable. The fact that he was an incurable romantic was anathema to post-war critics. Anything in such a vein was suspect and open to attack from pedants like F. R. Leavis. 'Q' was not slow to react. He belittled T. S. Eliot's poetry as unpalatable and muddled, while

Bloomsbury cliques got short shrift. Inevitably with such polarized views, partisan admiration and abuse were attracted. Evaluated dispassionately, there was much about 'Q's work that was solid achievement. Knighted in 1910, he had the satisfaction of establishing an independent Honours School in English and was largely responsible for founding an English Tripos at Cambridge. He succeeded in making the theme of literature not only uplifting, but adventurous by his spontaneous enthusiasm that won response from listeners and readers.

As to 'Q' himself, he was something of an enigma, reluctant to reveal what he was like and how his mind ticked. In that sense the time spent with him in the Interim Club and occasionally in the privacy of his room in Jesus College on C Staircase was rewarding. Sadly, it invoked the thought that what might have been his most absorbing book was never written. The tragic accident that cost him his life in 1944 meant that the autobiography was left unfinished – chapters that would have given insights into the lives of many famous literary and artistic figures in his life. A glimpse of these cropped up from time to time in his reminiscences.

In an age when 'characters' are rare, 'Q' was outstanding. A man of panache, he was often flamboyant in dress. During the May Races he entered into the mood of the week in yachting trousers and reefer jacket, but in the lecture room he was a stickler for academic correctness and always wore morning dress. University rules had to be meticulously observed, so much so that women students in the audience were ignored as he addressed them as 'Gentlemen'. Even in the war when masculine representation was almost nil, the form of address remained the same. Women as such in the academic sense, did not exist, though in no way was he a misogynist. On the contrary he never discouraged feminine attention.

The Interim Club musings were varied. He harked back to the days when he was assistant editor of the *Speaker* with a staff that included W. B. Yeats, L. F. Austin, Augustine Birrell and J. M. Barrie and recalled how the layout used to be finalized in a room at the Craven Hotel. The paper itself was printed at La Belle Sauvage in Ludgate Hill, where Oscar Wilde, then editing *Woman's World* often joined them for lunch. Barrie was a close friend and often stayed in Cambridge, their joint pleasure being long walks on the bank of the Cam. 'Q' described visits to Boxhill with Barrie and Conan Doyle to lunch with Meredith, whose style he regarded as dandiacal, particularly in *Modern Love*, a bleak commentary on human relations based on his marriage. On other visits to Boxhill he met Swinburne and Rossetti. He also described watching John Sargent as he painted the famous picture of Ellen Terry as Lady Macbeth in his studio. There were innumerable word-vignettes, like Ruskin replete in velvet cap, Jowett's early morning jog round Trinity Garden, and Matthew Arnold at Balliol. The reminiscing was endless and always in good humour.

As to personal matters, 'Q' admitted that the Cambridge professorship was accepted with a degree of hesitancy, because having failed to win a fellowship at Oxford, where he read classics, he had turned to journalism, popular novels, essays and short stories, in fact everything that dons frowned upon. A redeeming feature was editing the *Oxford Book of English Verse*. Even so, alongside many colleagues, he felt unqualified. Such fears were groundless. Rarely has any professor commanded the respect of so many generations of students. He became an integral part of Jesus College. Oxford was his first love, later supplanted by Cambridge, but first and foremost he was a Cornishman. He confessed that only in the crooked streets of Fowey and the creepered house called The Haven that was his home for so many years, did he really know happiness. When he wrote *Troy Town* he enshrined Fowey and it was fitting that this little town should show its appreciation by making him Mayor and then adding the Freedom of the town.

As an academic 'Q' was one of the best-loved figures in Cambridge. In many ways he epitomized what his novels expressed. Their pages contain more about him than he realized.

H. W. Tilman

To the general public Major Harold Tilman CBE, DSO, MC was an unassuming and retiring individual who preferred an anonymous role. No impression could have been more misleading. Few men have equalled his audacious spirit in search of adventure. By instinct he was a pioneer. After the First World War he spent fourteen years in Kenya, and while in Africa seized the opportunity of climbing many well-known mountains. He took part in the Kenya gold rush, and closed the African chapter by making a remarkable trip across the continent from Kenya to the Cameroons, a distance of 3,000 miles, on a push-bike.

It was, however, his exploits in the Himalayas that brought his name to the public. In the summer of 1934, he and Eric Shipton, the mountain explorer, accompanied by three Sherpa porters, were the first men ever to penetrate the inner Nanda Devi basin, that seventy-mile barrier of the twelve peaks of over 21,000 ft with no depression lower than 17,000 ft, except in the west where the Richganga River runs through one of the most terrifying gorges in the world. It is identified by Hindu mythology as the last earthly home of the Seven Rishis. The small party forced its way across the chasm and carried out an invaluable survey of glacier systems in hitherto unknown territory, an exploit of mountain exploration duly recognized by the Royal Geographical Society with the Gill Memorial. One incident during their hardships was frequently recalled by Tilman, partly because of its unexpectedness. After the tough river crossing, they climbed the gorge to find themselves, like the characters in *Lost Horizons*, in a region of rolling grass-slopes and alpine flowers.

Close on the heels of this successful expedition came further achievements. Harry Tilman and Noel Odell scaled Nanda Devi (25,645 ft), the highest mountain in the then British Empire and the highest peak mastered by man. The feat marked an epoch in the annals of mountaineering. It was the first time that one of the generally acknowledged major peaks in the Himilayas had been mastered, the gradient was the steepest in the world, and no mechanized aids were used, no oxygen apparatus employed, which confirmed that man could scale such heights unaided. A sidelight on Tilman's character was reflected in the way the news of their success was relayed to the outside world. A laconic cable was dispatched – 'Two reached the top, August 29'. That was all. No names. No credit allocated to a single individual. As a team they set out. As a team they triumphed.

Apart from the challenge to conquer Everest, there was and still is an unsolved mystery associated with the mountain and others in the same range. For years natives have talked of the existence of a peculiar creature called the Mirka or Mi-Go, more familiarly known to Europeans as the Abominable Snowman. Rumours say that this creature, still unknown to and unrecognized by science, is massive, ferocious and carnivorous, and roams the uncharted Himalayan wastes. Critics tend to scoff, but its existence has been confirmed on evidence submitted by many exploring moun-taineers. I became convinced after listening to Tilman.

He described how one night he camped at an altitude far above natural sources of subsistence, in a region where all life was dead, yet emerging from the tent in the morning, he found enormous tracks embedded deep in the snow, an unusual feature being that they followed a dead-straight line like a bird. The imprints were several inches deep and had been made by an exceptionally heavy body. The Sherpas identified them as the Abominable Snowman and refused to move, believing that even to see the creature meant instant death. Tilman's description was corroborated in a tele-vision discussion on the subject that I had with Eric Shipton. The deep imprints were the same with one significant difference. The trail led to the sheer face of a cliff that was virtually unscalable, yet could be seen in the snow above the ice-cliff continuing upwards. Photographs taken by Shipton visually confirmed the story. It would seem that unusual creatures do not exist above the snowline in these remote regions. Up to now none has been captured, but time is on man's side. Eventually one will fall to his hand and maybe the 'missing link' will be found.

In later years Tilman lived in Barmouth on the Welsh coast where he was instrumental in creating the Three Peaks race that involves the gruelling combination of sailing and climbing, a week-long ordeal ending some 350 miles away at Fort William. By then the entry, usually about twenty boats, will have moored three times along the coastline so that two of each crew can scale the highest peaks in Britain, Snowdon, Scafell Pike, and Ben Nevis. Roughly speaking it means running seventy miles and climbing 11,000 ft. By Tilman standards it seems small fry; nevertheless the race calls for considerable experiences of sailing in rough seas by skippers and navigators and stamina in plenty from the runners.

Tilman described the difficulties in greater detail. The first stage takes the boats from Barmouth some seventy miles up the coast to Caernarfon, about a day's sailing. The crew then have to navigate the rocky and dangerous entrance to the Menai Straits before landing the runners to tackle Snowdon, 3,560 ft. After the athletes' return, the boats set off through the Menai Straits on the 150-mile leg to Ravenglass. Timing is vital. It is important to arrive on the tide, otherwise valuable time is lost waiting to get into shore. The runners have to return smartly to avoid being stranded at Ravenglass until the next tide. Once the 3,210-ft Scafell Pike has been conquered, and provided the boats have a clean get-away, all is set for the dicey 220-mile trip in the Irish Sea to Fort William. Roughly eighty hours are needed to complete the last leg in strong tidal currents. Ben Nevis, 4,406 ft, has to be climbed. The first runners to clamber on board are the winners. The event appealed to Tilman's imagination and has had enormous support.

Sadly, Harry Tilman resented the curbs imposed by advancing age. Three small bases on his mantelpiece were reminders of the past. One had a stone taken from the top of Kilimanjaro, the highest mountain in Africa; the second a piece of rock from the summit of Nanda Devi, for many years the highest mountain climbed by man; the third was empty. On it he had hoped to place a stone taken from the Everest summit. It was not to be. I once asked him why he had felt the urge to take up the challenge of Everest. His reply was simple and almost echoed the thoughts of F. S. Smythe: 'I wish I knew – only, in discomfort, in storm, in the beauty and grandeur of the mountains I discovered something very much worth while, and like a magnet this indefinable something will draw adventuring pioneers back to the scene of former triumphs and disappointment – maybe to fresh conquests – maybe death.'

Tilman once told me that he had no intention of dying of old age in bed. The wish was granted. Somewhere in the South Atlantic he died in those cruel waters, probably on his eightieth birthday, striving for the impossible. It was a sad but fitting end to a remarkable life.

Dame Barbara Hepworth

My first meeting with Barbara Hepworth was shortly after the outbreak of war when she was evacuated with her family to Cornwall. That temporary stay became permanent and it was always in St Ives that we met. On the last occasion I asked why she had remained so faithful to this remote corner of England. She replied by saying that I had given one of the reasons. Out of season it was remote and withdrawn and she had grown to love the background, the legends and the locals. It was like being in several worlds. In the old days St Ives was divided into the Stennards and Down-along. The miners, who formed a large part of the community, lived in the Stennack. The fishermen were congregated Down-along by the wharf, among the narrow streets that twisted from the harbour to the Digey and the edge of the island. No miner ever settled Down-along, no fisherman had a house in the Stennack.

But times had changed. The cobblestones were still rough, the steps still slippery, and cats still prowled among the alleyways, but the partition between the Stennack and Down-along no longer existed, although there were still such corners as Teetotal Street, Virgin Street and Salubrious Place. What had happened was an invasion by artists, an impulse that began as far back as when Whistler and his friend Walter Sickert stayed in St Ives. From her point of view the colony had brought fresh creative minds into her life from such people as Bernard Leach, Adrian Stokes, Gabo, and many others.

She had always found that inspiration was fired by the enthusiasms of others. It began when having won a scholarship to the Leeds School of Art at the age of seventeen, she came into contact with Henry Moore, who was also a student. Although five years her senior, his encouragement had meant a lot. They both went on to the Royal College of Art in London and shared similarities of expression in sculptural terms, a likeness that persisted throughout their careers, each drawing on the symbolic relationship of the human form to the landscape.

In this connection Barbara emphasized how important Cornwall had been in using abstract form as a means of conveying something about nature. The influence of external setting and atmosphere left its mark from her childhood in Yorkshire. Looking back, her recollections were slag-heaps, cobbled streets, warehouses, foundries, ugly houses, smoke, dirt and smells. It was like a nightmare montage of nineteenth-century industry. In Cornwall the background was different, almost a revelation. She never tired of the granite moorlands of Bodmin, the landscape near Land's End sprinkled with megalithic remains, the coast country so desert-like and desolate in appearance, the Cornish megaliths, *Men-an-Tol*, the massive neolithic dolmen called *Chun Quoit*, and the fantastic rock formation, the *Cheesewring Rock*, balancing on the edge of a quarry. These and many other prehistoric monuments had affected the spirit of her work, like a compressed sculptural statement with a challenge to keep massive forms light, poised, almost weightless, yet suggesting strength and muscular power, with a hint of the mythological quality of a *genius loci*.

In the cell-like calm of her room in St Ives, Barbara would chat readily about those early influences, of her life with Ben Nicholson, the triplets, the impact made by the simplicity of Brancusi's forms, the problems of capturing the evocative spirit and mood of figures and environment, and the relation of mother and child, and about more mundane matters, like converting the old St Ives cinema into a suitable setting in which to show her work.

Tragically Barbara's life was cut short in a fearful fire. There was still so much she wanted to do, concepts never to be developed, but she is remembered as the most purely idealistic of English sculptors who employed abstract forms as a means of conveying something dramatic about nature. Her unflagging creative energy and versatility were in a class of their own.

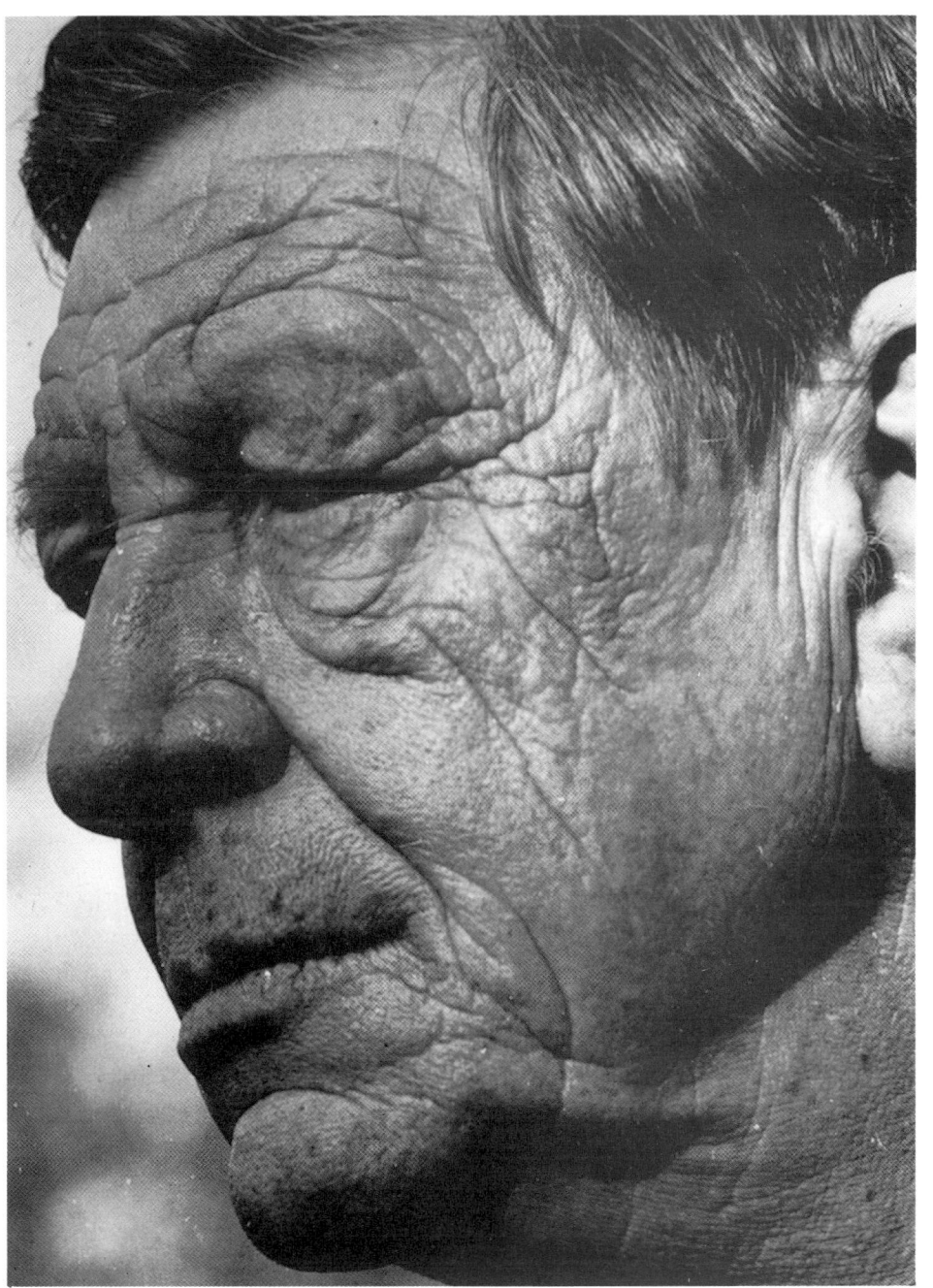

W.H. Auden, a man of moods

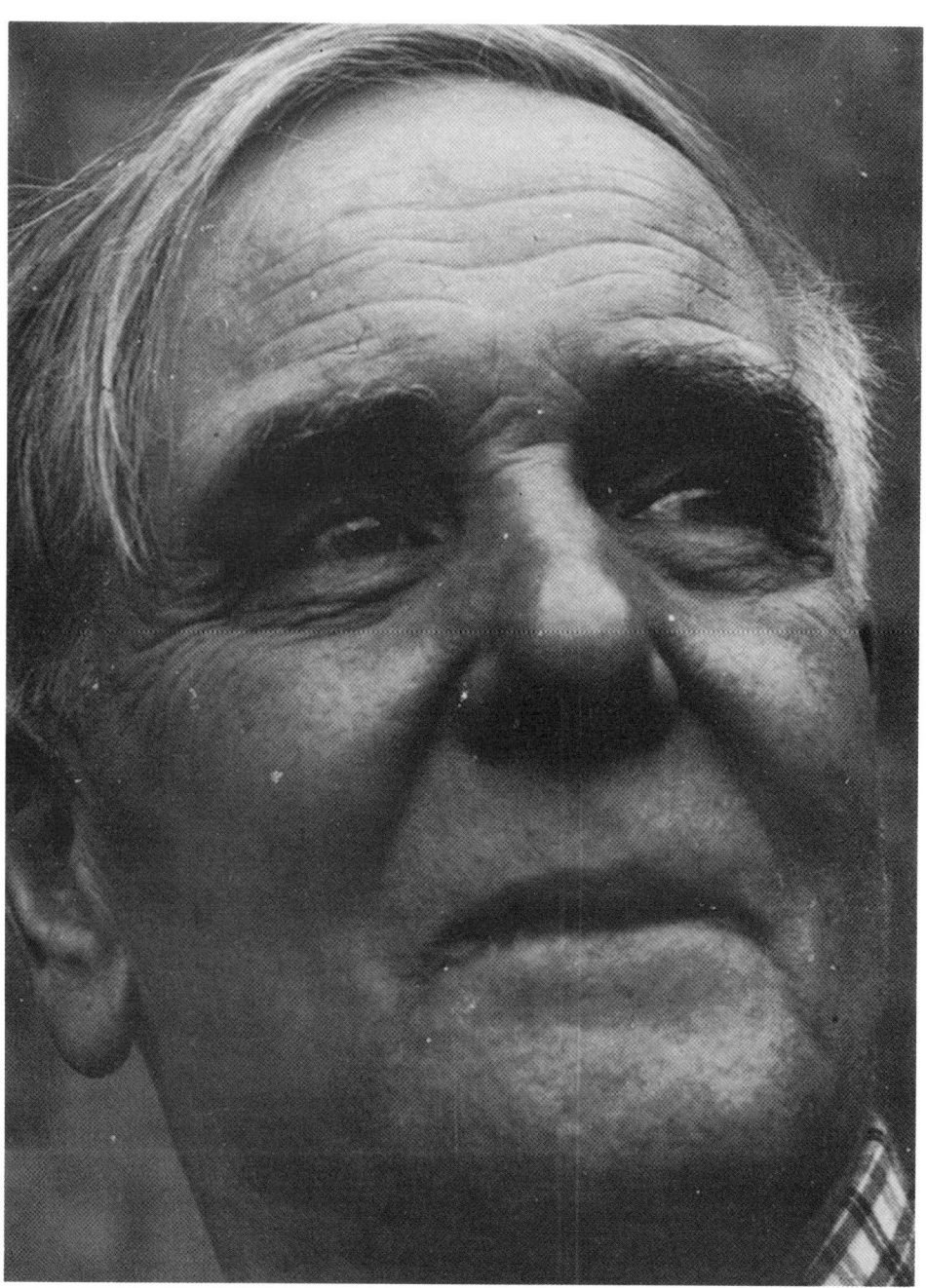

Peter Kapitza, the brains behind Russia's first A-bomb and satellites

Gordon Craig, last of the great Edwardians

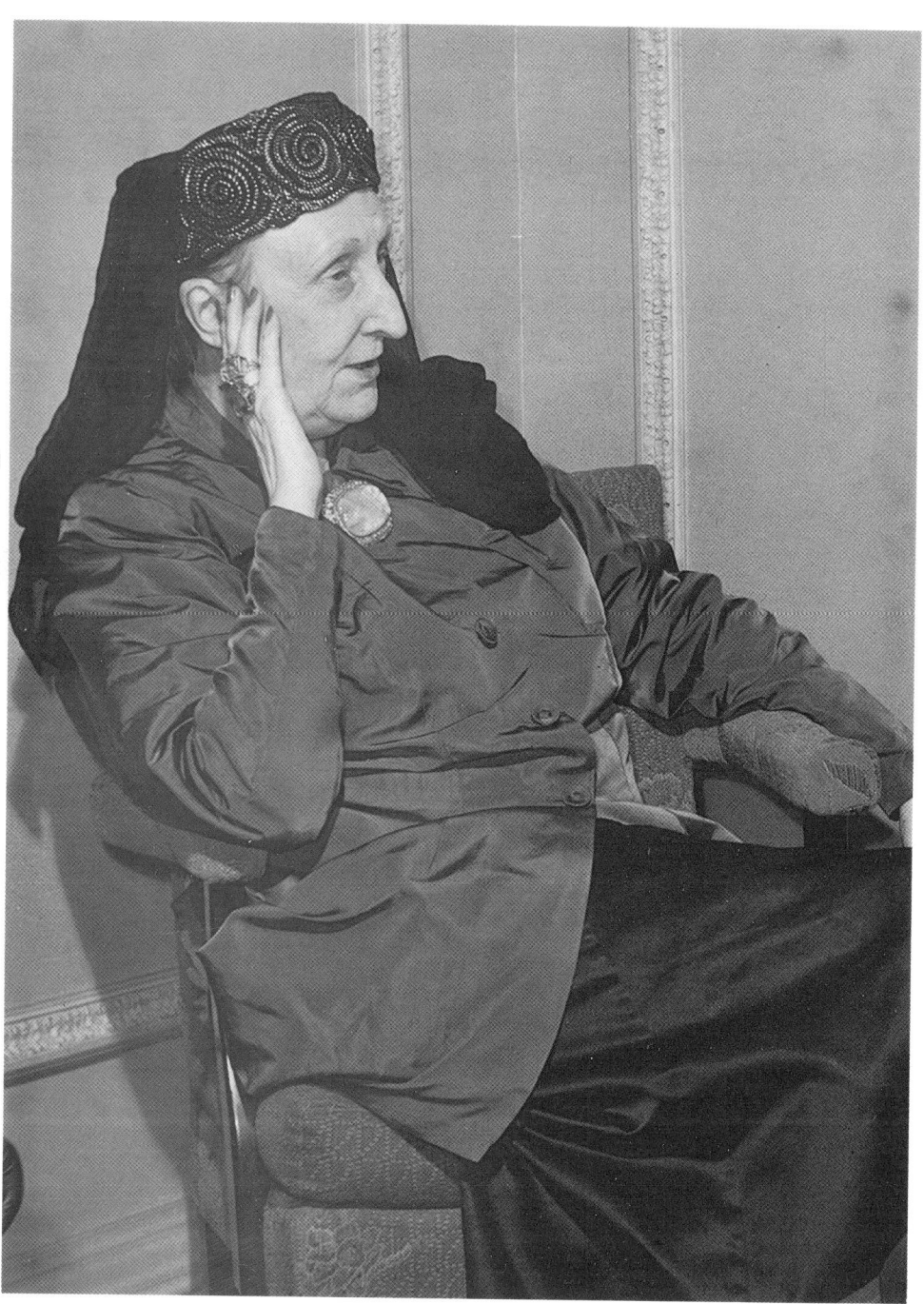

Dame Edith Sitwell defied all categories

Artistic tranquillity came easy to Ralph Vaughan Williams

John Foster Dulles, the Don Quixote of
American politics

The aesthetic school disliked the
selection of a realistic Laureate like John
Masefield

Tom Mix, the veteran film star had been
a soldier of fortune in the Boer War

The exploits of H.W. Tilman were
remarkable

Lord Beveridge crusaded persistently on a national scale

W. H. Auden

Wystan Auden, versatile poet, essayist and librettist, was a man of moods, instinctively reticent, quickly on the defensive, but reacted to his surroundings. If the company was congenial and on the same wavelength, he thawed and became animated. If not, he was phlegmatic and poker-faced, wrinkles converging into crossroads of irritation. This chameleon mixture was part of his appeal.

On a visit to the Old Mill House, Auden was in a talkative mood. After lunch I said that at some time in the future I hoped to write a pen-portrait of him. The literary side would be straight-forward, but the personal side presented certain problems. It would be much easier if he could answer three pertinent questions. Auden's reaction was clear: Ask by all means, but don't be disappointed with the answers.

I asked whether he could recall what had been his biggest disappointment. After reflection Auden narrowed it down to an incident of hurt pride. After Cecil Day Lewis died, he half-expected an invitation to become Poet Laureate. It never came. The reaction had been pique rather than disappointment, but it niggled. Another disappointment had been his return to Oxford when Christ Church made available a grace-and-favour cottage in the grounds. The years as Professor of Poetry at the University had been happy, but it was not the same. Oxford had changed. Attitudes were different. It was never possible to go back in the guise one imagined. If you do, memories are often murdered. They were in this instance.

I felt my second question might be too intimate. On being told not to be ridiculous, I asked when he first became attracted by homosexuality and how it had affected his life. There was no hesitation in answering. The first awareness of the undercurrents of homosexuality came when he was a student at Christ Church in the 1920s, a period of decadence when the appeal was more platonic than physical. The real awakening came in 1939 at a poetry reading when the subliminal turned into the consummated through meeting Chester Kallman. The physical attraction he felt for this Jewish Brooklyn youth was something he had never experienced before, a reaction that was mutual. The intense relationship lasted for two years, and after that passion gave way to companionship. Inevitably there had been arguments, rows, even scenes in the same way that clashes occur with any couple living together, but they were only surface differences. They had become dependent on each other with a way of life that in many ways had everything. Spring and summer in Austria, autumn and winter in New York. Few could ask for more. Auden made the relationship sound stable, but he was silent about the pain of jealousy through Kallman's waywardness. He had a reputation of acting like a predacious pederast with other conquests, but a special kind of loyalty refuses to acknowledge such unfaithfulness.

The third and last question was whether he could recall his most irresponsible act. It took time to answer because, as Auden said, there had been so many. In the end it concerned a friend of Christopher Isherwood in Amsterdam. The lady was Erika, daughter of Thomas Mann, who was horrified at finding herself on the Nazi list of wanted enemies. Fearing detention, she was desperate to marry an Englishman so as to become a British subject. Isherwood declined, but suggested Auden as a possibility. In a moment of mental aberration, Auden agreed to marry her – somewhat rash as he had never seen the girl. The ceremony took place at Ledbury in June 1935 and she was still legally married to him at the time of her death in 1970. Considering Auden's sexual preferences, it was a gallant if irresponsible act.

Auden died unexpectedly in Vienna in the autumn of 1973. He was buried at Kirchstretten, and remembered in this country by a memorial stone in Westminster Abbey. More personal was the tribute paid by Geoffrey Grigson in his poem 'To Wystan Auden':

> . . . there was a time –
> I recall – when you were not. Once more
> You are not. But time, after you, by you
> Is different by your defiance . . .

Frank Debenham

The feat of three young Britons who trekked 883 miles to the South Pole in the footsteps of Captain Scott's ill-fated journey captured the imagination of the public. It appealed because it was the real thing, man against nature, without sophisticated back-up resources that so often make modern expeditions into a 'wish you were here' performance. Equipment was modest, like the compass bought for a tenner, while distances were measured with a wheel. By comparison three meals a day of freeze-dried chickens, soup, eggs, butter and chocolates were five-star luxuries, but the motivation was the same, the blending of adventure with scientific discovery was in the same league as Scott's expedition, even to the naïve link of setting out from their base at Camp Evans seventy-four years to the day after Scott's departure.

Their endeavours would certainly have been applauded by Frank Debenham, survivor of the Scott expedition, the first Professor of Geography at Cambridge and founder of the Scott Polar Research Institute. During his years at Cambridge, Debenham became something of a folk legend, a role that appealed to his Australian temperament. During term time he would often hold court in an upstairs café in Regent Street that brewed excellent coffee and crispy rolls. Occasionally Edward Welbourne, Master of Emmanuel, would join our table and invariably act as devil's advocate in any discussion just to be bloody-minded. The only one to take the bait would be Gordon Manley, the President of the Royal Meteorological Society and expert on polar climatology. One of Welbourne's corny remarks was that Debenham only joined Scott by the back door. In a way it was partly true. When Scott and Dr Wilson visited Sydney on their way south for their journey to the Pole, Debenham was working as a geologist at Sydney University on the results of the Shackleton Expedition. Scott anxious to involve Australia in the project and at the same time strengthen the scientific side, invited Debenham to join the team.

No man could have brought more enthusiasm. The recollection of those days never left him, the sense of challenge was kept fresh. He used to say that stay-at-homes could not visualize the hazards, the fact that Antarctica is a continent larger than Europe with an area of some 5,450,000 square miles, or sixty times the size of Britain. The Fuchs Expedition was like a red rag to a bull. He felt the coverage by the media was over-dramatized. When the scare was raised as to whether the journey back could be made within the safety time-scale, Sir Leslie Martin, the architect, asked over dinner whether the fears were founded, and how the situation compared with Scott's plight.

Debenham pointed out that such a comparison was difficult because conditions were so different. He felt that Fuchs was feather-bedded. They only had to take equipment and provisions for the journey to the Pole where they would find shelter at an American research station. They had at their disposal mechanical snow-cats, tracked vehicles, radio links, even plane surveillance. As regards the return journey, once the polar plateau and the formidable Bearsmore Glacier had been conquered, everything should be plain sailing. His outline of the route was so detailed it felt like plotting a journey from Liverpool along the M6 coping with Spaghetti Junction on to the M1 and home.

The Scott expedition had set off on 2 November 1911 on a round journey of more than 1,700 miles without radio links and largely without maps. Beyond the Beardsmore Glacier supply caches had to be set up *en route*. The men were on foot because the dog parties had been sent back. Then came the terrible disappointment when they arrived at the Pole on 17 January 1912 at seeing the fluttering Norwegian flag planted by Amundsen a month earlier. They retraced steps in worsening weather, with the necessity to reduce rations, suffering appallingly in the blizzards that never lessened. Then followed the accident to Evans that led to his death through the injuries, the gangrene and frostbite that caused Oates to leave his tent during a blizzard to certain death, the weakness that sapped the strength of Scott, Wilson and Bowers when only eleven miles from the One Ton Camp, and the blizzard that never abated for ten days during which the three men perished.

To Frank Debenham that saga was engraved in letters of gold. Fuchs fell short of that imaginative expedition, but he would have paid tribute to the enterprise of Robert Swan, Roger Mear and Gareth Wood who were cast in the same mould.

Ralph Vaughan Williams OM

When I looked on Ralph Vaughan Williams for the last time, he was in a spacious white room in Hanover Terrace, white hair gently waving in a soft breeze that came from the open window as he stood by the balcony. The composer, a majestic, leonine figure with noble features, looked across the trees as if remembering. Artistic tranquillity came easy to Vaughan Williams. His difficulty perhaps was to find sufficiently strong feelings to remember. He had all his life, it seemed, been more interested in examining the wrinkles in the sand left by the tide than in bathing in the sea. His genius was a genius for reverie: phase after phase in his own life, reflection after reflection, image after image, turned and evaporated like wreaths of smoke. His mood of reverie was a quiet, patient one; poignancy of emotion was foreign to it.

Vaughan Williams's background was a major factor in shaping his outlook. Born in Down Ampney, he retained traces of a Gloucestershire accent; in fact, the West Country influence never left him. It went with him to Charterhouse, Cambridge and the Royal College of Music in the same way that Dvořák took Bohemia to New York. In this respect Vaughan Williams could be likened to Thomas Hardy. Both found that independence of vision was first generated by locality rather than personality. I would extend the comparison and liken the composer to Milton, William Blake and Shakespeare. Milton's landscape is primarily English and behind Vaughan Williams's music there is a similar vision of the English countryside. The influence of the English scene persists even in works whose avowed setting is a foreign land: for instance, there is no trace of the East in *Job*; the flocks are in an English pasture. Shakespeare's dramatic range is found not only in the composer's operas, but in the *London Symphony* and *Five Tudor* Portraits with occasional flashes of typical Shakespearian wit and warm sympathy. In Vaughan Williams you find the imaginative drawings of Blake's designs, his Biblical imagery and remote mysticism. Milton, Shakespeare, Blake and Hardy are distinguished names in our English tradition. Vaughan Williams was at ease in their company – a great Englishman composing music magnificently, serenely and simply.

Yet in many ways he was a contradiction. The man who cared so passionately all his life about hymns and carols and spent so much of his time in setting to music Herbert and Bunyan, the Bible and the Liturgy, even the Catholic Mass, was a youthful atheist and lifelong agnostic. On the maternal side, he belonged to the illustrious Wedgwood–Darwin clan and delighted in describing one of his earliest memories. He asked his mother about the *Origin of Species* controversy. In reply, she told him, 'The Bible says that God made the world in six days. Great-uncle Charles thinks it took longer; but we need not worry about it, for it is equally wonderful either way.'

Analysing Vaughan Williams's works means assuming the reader's knowledge of his music, a questionable assumption, for in England there are many who know much about music, few who know much music. The average repertoire is very limited. In a way the hesitancy is understandable for in parts his music is impolite. Half a century of composing conferred immense international stature on Vaughan Williams, though the meaning of his utterances is still in proportion to one's knowledge of music.

The beginning of Vaughan Williams's search for musical truth occurred when music in England was courted through foreign channels. Singers struggled to master any sound except those found in the English vocabulary. The first choice was Italian, followed by German, and into this welter came Vaughan Williams, conscious that, while the English people were prepared to accept the Russian in Tchaikovsky, the Dauphinois in Berlioz and the Basque in Ravel, they were reluctant to acknowledge the Englishman in their own composers. Vaughan Williams always had an insatiable curiosity about new works and any possibility of utilizing instruments currently used in the classical armoury. He was criticized for the use of the vibraphone in his Eighth Symphony but justified the choice because it made a lovely noise. And there was the care he took in mastering the technical possibilities of the harmonica when he wrote that charming piece for Larry Adler. There was never any reluctance about expressing views. Remarks made many years ago by Vaughan Williams still have relevance to the current state of music in England. He argued that we were too fond of looking on music as a matter of detached appreciation. The English amateur believes with Rossini that there are only two kinds of music – good and bad. If he could afford it, he preferred to import, together with the best brands of cigars and champagne, and the best brands of music. He felt the connection between music and everyday life was entirely severed. Music, the subtlest, most sensitive, and purest means of self-expression is supposed to be on a plane by itself, detached from its surroundings, a mere sensation to be enjoyed by the epicure. Such were the views of the composer spanning some forty years.

The composer developed the argument. He felt that when the English people realized that the composer was their own voice speaking through his art those things that they could only dimly grope for, then indeed the English composer would be wanted if only he were ready. He thought that too many composers thought of composition as a series of clever tricks that could be learnt and imitated; were content to write operas which only equalled Wagner in length, symphonies made up of scraps of Brahms at his dullest, or pianoforte pieces which were merely crumbs from Debussy's table. It was all very well to catch at the prophet's robe, but the mantle of Elijah was apt, like all second-hand clothing, to prove the worst of misfits.

Vaughan Williams was fascinated by folk-song and regarded it as a worthy study for all musicians, the germ from which all musical developments ultimately came. Instead of going to concerts to hear the finished product, composers ought to be concerned with the raw materials, such as the lilt of voices joining in a popular song at a music-hall, the fervour of an evangelistic hymn, a great choir singing at one of the Festivals, Welshmen singing a hymn at Cardiff Arms Park, and innumerable other occasions when music gives full expression to the emotions. We should cultivate a sense of musical citizenship. It was wrong for a composer to shut himself up and think about art. He should live with his fellows and make his art an expression of the whole life of the community.

He certainly applied this method to himself. His art grew out of the very life of the community in which he lived, the nation to which he belonged. His years of composition were one long process of development. His work showed his Englishry most firmly and at one time looked as if he would establish a national school, but fortunately avoided such a *cul de sac*. Vaughan Williams preferred independence and individuality. In that sense the public mask and the private life were one and the same. He evolved a musical style that was comprehensive, though he could be a remote composer, as in *Flos Campi*, in the *Magnificat* and the Piano Concerto, but apart from these his music was saturated through and through with the English people, with all the limitations of their odd, complex character. He recalled being told that some of the English music, which appealed to us at home, was considered smug by foreign critics. He was delighted because it suggested that our English composers had some secret which was for our ears alone. Maybe it was an insular reaction, but it confirmed the tenet that national music is personal music tinged by the cultural background of a nation.

Every genuine artist has an individual speech. Hearing the music, we know something of the man. The music of Vaughan Williams uses dissonance, not as a new language, but as an enrichment of the old. It admits tension but accepts repose as something due to the mind. There is in much of his music something that recalls the English countryside, where there is often no challenge to the eye but a pervading tenderness of harmony and outline. The works that confirmed Vaughan Williams's passport to fame and reflected his image must include the visions of conflict and violence in the Fourth Symphony and much of the Sixth; and of desolation in the finale of the Sixth as in the shining solemnities and profundities of the Fifth, which is perhaps the most characteristic and successful of all his works. He was denied real success in the opera house, the conception of the *Poisoned Kiss* being impossible to realize. Only once when he set Synge's beautifully shaped *Riders to the Sea* did his genius fully emerge in this field and in *Job* he wrote one masterly ballet. It was *Job* which by virtue of its grand scope and its good-and-evil conflicts paved the way for the crowning achievement of the three central symphonies, nos. 4, 5 and 6. These works together with a few smaller scores, such as *On Wenlock Edge*, the *Tallis Fantasy*, and the *Serenade to Music* are more than memorable.

Ralph Vaughan Williams was part of England. His nationalism was not conscious. There was no pastiche, no affectation. In that sense he had no division between public and private life. Like his music, it was a breath of the open air of England. This was often demonstrated in practical fashion at the Cheltenham Festivals, where every morning at 10 o'clock the great old man eagerly waited to hear the works of young men, many comparatively little known, without prejudice and always with helpful intent. His last Cheltenham Festival closed with his *London Symphony*. He was given a wonderful ovation that night which moved him deeply. It was a tribute, not only to his work, but the kindliness and sensitivity behind the shaggy grandeur of this much-loved composer.

John Foster Dulles

John Foster Dulles was, beyond cavil and question, a pivotal figure in American – indeed, for a time – in world history. At the core of his character the will and purpose were like granite. It was that which gave him the strength to master opposition, and he had plenty during his lifetime. Shortly before meeting him in California, I was with Adlai Stevenson in Chicago. His evaluation of Dulles was cryptic: 'the original misguided missile, travelling fast, making lots of noise, and never hitting the target', a description that fitted several of his successors. Against that must be set Eisenhower's tribute to Dulles as a great Secretary of State.

Opinion in England was just as incisive with no punches pulled. Many felt that he tried to disrupt the British Commonwealth and reduce Britain to the status of a purely European power. Certainly he had little sympathy with British policy aims in the Middle East. The main criticism was not brinkmanship or playing Russian roulette with world peace, but of dithering, and international dithering is dangerous as the Reagan administration showed. Dulles used to demand that Soviet integrity be proved by deeds, not words, yet, when Russia began to supply Egypt with arms, he discovered that Russia had a legal right to do so. When the threat to Middle East oil supplies caused British to side more with Israel, attempts were made to bring America into the picture under the 1952 tripartite declaration. Dulles skirted the issue, invoked the United Nations, and left the door wide open for Russian interference in any settlement.

I can think of many instances of Dullesian two-faced strategy. On the domestic front, he hardly came out of the trial of his nominee, Alger Hiss, with enhanced reputation. Dean Acheson at least had the courage and honesty to say, 'I should like to make clear to you that whatever the outcome of any appeal which Mr Hiss or his lawyers may make in this case, I do not intend to turn my back on Alger Hiss.' When the incriminating papers were found, Dulles was vulnerable to criticism because of his past association with Hiss. He had nominated him with glowing recommendations for the position of Director of the Carnegie Endowment. At both of the Hiss trials Dulles appeared as a prosecution witness.

In foreign affairs, during a visit to Pakistan, Dulles told members of the SEATO alliance that allies of America received more favourable treatment from the United States Treasury than non-allies, and quoted figures to emphasize the point. A week later he changed his mind for the benefit of the non-allied Indonesians. He maintained that there was no truth whatsoever in the belief that membership in a military security pact with the United States meant increased financial aid. How could there be when India and Ceylon, neither of whom were allied to America, both received aid? Then when Dulles met Pandit Nehru in New Delhi, he had to assure the Prime Minister that his earlier reference to Goa as a province of Portugal was not intended as an unfriendly attack on India.

Any skill that Foster Dulles possessed for disentangling himself from embarrassments came from long practice. The Korean War provided further characteristic examples. Just before the outbreak of war, the Secretary of State visited South Korea and stated that in the event of attack they would not stand alone. At a press conference in Washington he confessed that President Truman's action in moving United States troops into action came as a relief, for otherwise his promised support would not have materialized. Dulles upheld the Truman decision to enter the war until the 1952 campaign. He then became highly critical and remained so until the 1954 mid-term elections left a Democratic majority in control of the Senate.

Dulles was proud of his brink-of-war decision. He liked to believe that his audacity saved the peace. His own version of how he got the Chinese Communists to agree to a truce in Korea lost no detail by constant repetition. In India Dulles told Nehru that if the truce attempts failed, America would carry the war across the Manchurian frontier, the inference being that Nehru immediately informed Peking of the warning, and the truce was signed as a result. Nehru always denied that such a remark was made, adding that even had Dulles said it, he would not have taken it seriously.

Most of Dulles's rich-sounding phrases became the clichés of an empty pose. Warnings that sounded like an ultimatum were common, but never came to anything, like the occasion when the American Seventh Fleet steamed westward backed by the Formosa

Resolution. Formosa would be saved, declared Dulles, even if it meant war with China. Not a shot was fired at the Communists on the China coast. The Chinese Nationalists were evacuated from the Tachen Islands, and the fleet sailed away.

Dulles's policy became blunted compared with the promises made at the outset of his term of office. Then he stated that the policy of Acheson's containment would be changed, forthright action would follow, enslaved peoples under Soviet domination would be liberated, and the Iron Curtain rolled back. Vacillation turned Dulles into a diplomatic ostrich. The confusion that surrounded Dulles's career was largely self-caused. It may be that his background influenced outlook and tactics. Both his maternal grandfather, John W. Foster, and his uncle, Robert Lansing, achieved distinction as Secretaries of State of the United States. His father was a highly conscientious Presbyterian clergyman. This urban preacher's son made the grade by way of the legal profession. He became the most highly paid corporation lawyer of New York City. As a lawyer his ability to 'make a case' was marked. And he carried the same principles into his conduct of American diplomacy.

Unfortunately Dulles did not see that this legal method cannot be applied in a revolutionary situation, for it presupposed a framework of agreed rules within which negotiating skill could be exercised. It is not the process of negotiation as such which accounts for the settlement of legal disputes, but a social environment which permits that process to operate. To the Soviets, both then and now, the key to their ultimate triumph resides in their superior understanding of 'objective' forces and the processes of history. When Dulles suggested that a change of Soviet tactics implied a surrender of Marxism, Krushchev stated, as Gorbachov and Shevardnadze would echo, 'If anyone believes that our smiles involve abandonment of the teaching of Marx, Engels and Lenin, he deceives himself poorly. Those who wait for that must wait until a shrimp learns to whistle.' Dulles countered every Soviet thrust like a pedantic professor sure of his self-righteousness. He forgot that the world is not moved by legalistic phrases.

I talked with the Secretary of State in San Francisco and in Vienna during the signing of the Treaty of Independence. Each time I came away convinced that he was preoccupied with the ranking of John Foster Dulles in history. He was intelligent, but not as shrewd as many people imagined. He could plead a case with conviction. He liked to imagine that he embodied the

Department of State. For all practical purposes, the American Policy Planning Staff might just as well have played golf at Augusta in Georgia with the President. His knowledge of the complex problems of foreign policy was considerable, yet in the background were signs of uncertainty, as if he was conscious that he lacked the stature and ability of his grandfather.

John Foster Dulles was the Don Quixote of American politics; a Secretary of State who took more risks on the brink of appeasement than on the brink of war; who accepted America's position as a Great Power, but refused to move into world politics; who adopted a policy of indifference, vacillation, and embarrassing inconsistency. History remembers him as the American Secretary of State who rode foreign policy backwards.

Joan Collins

Having Joan Collins as a guest for the Monaco Grand Prix was an illuminating experience, if only to watch her strategy with other people. She has the assurance of someone dealing herself a fifth ace in a card game with children, an attitude hardly surprising in the Indian summer of her career that produces an incredible income per episode of *Dynasty* to say nothing of a fortune for allowing Cinzano to be poured down her cleavage.

By no stretch of the imagination could Joan Collins be described as a motor-racing enthusiast. She watched the Grand Prix but hardly enjoyed the experience. The thunderous volume of sound on the island-pit nearly had her screaming, but she recovered quickly. The gala dinner held promise of a meeting with Princess Grace that might have caustic overtones, at least on Joan's side. It coincided with her birthday so I arranged for the chef to bring in a birthday cake after the main course. One candle would be lit, otherwise it would have been too big, with orchestral and vocal accompaniment setting the mood. The cake was cut with due ceremony and Joan had a slice taken to David Niven who was sitting next to Princess Grace. Afterwards Niven came to the table and told Joan that Princess Grace had warned him not to eat anything from 'that bitch'. It would probably be poisoned. Even so, both stars greeted each other later with affectionate insincerity.

Joan is an ageless fantasist who has developed a maximum of straight animal magnetism. The only image she recognizes is the reflection in the looking-glass, in other people's eyes, and she knows exactly what that reflection looks like. She is the original with immense dark eyes that widen as they absorb everything, scarlet claws, high lip-gloss, the lot. For a woman of over fifty, her face and figure must give hope to thousands of women. Success returned when she was like a chameleon clinging to a slippery perch. Her long film career was drawing to an uneventful close when her sister, Jacky, wrote two novels, *The Stud* and *The Bitch*, that were turned into films. Joan's comeback became the springboard for *Dynasty* and Hollywood once more, although she resents the 'Superbitch' label. Off camera Joan is unselfconsciously natural.

During her marriage to Ron Kass, who laboured tirelessly in her interests and played no small part in the revival of her fortunes, their home in London reflected joint interests. Ron specialized in music, Joan was an avid collector of art nouveau pieces that in style mirrored her tastes. Certain items had special significance, recalling her friendship with the Kennedys. Treasures bought at Christie's and Sotheby's had pride of place. The bedroom was worthy of Alexis with silk wallpaper, pleated silk circular ceiling, ornate mirrors, several alluring photographs of Joan, an enormous water-bed with exquisite covering and a sauna in an adjoining room.

Her two children by Anthony Newley were motor-racing fans. In the basement was garaged a BRM go-cart that was polished daily. At Silverstone the high spot was to sit in the BRM cockpit. Both are now in their teens, Sacha at school in England and Tara in Paris. Ron's child Katy, narrowly escaped death in a car crash and was lovingly coaxed back to life by the joint devotion of Ron and Joan. Unfortunately the high-pressure artificiality of Hollywood and the publicity disadvantage of a settled domestic background proved too much and contributed to the break-up of the marriage.

In her London home Joan used to be utterly relaxed, casually dressed in a leotard and tracksuit with minimum make-up, yet still looked lovely. Both in public and private her image ignores the toll of time. How many women over fifty would dare to risk a *Playboy* feature-study, yet for sheer beauty the result was incredible. In *Dynasty* her predatory claws may be unsheathed in contrast to the deep-blue eyes and dazzling smile of Krystle Carrington from under a golden fringe, yet in reality both women are equally feminine. Alexis libels the real Joan Collins.

John Masefield OM

The duties of the Poet Laureate are open to debate. The popular view is that the public expects him to signalize in verse any occurrence of national importance. The minority identify the office as official recognition of poetic ability with no duty attached to it other than to continue to produce the quality of poetry that earned the award. Tennyson as Laureate was eminently successful in the first role. He adapted his powers to public themes by stimulating public imagination without incurring the displeasure of the purists. The precedent was too formidable for his successors. Robert Bridges took a strong line and antagonized the popular Press by arguing that the Laureate should not be expected to write poetic journalism.

When Bridges died in 1930, the Prime Minister had the difficult task of selecting a new Laureate from at least six well-known poets, any of whom could worthily have filled the office. Ramsay MacDonald played safe. He chose a poet of the people, one who was thoroughly English. Even so, John Masefield's succession to the Laureateship had a mixed reception. The reaction was nothing new. When Bridges succeeded Alfred Austin, an able journalist and innocuous versifier, the academic world was delighted, while the man-in-the-street asked, 'Who *is* Robert Bridges?' There was an equally petty reaction in some quarters when John Betjeman was made Laureate. He introduced an all-embracing range of subjects that he immortalized in verse: such diverse topics as chintz tea-shops, old churches, lilacs in the crescent, the Co-op, wrought-iron railings, branch railway lines and Metroland, seaside golf-clubs and Woolworths – his affectionate treatment of such unlikely themes had a charm of its own. His people were just as familiar. We all know

> Miss J. Hunter Dunn, Miss J. Hunter Dunn,
> Furnish'd and burnish'd by Aldershot sun,
> What strenuous singles we played after tea,
> We in the tournament – you against me!

Now, after Betjeman's death, we have the shy and retiring Ted Hughes as Poet Laureate. From the rural seclusion of a Devon farmhouse, he shuns the media, while the unpoetic majority enquire, 'Who *is* Ted Hughes?' The wheel has again come full circle, a repetition of the days when the academic world or, more accurately, the pseudo-intelligentsia asked with ironic emphasis, 'Who *is* John Masefield?' The aesthetic school disliked the selection of a realist as Laureate. Their opposition to Masefield was increased because he had made a bold attempt to widen the realistic class of poetry. Admittedly he was no poet for those who looked for purely aesthetic beauty. Critics who visualized poetry only in terms of static beauty and refused it any interpretation beyond itself, found it difficult to approach Masefield with sympathy. He dealt with a raw, rough world beyond their ken. At times his work was a contradiction in terms. It was not easy to assess a poet who could mix sublimity, crudeness, bathos and even trite triviality within a few stanzas, or even sometimes in a single stanza itself.

That first-class narrative poem, *The Everlasting Mercy* – probably the turning-point in Masefield's career – was his most characteristic achievement. It created a stir in 1911 similar to that produced by Byron's *Childe Harold* in 1812, or, perhaps a better parallel, by Swinburne's *Poems and Ballads* in 1866. It is one of the ironies of literary history that two poets as dissimilar as Swinburne and Masefield should have stirred up the same kind of sensation in their respective generations.

The originality and power of this study in conversation are undeniable. In stark realism, it depicts Saul Kane, the blackguard of a small Herefordshire town as he was before his redemption. In those days it was an innovation for poetry to follow a scoundrel into a pub, but actually to reproduce his blasphemies was unthinkable. Bernard Shaw's Eliza Doolittle had yet to shock polite society. Masefield went one better. He not only called a spade a spade, nor even a bloody shovel: he outraged current realism itself by such lines as:

> I'll bloody him a bloody fix
> I'll bloody burn his bloody ricks

As St John Adcock commented, no ruffian was ever heard to speak quite so elliptically. Still, it was a step in the right direction. Masefield had achieved the impossible. He made the British public read contemporary poetry, an event which had not occurred since the death of Tennyson. Here at last was a man who took Synge's advice and infused into his poetry the life he knew. Synge had said that before poetry could be real again, it must learn to be brutal; that there was no true poetry which had not its roots among the clay and the worms. Masefield faithfully followed the prescription and the foundation of his fame was laid.

Masefield was regarded by half-fledged intellects as antediluvian. Much of the criticism was superficial, part the reflection of genuine uncertainty. Masefield ignored cut-and-dried labels. Rigid traditionalists distrusted his experiments. Modernists found him too traditional. Lovers of beauty questioned the hesitant touch. Those who admired religious lyricism were hurt by his frankness. Masefield's career was one of extremes, both in his work and public reaction to it. There was never any half-measure about the criticism of his writing.

In a way the conflict was linked with the circumstances of his life and personality. An unhappy childhood in a lovely countryside made him realize the contrast between beauty and the things that mar it. The sea and seafaring folk made a mark upon the impressionable years of adolescence. Youth and early manhood left bitter memories. He had to fend for himself and live among people who toiled hard for their living by earning his own amongst them. It gave Masefield a lifelong, passionate sympathy with the under-dog and the unprivileged.

For years Masefield worked as a journalist and developed a quick, nervous prose which affected the whole of his literary activities. His output was tremendous. His collected poems are bulky. He wrote novels and a number of other prose works. The theatre knew him as historian and playwright. To these could be added his official efforts as Poet Laureate, conscientious poetic journalism limited in interest to the occasion that evoked them. Viewed in its entirety, the standard of his work fluctuated. Honesty compels the admission that Masefield was one of the most uneven writers of this century. That can be a sign of genius. Creative work in large quantities is bound to be uneven. No writer is judged by his minor work. Sibelius produced mighty symphonies. He was also responsible for innumerable *salon* pieces which Sir Arnold Bax described as not even vulgar. Masefield had obvious limitations, but throughout his work one dateless quality persisted – it was fervour. Hardly a poem was unmarked by it. The feeling swept through his writing like a mighty wind, spiced and heavy with sea-salt. Masefield's intermittent genius was that of a vigorous craftsman who never stopped work for fear of making a mistake.

When Masefield gave of his best and reached the peaks of inspiration, he found the mainspring to be his love of life and compassion for all that live it. In *Reynard the Fox* we have the finest English narrative poem of this century, and one of the greatest in our language. In itself it could epitomize a lifetime's work. The subject and setting gave Masefield full scope for all his powers. It is a sustained paean of fox-hunting with certain aspects that are puzzling. During one visit to his secluded house in Abingdon, we sat on his favourite bench by the river that flowed by the garden and I asked why he had avoided any reference to cruelty in this poem. In it the question is not discussed nor even mentioned. The hunt is neither attacked nor defended. It is accepted as a traditional English institution. To a question why he wrote the poem, Masefield explained that the fox-hunt gives an opportunity for a picture, or pictures, of the members of an English community. At a fox-hunt, and nowhere else in England, except perhaps a funeral, could you see the whole of the land's society brought together, focused for the observer as the Canterbury pilgrims were for Chaucer. It is impossible to gauge how posterity will assess this poet, but the odds are that this extrovert English poem will survive the years.

Sir Ralph Richardson

Ralph Richardson is remembered with affection. He was an eccentric in so many ways, unpredictable, tender, with an excitable voice that lent itself to extremes, and a ripe face compelling attention. As an actor he fell short of the sensitive interpretations of Lord Olivier and Sir John Gielgud, but in certain roles he was superb, as in Peer Gynt and Cyrano de Bergerac. The greatest performance was as Falstaff at the New Theatre when the Old Vic returned in 1944 from war exile to London. It was a peak of perfection.

In the seclusion of his delightful Regency house in a Nash terrace, Richardson was more relaxed. At such times he had an almost episcopalian appearance as he meandered round in benign fashion looking for a biretta. Maybe it was a throw-back to early days when his mother, who was a Catholic, hoped he would be a priest and sent him to a Jesuit seminary, but it didn't work out. That life was not for Richardson, yet he remained attracted by ritual.

Richardson had three enthusiasms. One was for his collection of antique pistols, for he had an intimate knowledge of early firearms. He would describe how the smallest type of firearm designed to be fired with one hand, was introduced about 1520, fitted at first with a wheel-lock, later snap-hammer, flint- and percussion-lock, but never a match-lock in Europe. There was so much to learn, so much to tell, even if the listener did not always appreciate the finer points of producing a revolving pistol and the fact that none was really successful until the invention of the Colt percussion revolver patented in 1836. He would say that nineteenth-century parsons were far more practical than their current counterparts, citing the Reverend Alexander Forsyth who took out the first patent for a percussion lock in 1807, the Church militant in action.

His affection for pets was pronounced. During the filming of *Dr Zhivago* in Spain, he became attached to a parrot and decided to buy it. The form for an import licence required a name to be given.

The bird was formally christened José Parrot and as such was always known. Other additions included a ferret known as Eddie, whose life-span was not long and was duly buried in the grounds, while a tame rat belonging to his wife, Meriel, was treated with loving care. In keeping with this love of animals, Richardson would recall in terms of horror how on going to the Oliviers' for dinner, he sat down heavily in a chair, thought it was exceptionally soft, and found he had killed their cat.

But Richardson's greatest joy outside the theatre was his 750-cc BMW motor cycle. Appreciation of speed came somewhat late in life. Not many turn to this form of travel in their seventies, but he would don a crash helmet, pipe stuck in his mouth, and roar off on the monster to exceed the ton-mark. Even on occasions he could be seen in the park with José Parrot perched on his shoulder, chugging along like a twentieth-century *Treasure Island* character. In his heart that was a natural role.

Peter Kapitza

It is not often that a leading Russian-born atomic scientist is welcomed to this country with genuine affection, but such was the experience of Peter Kapitza, the brains behind Russia's first A-bomb and satellites.

At the end of the 1914–1918 war Kapitza was sent by the Russian authorities to visit various laboratories on the Continent and buy or note any apparatus which might be of value to the Soviet Union. One such visit was to the Cavendish Laboratory in Cambridge where he met Professor Rutherford, who agreed to accept him as a research student. He made such spectacular progress that he was elected a Fellow of Trinity College five years later and eventually a Fellow of the Royal Society. Kapitza's work produced a magnetic field of far greater intensity than earlier ones. He constructed novel apparatus that could produce liquid helium and liquid hydrogen at temperatures near absolute zero. This, plus many more experiments were recognized by the Royal Society's appointment of a personal professorship and a grant from the Ludwig Mond Bequest for the building of the Mond Laboratory designed in particular for Kapitza's special work.

From 1926 onwards Kapitza made several visits to Russia leaving his wife and family in Cambridge, but always getting a written assurance from the Russian authorities that he would be allowed to return on a specified date. In 1934 he again visited Russia to attend a conference to honour the Soviet scientist Mendelleff, only this time he was ordered to stay and work in Russia, where he continued his researches, and in 1944 was awarded the Order of Lenin and in 1955 the Stalin Prize; but it was evident from letters that he resented his enforced status.

Thirty-two years later Kapitza returned to Cambridge, where he received a warm welcome from the Cavendish scientists and the handful who had previously worked with him. He described how he and his wife had tried to create an English style of life. A magnificent villa had been specially built near Moscow, surrounded by a rose-garden, a very English lawn and a tennis court. It was an attempt to capture something of the atmosphere of Newnham Cottage, Lord Rutherford's pleasant house with a large garden. In his study was a huge polar-bear skin on the floor, again repeating a Cambridge touch, while next door had been built a specially equipped laboratory. One luxury denied in Cambridge was a car and chauffeur, but at heart he preferred his old bike that he used to pedal along the Backs.

On thing he had not been able to copy was Rutherford's 'Talking Foursome', a group that used to play a form of golf on the Gog Magog course. There were eight members of this select company: Francis Aston, chairman of the International Committee on Atoms and Nobel Prize winner for Chemistry; Charles Darwin, Master of Christ's College; Charles Ellis, Wheatstone Professor of Physics; Ralph Fowler, Plummer Professor of Applied Mathematics; Frederick Mann, Reader in Organic Chemistry; Francis Roughton, John Humphrey Professor of Colloid Science; Richard Southwell, Rector of the Imperial College of Science; and Geoffrey Taylor, Yarrow Research Professor of the Royal Society. As Kapitza remarked, rarely could such a battery of brain-power have been applied to mastering the art of golf. The fact that they failed was some compensation, for on the two occasions that he played the results were catastrophic, possibly accentuated by the fact that he always took up a stance on the tee some forty-five degrees to the right of the required direction. A consequence was that he visited parts of the course that the others never knew existed. Judging by the tactics adopted by this academic eightsome, it would seem that Stephen Potter's gamesmanship had been anticipated.

Lord Beveridge

When Norman Fowler, as Social Services Secretary, published his proposed reforms, he described them as 'the most substantial examination of the social security system since Beveridge'. Whether the comparison meant much to the average person was a moot point. Not many know anything about the original Beveridge Report and even less about its architect, which is a pity for William Beveridge was a remarkable man, a visionary and tireless worker with Teutonic respect for detail and a highly developed awareness of the value of publicity if it helped him to get his own way.

When Fowler's Report appeared there were no queues at the Stationery Office, but the Beveridge Report, dryly entitled *Report on Social Insurance and Allied Services*, was a best-seller overnight. That response did not happen by chance. The timing of its release was psychologically right. British troops had just won their first major victory of the war at El Alamein. Beveridge sensed the mood of euphoria and launched a nationwide attack on the evils of want, disease, squalor, ignorance and unemployment. Acceptance of his Report could be the answer. It would substitute the haphazard approach to these injustices with a guaranteed free national health service, family allowances and a comprehensive system of social insurance with benefits paid at subsistence level as a statutory right. Public assistance would be transferred to the national exchequer, the whole system of income maintenance being supervised by a new Ministry of Social Security. The hated means test would wither away.

Beveridge crusaded passionately on a national scale, a campaign that displeased Whitehall overlords who deplored the chairman of a government enquiry using such publicity-seeking aids as well as his high-handed treatment of officials. Beveridge ignored the rebuff and persisted until the bulk of his proposals were made law by the post-war Labour Government. Its very success ensured continuation whatever government was in office. Beveridge was the father of the welfare state, though its growth has been different trom that which he visualized. For one thing, he did not advocate free hand-outs and was explicit about aims, assumptions, methods and figures. The target was abolition of want, which he measured in terms of weekly needs and costs throughout the life-cycle, but he also recognized that needs as well as costs would change with the times. There were obvious limitations to the blueprint, but it was strategic thinking on a grand scale. It had a touch of magic that captured the mood of the moment and still persists. Beveridge believed that the people of Britain wanted benefits in return for contributions rather than a free allowance from the State.

As to the man himself, Beveridge was many-sided. He never forgot the advice given to him by Edward Caird, the Master of Balliol: 'When you have learnt all that Oxford can teach you, go and discover why, with so much wealth in Britain, there continues to be so much poverty, and how poverty can be cured.' Beveridge took it to heart, not that hardship had ever been part of his life. Born in Rangpur, Bengal, he was a son of the Raj in a household run by twenty-six servants who looked after the needs of his father, a Judge on the district sessions, and his strong-minded mother described by George Bernard Shaw as 'the cleverest woman of my acquaintance and the wickedest in my opinion'. Be that as it may, there was no doubt about the formative influences of those early days. What emerged was not what his parents expected. At Oxford Beveridge distinguished himself academically as a scholar with a first in Greats, then he decided to become a social worker in the East End of London. Here it is necessary to define Beveridge's idea of social work. It was not a Ken Livingstone ego-trip into repressed minority groups or a bout of personal do-gooding, but an analysis of the area's social difficulties with a view to proposing solutions.

Once over a meal in his Oxford home, Beveridge recalled some of the personalities and events of those early years. He recalled his involvement in the problems of casual labour in the docks that led to Churchill summoning him to Whitehall where he created what became the Ministry of Labour and the first Labour Exchange; how during the First World War he was transferred to Munitions and later Food, where he introduced the system of rationing and price controls; and how Harold Wilson once worked for him as a researcher in the 1940s. In 1919 through his friendship with Beatrice and Sidney Webb, he was persuaded to become Director of the London School of Economics. He described it as a challenge, not always a happy one as he continually crossed swords with the left-wing LSE prophet, Harold Laski, a formidable opponent who never conceded. About this time he also clashed with Maynard Keynes. In the sphere of economics, theoretical and applied, Beveridge and Keynes were interesting contrasts, approaching their subject from different angles – Keynes the deductive economist beginning always from first principles, Beveridge always indirectly. Only on a few issues could he recall they had agreed.

Beveridge was generous in his praise of G. D. H. Cole, the Reader in Politics at Oxford, who unquestionably coloured his views during the years in the Master's Lodge at University College. The ambience there was gentle and he admitted missing the immediacy of politics and current affairs. In spite of his record, Beveridge was not a good committee man. He was too much a loner, both in public and private. A good example was the spell with Ernest Bevin when drawing up the schedule of reserved occupations. It was a turbulent association. Beveridge felt they were too abrasive to achieve any real rapport. Janet Beveridge, his dour Scottish wife, added that even Chruchill was wary of her husband. He acknowledged his brilliance but found him awkward and difficult. In 1941 Beveridge was relegated to committee work on social insurance in the hope it would keep him quiet. Instead with drafting skill and crusading vigour, he evolved the plan to provide government support from cradle to the grave. Unfortunately, four decades later it has grown out of hand. Taxpayers baulk at the rocketing costs, while those in need are often bewildered by its complexity. Critics argue that it saps individual drive and responsibility, while poverty persists in pockets and unemployment figures soar. It is these disturbing trends that Fowler attempted to stem and many aspects of his plan for a new, leaner welfare state would have met with Beveridge's approval.

Beveridge had a long life, but never thought of retiring. Before he died at the age of eighty-four he was still talking of future projects. I recall an occasion in the modest lounge of his Oxford flat with spring sunshine pouring through the windows. In an armchair sat a white-haired man with lean, ascetic features, gentle of voice and courteous of manner, a figure outwardly more suited to the study and college common-room than a political platform, but the truth was different. Political ambition had made him Liberal Member for the Berwick-upon-Tweed Division of Northumberland, but it was of short duration, an all-too-brief spell in Westminster when he made eight telling speeches in the House in six months. It was ironic. He surrendered two attractive posts with salaries and other amenities for a political career, then ten months later he was in the wilderness without an income and cut off from former occupations and friends. Even Edinburgh was too remote from London. His dilemma was almost anticipated in his farewell address to undergraduates at University College when he said that what he had planned to do in life had again and again been prevented by events beyond his control, yet on each occasion he found something else worth doing.

This train of thought came out in *Power and Influence*, a fascinating book that mirrored Beveridge's mind and character, but stopped short of self-portraiture. Not a line expressed hesitation, not a page let us watch him making up his mind. It was always made up when he put pen to paper. He explained motives and reasons for having acted in a certain manner, but we were given the results rather than the processes of deliberation. That Beveridge was extraordinarily impartial, that he was a scholar was clear to everyone, yet it would be wrong to suggest he was a scholar pitch-forked into active life. The cast of his intellect and imagination was essentially that of a man of action. I have mentioned his courteous manner, yet at times he surprised by the dryness and curtness of his comments. He had a knack of brushing aside what was insignificant. The reluctance, in private as well as public, to discuss what was not clear to him was the manifestation of a fundamental characteristic, namely a perfect integrity of mind. Many men's writing is the spoken word on paper, merely titivated commenting. Beveridge actually spoke the language of the pen. It left the listener with nothing to do but understand.

On my last visit to him I caught a glimpse of another side to his nature, a personal introspective aspect, reflecting the essence of what he really believed. He described how he was brought up as an agnostic without acceptance of any Christian dogma. The doctrine of personal immortality, 'perhaps the most pervasive of all Christian beliefs', meant little to him. On the other hand, belief in the impossibility of escaping what Samuel Butler of *Erewhon* described as vicarious immortality seemed to him to be important, ever since he read the doctrine set out in one of Butler's sonnets which he quoted:

> Not on sad Stygian shore, nor in clear sheen
> Of far Elysian plain, shall we meet those
> Among the dead whose pupils we have been,
> Nor those great shades whom we have held as foes.

We shall not argue saying, ' 'Twas thus' or 'Thus',
Our argument's whole drift we shall forget;
Who's right, who's wrong, 'twill be all one to us;
We shall not even know that we have met.
Yet meet we shall, and part, and meet again,
Where dead men meet, on lips of living men.

Beveridge felt that belief in vicarious immortality was a strong moralizing doctrine. It discouraged selfishness, idleness, arrogance, vulgar ambition and cruelty. If we wanted our successors to think kindly of us when we were dead, we had to act kindly in our lives. But though the Christian dogma never meant anything to him, the personality and spirit of Christ meant much. He recalled how towards the end of his undergraduate days at Oxford, Edward Caird told him of a sum of money which the College had at their disposal to promote serious study of Christianity. Beveridge was asked if he would like to be endowed for this purpose. The offer was declined, but the suggestion led to making for himself a study of the life and character of Christ as shown in the Synoptic Gospels. He came to feel that here was one of the greatest personalities in human history with a greatness the more impressive because it had to be seen through the minds of very ordinary men. He described how he happened from Monte Mottarone in the Italian lakes, to see Monte Rosa twenty-five miles away shining through drifting mists, and looking all the larger and more overwhelming because of the mists. He made the simile that Christ was all the more superhuman, if ever any man was, by the way he shone through peasant minds.

Beveridge is remembered by those who knew him for his buoyant freshness. Nothing is more precious than a radical voice, influential and persuasive enough to command a national audience and force politicians to pause and think again. Taking decisions on his initiative was the breath of life. One possible weakness might be mentioned: it was a refreshing, if tactless habit when exasperated of not hiding his opinion of people he was working with. If there were reactions, he would shrug his shoulders and get on with the job in his own way and always got it done. Invariably the rebuke was justified.

Gordon Craig

Gordon Craig was the last of the great Edwardians. His influence on the theatre was so far ahead of its time that even today some of his ideas would be considered too daring to be economically viable. He maintained that true drama should be the creation of one man, who would be responsible for the words, décor, lighting and music, the designer ranking above actor or dramatist. He put such theories to the test. *The Lady from the Sea* gave a glimpse of a new sense of beauty and imagination and emphasized the potential loftiness of theatrical art by creating with pure simplicity, shadowy settings with soaring arches. It was a revolt against the extravagant staging of his time, its realism and lack of imagination. Craig had a rare diversity of genius in practical affairs. His ambition was to have a theatre like Henry Irving and the Lyceum but that needed finance and no manager was prepared to take the risk – at least in London. Continental reaction was different. Across the Channel, Craig was recognized as a brilliant and seminal theatrical designer, who had introduced a fresh element in interpretation.

His style and theories were unmistakable and had influenced men like Reinhardt and Stanislavsky. Particularly outstanding was the staging of *Venice Preserved* in the Lessing Theatre in Berlin; Eleanora Duse in *Rosmersholm* in Florence, and a revolutionary modern production of *Hamlet* at the Moscow Arts Theatre. W. B. Yeats declared that Craig's purple backcloth made the *Dido and Aeneas* of Purcell seem like wandering on the edge of eternity.

This type of artistic work was not what had originally been planned. His mother, Ellen Terry, whose illegitimate son he was, felt that he had real talent as an actor. For eight years he was a member with his mother of Irving's company and went on their second tour of America in 1885. Eventually Ellen Terry gave him the chance of producing *The Vikings* by Ibsen. It won praise from Count Kessler for its beauty, but the show lost money. The same thing happened with *Much Ado About Nothing*. That was the last time Craig produced a play in England, though he had the possibility of doing so years later when C. B. Cochran invited him to tackle a new play of his own devising. Unfortunately they could not agree on terms and Craig left these shores for good. His home thereafter was to be with foreigners.

It was exile in pursuit of his ideal theatre. In this direction Craig's influence was through such books as *The Art of the Theatre* and *Towards a New Theatre*, the periodical *The Mask* which he issued from Florence between 1908 and 1929; through designs like those in an edition of *Hamlet* published at Weimar in 1930; through graphic work, lectures and broadcasts. During the First World War he lived in Rome. He was in France in 1939 when the Nazis arrived. He was interned but later released by the intervention of a German Intelligence officer who was sympathetic to Craig's work, and spent the rest of the war in his Paris studio. In later years he moved from Rapallo to Saint Germain-en-Laye, and then to Vence. It was there that I met him for the last time.

Parking the car by the Place du Grand Jardin, I entered the town by the Porte de Pyre and found myself in the forum of the Roman city of Vinticum, now a delightful little square with a fountain in the shape of an urn and a high square stone tower. Vence has a history of its own. Here it was that D. H. Lawrence died of tuberculosis after being rushed from a nursing-home in Bandol. Its bishops have included two Saints in St Veran and St Lambert, as well as a future Pope in the famous Alexander Farnese, better known as Paul III. Also linked with it is the convent of White Sisters, Dominican nuns who nursed Matisse through a long and serious illness. Though a freethinker, Matisse built the Chapel of the Rosary as a token of his gratitude and decorated it himself. The Chapel was consecrated in 1951 when Matisse was an octogenarian.

To this august company was added the name of Gordon Craig. Although a great age, he still had grace of manner, courtesy and charm. Deep lines etched his features, the body was slightly bent, but his mind was active, almost over-active. Words tumbled out in bubbling enthusiasm. The famous Terry voice added to the effect. The house was insignificant, a small *pension de famille*, with his room cluttered with memorabilia. Every item had significance. Masks he had carved hung on the walls. There were books on the Italian theatre, day-books and journals; notes written in fine calligraphy with tiny thumbnail sketches; prints, letters and designs; miniature model theatres; his printing press surrounded by a clutter of pencils; and Irving's walking-stick that he thumped to get silence on the Lyceum stage. On a shelf by a brass bedstead was a photograph of his lovely mother worthy of the description. Gordon was the second child of Edward William Godwin, an architect, but when the relationship soured, his mother married Charles Clavering Wardell, and it was as Edward Wardell that Craig went to school near Tunbridge Wells, later to Bradfield College and Heidelberg. *Craig* was adopted as a stage name after the island Ailsa Craig.

Conversation in that room of shadows was like a commentary, interspersed with questions about England. Although a self-imposed exile, it was obvious that past associations were still meaningful, Knowing of my links with Cambridge, he talked about Clive Bell, E. M. Forster, Gwen Raverat and George 'Dadie' Rylands of King's. He switched the topic to Stevenage. Did I know that he was born in Railway Street in 1872? He was quite sure that Stevenage Council neither knew nor cared about the fact. After all, plenty of people had been born in that mean little street. He talked about Denham where he lived after his first marriage when it was little more than a village. It was there that William Nicholson taught him how to use a wood-engraver's block and tools and print proofs, tutelage that inspired more than 500 wood engravings for scenes and costumes in his books. He also recalled with pleasure the hours spent as an unknown young man with W. B. Yeats in his room off the Euston Road, evenings spent discussing poetic drama – it was all so long ago.

Age had not dulled other memories. Details were clear. Even by *Dynasty* and *Dallas* standards, Craig's private life was colourful and tempestuous. Women were attracted to him like bees to honey. Fated to have a series of liaisons, he was not a man to side-step a challenge. His first marriage was a disaster, but May Gibson, an actress, still produced four children in four years before it broke up. Then Elena Meo, a violinist, took over and came to live with him. The relationship was happy, a son and daughter were born, until a split was caused by a whirlwind affair with Isadora Duncan, an infatuation that added another daughter. Isadora was an inspiration, the most vital creature in Craig's life. Isadora expressed her feelings in writing: 'He was one of the few people I have ever met who was in a state of exaltation from morning till night. Even with his first cup of coffee his imagination caught fire and was sparkling, even though he talked incessantly . . . he was one of the most extraordinary geniuses of an epoch, a creature, like

Shelley, made of fire and lightning.' There were other emotional entanglements, but by comparison none of lasting effect. Craig never married Elena, but when she died in 1957 in England, the memory of the affection was kept alive when their daughter came to live with him in Vence.

It was ironical that this isolated, ill-furnished room should have been the final resting-place of a man of such profound scholarship, a genius who created a legend bigger than himself. At least he had the satisfaction of knowing that his methods had borne fruit all over Europe. His staging of Ibsen's *The Pretender* in Copenhagen had been rewarded by the Order of the Knight of Dannesburg in 1930, then in 1958 he was made a Companion of Honour, but regretted he did not receive the royal bestowing personally because he could not afford the fare to come to England. Even so, there was no bitterness or pathos at being neglected. After all, as he said, be brought it on himself, but the recollection of the public banquet given in his honour in London in 1911 still gave him satisfaction. They were all there, he chuckled, all 200 of them, artists, musicians and men of letters. Among those who paid tribute to his work, he singled out Augustus John, H. G. Wells, Max Beerbohm, Laurence Binyon, W. B. Yeats and his mother. That night compensated for many barbed comments.

When I asked how he would like to be remembered, Craig's answer was simple: 'As the first prophet of a new order in the theatre.' That wish was realized.

Dame Edith Sitwell

Edith Sitwell was the most unusual woman I have known. She defied all categories. Completely uncontemporary, she was like a Plantagenet time-capsule, living the role and playing the part. In appearance she was unforgettable. A tall woman, slightly bent, with distinguished nose, rare Gothic head, grey-green eyes, slender hands bedecked with enormous rings of semi-precious stones and features carved as if out of alabaster. Very conscious of her aristocratic lineage, she could have been a stand-in for Elizabeth I.

Throughout her life Edith Sitwell was a controversialist in the class of Whistler. Life was a battle and she never laid down her arms. At times she could be witheringly cold, but the other side of her nature, shown only to close friends, was light-hearted, eccentric to the point of absurdity and revelling in a gift of fantasy particularly when planning new ways to annoy Dr Leavis. There was also a tenderness of heart that repeatedly came through her poems. There was nothing snobbish about her and she was entirely without arrogance. Her real image was obscured by a misleading, contradictory public persona.

Edith Sitwell had a long memory. To the end of a life rich with honours, she never forgot the bitter recollections of childhood and youth. Her father, the trying Sir George, resented her sex, her mother disliked her unconventional beauty. If only Edith had been a son and heir or even a pretty débutante, but she was neither. She was not conventionally pretty nor conventional in any other way. As a result, childhood was remembered as a hell. It left her a lonely, vulnerable, high-bred child fighting for identity and independence, but in the end it was a losing struggle to assert herself as a poet in the social milieu of her family home. Only when her gifted brothers grew up did she receive sympathetic under-standing and support. There is no doubt she suffered intensely from these disagreements.

Her poems are not always easy to understand. The flights of

metaphor at times are difficult to interpret. Yeats summed it up when he said she brought back into literature the rare quality of fantasy, wit and verbal dignity. A tenderness of heart runs constant like a golden thread, while her later poems are pre-occupied with the conflict of life and death. Over-emphasis on how she fought back as a poet against the philistines tends to overshadow the vital part she played in the literary revolution of the 1920s against the dead patterns of the Georgian poetry of that time, and how perceptive she was in her early championship of young poets like Dylan Thomas and Pavel Tinilitehin. Her association with Sir William Walton, who wrote the music for the poem-sequence *Façade*, resulted not only in a setting to music, but a fresh satirical-fantastic invention that still delights by its gaiety and freshness of imagery. This poem-cycle was first performed privately at the brothers' home in Chelsea. The private hearing was so well received that Osbert Sitwell was persuaded to stage a public performance at the Aeolian Hall in 1923. So that the audience should not be distracted by the personality of the reciter, a curtain was painted with a design of three primitive archways. In two of these were masks with stentorphones in their mouth. Behind the centre one of a huge female with closed eyes and open mouth, Edith Sitwell was stationed. Osbert stood behind the smaller mask. His task was to make announcements and explanations. Edith Sitwell's recitations were accompanied by the Walton music. Uproar broke out among the audience. *Façade* was not repeated until 1926 when the public reversed its opinion. In July 1952, Edith Sitwell received a tremendous ovation from a huge audience when it was performed in the Royal Festival Hall, London. Such is the vindication by time, the arch-critic.

It is significant that few women in English literature have made their name as poets. Only four or five are worthy of mention, and of those in English poetry only Christina Rossetti can be placed in the same category as Edith Sitwell, who was acknowledged by all, except a handful of biased critics, as a poet whose work within its limits was the product of a master-hand. Such plaudits were not easily won. It was a long and obdurate fight with an uncompre-hending public. There were times when Edith Sitwell's work, as it developed along its individualistic line, tended to outstrip the general understanding. Insensitive hearing is responsible for much of the adverse criticism of modernist poetry. Many of her images startled, but only by such bold blending could thought be refashioned.

Apart from the satirical-fantastic inventions of *Façade*, it is interesting to isolate instances of Edith Sitwell's extreme sensitivity, the flashes of beauty, and at times the exquisite gentleness of spirit that finds expression in rich poetic fullness. The elegiac, romantic vein in *The Sleeping Beauty*; the nostalgia of *Colonel Fantock*; the haunting rustic elegy *The Little Ghost Who Died for Love* with its lingering sadness; and the sweeping rhymes and powerful rhythms of *Gold Coast Customs* that showed a different side to her genius. It was in effect a powerful poetic denunciation of the heartlessness of the privileged in a world where the unprivileged majority could be subjected to abominable suffering. Some indication of the range of Edith Sitwell's poetic powers can be seen in the cold irony of 'Serenade'; Marlowe's famous poem which opens with the line, 'Come live with me and be my love' is transposed into the vision of Europe at war. The lover is unfaithful because he is 'the cannon's mate' and 'death's cold puts the passion out', and the only serenade is 'the wolfish howls the starving made'. Compare this poem with the frightful symbolism of 'Lullaby', where the only thing left in the world is the monster, the Babioun, which sings to the abandoned child on a devastated earth:

> Do, do, do, do —
> Thy mother's hied to the vaster race;
> The Pterodactyl made its nest
> And laid a steel egg in her breast —
> Under the Judas-coloured sun,
> She'll work no more, nor dance, nor moan,
> And I am come to take her place
> Do, do.

On one occasion I had a meal with Edith Sitwell in a small hotel situated in a corner of George Street. Its quietness and feeling of routine continuity appealed to her more than the ostentatiousness of their West End counterparts. She talked of her fondness for metaphor, how some purists of slow imagination were unhappy when she maintained that 'the fire was furry as a bear'; that the rain was 'grey as a guinea-fowl, squawking down from the boughs'; that 'the morning light creaks down'. Such carpings were childish. I asked if she could isolate one poem as her favourite. The choice was one written during the air-raids on this country in 1940, and five lines in particular:

Still falls the Rain —
Dark as the world of man, black as your loss —
Blind as the nineteen hundred and forty nails
Upon the cross.
Still falls the Rain . . .

The interpretation was clear. The falling of the bombs as a rain she likened to the falling of blood from Christ's side, a symbol of punishment and redemption through suffering.

Whatever the source or the subject, Edith Sitwell always observed her poetic credo: 'I believe that a poem begins in the poet's head, and then grows in his blood, as a rose grows among its dark leaves.' In her appearance as in her poetry, Edith Sitwell was triumphantly herself. Her creative impulse was both quiescent and receptive. The physical and spiritual attributes essential to a poet were present. At times so deep was her emotional nature that she took upon herself an attitude of detachment which permitted her to view mankind against a vast background, and from that vision to satisfy her own soul. Her life added emphasis to the fact that poetry is a lonely occupation. Her public mask was an attitude of detachment that concealed an emotional nature. The difference between Edith Sitwell and her poetic sisters was that she hunted the Infinite alone, while they hunted in packs.

The few privileged to know this rare woman when that Gothic mask was lifted were indeed fortunate. Alas, I was not of their number.

Bernard Darwin

All lovers of elegant writing appreciated the pen of Bernard Darwin. A golfer of a later generation once asked if I could describe what kind of man he was, adding, 'He must have been quite a character because older players talk so highly of him, yet I cannot find his name in the records as having won any of the major amateur events.' He was right. Darwin did not hit the headlines like many leading players but for many years his pen and voice were the essence of golf, while in his prime he was a player of distinction. I once tried to compose a pen-portrait of him for my own satisfaction. I let him see the jottings for his comments. Slightly modified, they provide the answer with Darwin's observations as a postscript.

'I am at Trinity,' said a Cantab to a Londoner. 'Trinity, Cambridge, or Trinity, Oxford?' asked the latter. The former, with insolent calm, replied, 'Trinity!' In like fashion Darwin eyed the *other place* ever since he was *in statu pup* in 1894. He was partisan and unashamed, particularly when it came to university golf, rugby football and the Boat Race. The current Dark Blue duplicity on the Thames would have left him speechless. Some people regarded such bias as madness but it was an honest frenzy and in your own kingdom you had the right to be mad. The Darwinian kingdom was a world on its own.

Golf knew Darwin as a writer. He wrote upon the game in *The Times* for over forty years, wielding his pen with the touch of Lamb and the vividness of Hazlitt. But there was more to Darwin than his essays. Eton, Cambridge and the Temple formed his early background. In the First World War he spent two-and-a-half years at Salonica. Although a barrister and fully qualified solicitor, he found the lure of golf too strong, not solely as a scribe, but as a performer. He was in the English team against Scotland on eight occasions, played for England against the United States in 1922 at Long Island, was twice semi-finalist in the Amateur Championship, won the President's Putter in 1922 and the

Worplesdon Foursomes in 1933 with Joyce Wethered. By any standard it was a proud record.

Every good writer tells you a great deal about himself though he writes ostensibly only about other people. Occasionally Darwin raised a corner of the curtain. In one delightful essay we were taken on a conducted tour of his small study in the house at Downe – a village in Kent which has seen the family name of Darwin become great in English thought and letters – and let the walls speak for themselves. 'You see what a domestic character I am,' said Charles Surface as he walked into his picture-room. 'Here I sit of an evening surrounded by my family.' The analogy was well chosen. We could say that as the Darwinian pen moved lightly across the paper the words were read by a goodly company of the champions of the past – prize-fighters, runners, walkers, a few cricketers and a single tennis player of surpassing elegance in a frizzled white wig.

It was Stevenson who said that one of the most deeply rooted things in the English character is the love of sailors and prize-fighters. The latter were certainly held in high esteem by Darwin; so much so that his quiet enthusiasm was almost naïve. At times no one would have suspected him of ever wearing his heart upon his sleeve. The polyhedral nature of that rugged organ does not lend itself readily to public exposure, but when Darwin took us into his confidence the effect was like a warm breath of the uncloyed pleasures of youth. I believe that as Darwin saw this company in his mind, so they lived outside and he refused to credit that they must have changed at times after their fights and sporting triumphs into shabby suits and greasy caps. He was not alone in his fantasy; most of us have moods of nostalgia, even for that which we have loved only by hearsay.

It would not be true to say that Darwin was without critics. A few belittled his writings on golf on the ground that his style was old-fashioned, verbose and overburdened with quotations. The attempts of these gentlemen to express themselves as they imagine golf should appear in print usually produces the type of journalism that justifies its own existence by the Darwinian principle of the survival of the most vulgar.

The charge of over-quoting must be examined more closely. A writer who lards his prose with the fat of other men is a sitting target for criticism. Anyone can go to a bookshelf and write an article round a handful of saws. Darwin was not of their company. His quotations enriched the reader's mind rather than embellished his own essay. Nor did he carry a Dickens concordance in his pocket. One point I was curious about. Some years ago the editor of a national newspaper told me that Darwin's quotations were sometimes a headache to *The Times* subbing staff. During the heat of a championship only the beginning of a quotation, not always accurate, was written. The gaps had to be filled in by some unfortunate underling in Printing House Square. I often thought of that libellous accusation as I watched Darwin writing his report by hand in the corner of the Royal and Ancient writing-room against a background of hubbub.

One of Darwin's favourite quotations was, 'Golf, thou art a gentle sprite, I owe thee much.' The words were written by the author of *The Golfing Manual* in 1857. Well over a century later we of this and earlier generations of golfers could have said to Darwin, 'We owe thee much.'

Darwin read my notes and penned this postscript:

Louis Stanley has bidden me write a brief postscript to his notes, giving my views of his views on myself. When the winner makes a speech after a tournament, he always begins by saying he has been very lucky and thereby he becomes a great bore. I will not imitate him by saying that Louis Stanley has been much too kind and flattering, although of course he has. There are two small points on which I may put forward not a defence but a mild suggestion. As to my being a Cambridge partisan, I certainly am and proud of it, but Oxford men know that my hatred of them, for just two days in the year, is at worst only skin deep. For all the other days I love them dearly and there is no honour I prize more than that which they paid me in making me an honorary member of the Divots.

Nobody has ever accused me of caring two pins whether an Oxford or a Cambridge man won the President's Putter. 'We don't recognize such distinctions here,' said Mr John Smanker at the Bath Swarry and there are certainly none such in the Society. That brings me to my other point. Of course I quote too much. Nobody knows it better than I do but it is the language I think in. But if ever my quotations reached *The Times* office in disarray, as has been hinted, it was the fault not of my memory but of my handwriting. The Post Office officials could not read it nor do I in the least blame them.

It was a sad day for golf when Darwin's pen was stilled.

Tom Mix

At the time of the Munich crisis, when Chamberlain thought he had checked Nazi aggression, I had occasion to show the veteran film star Tom Mix something of the sights of Edinburgh. Some actors and actresses are dumb without a script. Speech becomes a foreign language, a Pyrrhic victory over silence, but there was no such inhibition about the American. Still a dynamic figure, he had a zest for life, a healthy ego, and awareness of history as befitted a survivor from the Nickelodeon Era. He was a sucker for tradition. The pinnacles, towers, spires and turrets, the Castle and the Royal Mile became Scotland in miniature. He was fascinated by Canongate with its dark wynds, gloomy closes, stone courtyards and towering tenements with women shouldering baskets of clothes on their way to the public wash-houses. The nearest he had seen to this had been in Naples.

Ghosts of the past were everywhere. Here a Queen walked; there a Reformer thundered; that was where the Young Pretender passed; here was where Mary, Queen of Scots, spent her last night in Edinburgh; under that roof lived Robert Burns; in that cellar were signed the Articles of Union between England and Scotland; Sir Walter Scott dined there; Montrose was led past here on his way to execution; Oliver Cromwell lived in that house; over there was buried Adam Smith; here the small room in the Castle where Mary, Queen of Scots, gave birth to the infant who became James I of England and VI of Scotland; and in the courtyard of the Assembly Hall the fulminating figure of John Knox. It was all grist to Mix's imagination. Back in the Caledonian Hotel, we were joined by Dr Brasnett, one of Scotland's leading theologians, who, although not socially conscious, was always ready to talk about the world in general. It soon became clear that the name of Tom Mix recalled childhood memories, so much so that we were invited to lunch the following day to Coates Hall, the theological college of the Episcopal Church of Scotland of which he was Principal.

The meal in the austere hall brought together two contrasting personalities from totally different backgrounds. Brasnett, scholar and theologian, lived a cloistered life dictated by moral and spiritual disciplines, but curious about the happenings outside the seminary. Mix came from a world apart. Twice a real-life sheriff, Texas Ranger for three years, soldier of fortune in the Boer War, he fought in the American Army in the Spanish-American War and Boxer Rebellion. Mix described how he made his first movie in Oklahoma in 1910, when the Selig Company, out of Chicago, hired him as an extra, but the big chance came when William S. Hart, who preferred realism to the contrived, announced his retirement. Mix took over in more romanticized versions of the West, simple dramas of heroism in which he was cast as the puritan of the plains, distracted neither by scheming women nor good whisky. He was at pains to point out that he never used doubles for stunts, galloped his own horse, and handled cattle stampedes. Dicey at times, but the risk became an end in itself. Those days had gone for ever. There were no regrets. At times he felt they had never been.

The American was intrigued by Dr Brasnett, who looked every inch a parson and acted accordingly. He admitted that the Church had never figured in his life. Ministers of God were like professional spectacle-makers who tried to make sort-sighted folk see the invisible. Somehow it didn't work; maybe he was biased, possibly reaction to the influence of his parents who were puritanical in outlook, full of queer inhibitions, interpreted the Bible literally, and believed in miracles. That was a stumbling-block. He could never take those fairy tales. Why should God suspend the natural order by direct intervention?

The lessons life had taught him were not cheerful ones. He felt that cruelty played a major part in the make-up of the larger proportion of mankind and when suffering is widespread it generates callousness. He argued that nationalism had been a curse. He used to think that the American Declaration of Independence hit the right note when it says that all men are created equal; that they are endowed by their Creator with certain inalienable rights; that among these were life, liberty and the pursuit of happiness. It sounded fine, but proved unworkable. Instead of equality, there was diversity, social conditions deciding what was the right kind of life to live and the means to pursue it. The known was left to science, the unknown and unknowable to religion. He believed that Christianity and Buddhism had suffered by their isolation from each other.

Brasnett listened with interest throughout the meal and did nothing to stem the flow. Mix admitted that this was the first time he had ever talked in such detail about personal beliefs; in a way it had been a kind of confessional. His host was a stranger and a priest. Normally such thoughts were kept to oneself. Those who indulged in them looked set for a home. His creed was simple and had little to do with organized religion. He was often reminded of a beautiful legend known by the primitive natives of Australia. They believed that a conspicuous dark patch of the Milky Way in the constellation of the Southern Cross and known to seamen as the 'coal-sack', was the entrance into the star-lit dome of their heaven. The trail of a shooting star was believed to be the rope which a blackfellow climbs before he dies. He carries the loose end of the rope with him as he moves upward. When he reaches the roof he throws the rope down again as the streak of a shooting star to be grasped by another blackfellow whom it touches. It was a long climb to the top of the dome and difficult to get through the hole in it, but even after this had been done another journey, just as long, had to be made over the roof to come back again to the flat earth, this time as a black ancestor bleached by age into a whitefellow.

Mix felt that the story was symbolic of human life and its immortal spirit. Everyone has to climb up the rope and must throw the loose end down again for another to use. How high our heavens were above our earthly selves depended upon our conceptions of them, and the efforts made to reach them, measured not in terms of self-help but of service to others. Theoretically he believed such sentiments, but was conscious that he had fallen far short. Success plays havoc with good intentions. His home was more suited for a cattle baron than a cowboy. Originally his ambition had been to outdo the 'Falcon's Lair' of Rudolph Valentino and 'Pickfair' of Douglas and Mary Pickford, but such chapters were a thing of the past like the Keystone Kops and Blanche Sweet. Brasnett commented that there were allegoric truths in his legend, though possibly a simpler version might be to say that as a community we are like a ship in which everyone ought to be prepared to take the helm.

So ended a lunch that at least one of those present remembered for a long time.

Arnold Toynbee

The restricted vision of the human race is such that for most men experience is like the stern lights of a ship which illumine only the track it has passed. Among such men Arnold Toynbee was certainly not numbered. To many in England his name was only vaguely familiar, and frequently misplaced. This professional historian was far better known in America, where the abridged edition of his *magnum opus*, *A Study of History*, was a best-seller. I might add that Arnold Toynbee did not found Toynbee Hall. That honour belonged to his uncle. He was a Protestant, and not, as was often averred, a Roman Catholic. He came from a remarkable family in which every member displayed rare intellectual gifts. One uncle, Paget, was the great Dante scholar; another, Arnold, was the historian and economist; his grandfather was an eminent surgeon; his mother had several histories to her credit.

Arnold Toynbee, born in 1889, traced his career through Winchester, a Balliol scholarship, Classical Greats, and a Balliol Fellowship in Ancient History. He married the daughter of Professor Gilbert Murray. Three years as a don convinced him that he preferred scholarship to the grind of teaching, a conviction that altered the course of his career. Following a brief spell as Professor of Byzantine and Modern Greek at London University he turned to Chatham House in 1925 and became Director of Studies at the newly founded Institute of International Affairs. In time the names became synonymous. Chatham House and Arnold Toynbee were virtually one and the same. It was there that I first met him, against the background that became his life's work.

Quiet in voice and gesture, a stooping scholarly figure, with vivid white hair and noble profile, Toynbee possessed that graceful and endearing attribute *politesse du coeur* in such perfection that it was hard, for all but a few, to tell where courtesy ended and heart began. His attitude was that of a man who disliked and distrusted introspection, which could be daunting to anyone who would attempt to expound him. As in the case of other men of subtle intellect, his feelings were probably a great deal simpler than people found it easy to believe.

His talk was that of a man who had more faith in facts than theories, more interest in records than conjecture. Though he enjoyed cleverness, he never regretted its absence in a companion he liked. He seemed to suffer little from boredom, that common complaint of uncommon men. Many people's writing is the spoken word on paper, merely titivated conversation, but Toynbee actually spoke the language of the pen. His diction was plain, very accurate, succinct, yet full and rounded. It was formal and traditional rather than personal. It reflected not passing moods, but habits of thought and feeling. The senses contributed nothing to its vigour, which was intellectual, nor was it at all indebted to random meditation for richness. It aimed at definition rather than suggestion. He was extremely fastidious about the written word, giving everything he wrote the double polish; that which removed from the surface of style the roughness and inexactness of improvisation, and that which strove to obliterate traces of laborious care. He could conduct on paper a long train of reasoning with elegant eloquence. Toynbee's place among historians is assured. The double task of writing contemporary history in the annual *Survey of International Affairs* and universal history in *A Study of History* formed a unique undertaking and achievement.

After the First World War, Toynbee was a member of the British delegation at the Peace Conference. In the Second World War he again entered the Foreign Office, becoming Director of the Foreign Office Research Department, and in 1946 was once more a British delegate to a Paris Peace Conference. The experiment was not entirely happy and it was with a measure of relief that he returned to the more scholarly atmosphere of Chatham House, the Royal Institute of International Affairs, which, in striking contrast to the majority of established institutions in this country cannot lay claim to ancient lineage. Some sixty years have passed since its inception. Those years, however, have witnessed a series of momentous events in world history which have added significance to the activities of the Institute and have enabled it to establish a record of achievement, for the most part unknown to the general public, which qualified it to rank on terms of equality with better-known learned bodies of more ancient foundation.

One of the more positive consequences of the First World War was that an important change took place in the attitude of the great nations towards foreign relationships. It was to this change that Chatham House owes its existence. Before 1914 the governments of all the major Powers tended to assume that in the conduct of foreign affairs it was the duty of each to think almost exclusively in terms of national interest, and to frame its policy accordingly. In other words, in every country in varying degree, the tendency was towards thinking nationally rather than internationally.

During the Peace Conference of 1919 the necessity for a wider vision of international relationships became clearly evident. The need was recognized for a permanent organization for the collection, study and dissemination of accurate and specialized information about matters of international concern. As a result of the efforts of such men as Lord Robert Cecil, Lionel Curtis, Lord Eustace Percy and Geoffrey Dawson, the British Institute of International Affairs, as it was originally called, was inaugurated on 5 July 1920. The Institute opened its headquarters in Malet Street, Bloomsbury, in 1921, but moved two years later to St James's Square, to a beautiful old house, a historic building with appropriate associations, for among the famous people who had lived there at various times were the elder Pitt, Lord Chatham, and later, two great Prime Ministers in Lord Derby and Mr Gladstone.

Such was Arnold Toynbee's background. He used it to analyse in his writing the reasons for the widespread breakdowns that occurred in his generation. This capacity for incisive, almost prophetic insight and objectivity placed him alongside the leading historians of the nineteenth century – de Tocqueville, Acton and Burckhardt. In his first book in 1915 he predicted that another world war would result if Germany were deprived of the Polish Corridor. Elsewhere in the same book he put forward the suggestion that America should be responsible for the administration of the Black Sea Straits, a suggestion that found its echo in the Truman Doctrine. 1934 saw Toynbee anticipate a prostrate Japan dominated by America.

In the light of such predictions, it is interesting to recall some of the points in Toynbee's analysis of the future, as when at Princeton he spoke of the possible results of mankind having discovered how to tap atomic energy before we succeeded in abolishing war. Taking the pessimistic view that the future could be catastrophic, he prophesied that the future might well lie with the Tibetans and the Eskimos, because each of these people occupied an unusually sheltered position. By sheltered he meant sheltered from the dangers arising from human agency, not sheltered from the rigours of the physical environment. He pointed out that mankind had been master of his physical environment, sufficiently for practical purposes, since the middle palaeolithic age; since that time, man's only dangers had come from man himself. But the homes of the Tibetans and the Eskimos are sheltered no longer and could be drawn into a future Russo-American war.

If mankind was going to commit suicide in an atomic war, Toynbee looked ahead and speculated that salvaging of a fraction of the current heritage of mankind might centre on a remote peoples like the Negrito Pygmies of Central Africa. Their eastern cousins in the Philippines and in the Malay Peninsula would probably perish with the rest of us. The African Negritos were said by the anthropologists to have an exceptionally pure and lofty conception of the nature of God and of God's relation to man. They might be able to give mankind a fresh start; and, though we should then have lost the achievements of the last 6,000 to 10,000 years, what were 10,000 years compared to the 600,000 or 1,000,000 years during which the human race had already been in existence? The extreme possibility of catastrophe was that we might succeed in exterminating the whole human race, African Negritos and all.

Toynbee felt that on the evidence of the past history of life on this planet, even that was not entirely unlikely. After all, the reign of man on Earth – if we were right in thinking that man established his present ascendancy in the middle palaeolithic age – was so far only about 100,000 years, and what was that compared to the 500,000,000 or 800,000,000 years during which life had been in existence on the surface of this planet? In the past, other forms of life had enjoyed reigns which had lasted for almost inconceivably longer periods, and which yet at last had come to an end. There was a reign of the giant armoured reptiles which might have lasted about 80,000,000 years; from about the year 130,000,000 to the year 50,000,000 before the present day. But the reptiles' reign came to an end. Long before that – perhaps 300,000,000 years ago – there was a reign of giant armoured fishes, creatures that had already accomplished the tremendous achievement of growing a movable lower jaw. But the reign of the fishes came to an end.

The winged insects were believed to have come into existence about 250,000,000 years ago. Perhaps the higher winged insects – the social insects that had anticipated mankind in creating an institutional life – were still waiting for their reign on Earth to come. If the ants and bees were were one day to acquire even that glimmer of intellectual understanding that man had possessed in his day, and if they were then to make their own shot at seeing history in perspective, they might see the advent of the mammals and the brief reign of the human mammal, as almost irrelevant episodes, 'full of sound and fury, signifying nothing'. The challenge to us, in our generation, according to Toynbee, was to see to it that this interpretation of history did not become the true one.

At the Bampton Foundation at Columbia University, New York, Toynbee recalled Aldous Huxley's anti-Utopia, *Brave New World*, in which he pictured a world in which, in order to make human existence safe under comfortable material conditions, man had systematically and cold-bloodedly suppressed everything that from the higher point of view made human life worth living. He had got rid of war, disease, famine, but in getting rid of those ancient scourges he had also got rid of the soul. The moral of Huxley's penetrating piece of satire was that the price was too high to pay. Man, as pictured by Aldous Huxley in this brave new world, was living in what Plato called 'The City of Swine'. Toynbee commented that what we had to find was a path between catastrophe and a 'brave new world'. If we found it at all, it would probably be a narrow passage with formidable dangers on either side.

The principles upon which Toynbee lived and worked were those of a scholar to whom the esoteric side of Greek thought had been revealed. His work, with its fidelity, its conviction of the greatness of the civilization on which his own activities were a commentary, linked that classical past to the present day, and to the whole human society of tomorrow. Toynbee originally thought that religion existed for the sake of civilization. He became convinced that civilization existed for the sake of religion – a view that ran counter to the popular belief of Marxists and realists, and the academic historians. Toynbee was impervious to such attacks. In controversy he had at command a deadly ironic urbanity. After all, he used to say, it is the bitter and envious who wear themselves down soonest to weary passivity. Throughout it all Arnold Toynbee remained a quiet, dignified figure, unstained by the more dubious characteristics which are too often an ingredient of political and international life.

Robert Frost

My last meeting with Robert Frost was when he came to England to receive honorary degrees from both Oxford and Cambridge Universities. He was very conscious of the honour and pointed out with quiet satisfaction that the only other Americans to be similarly honoured were James Russell Lowell in 1873 – and that had been in part recognition of diplomatic services – and Longfellow in 1868 – 'but he didn't get both of 'em at the same time'. Not that Frost had any need for comparisons. He had received almost every American literary honour – the Pulitzer Prize for poetry four times: in 1924 for *New Hampshire*, 1931 for *Collected Poems*, 1937 for *A Further Range*, and 1943 for *A Witness Tree*.

Frost's refreshing vitality belied his eighty-three years. During his visit to Cambridge he found time to include my home, a 400-year-old mill house with matured grounds. It revived memories of the initial impact of England in 1912, the realization of an ambition of his wife to live in rural setting, preferably under thatch. Added to this was Frost's lifelong admiration for England's lyric poetry and the necessity to live cheaply so he could concentrate on writing. With that in mind the New Hampshire farm was sold and he took one in Gloucestershire. With a twinkle, he added that it all sounded much grander than it was. There were no rolling acres, just a cottage, small garden and a few hens, but it was what they wanted and it more than lived up to expectations.

The English years were significant. Frost recalled that his first volume of poems was published in this country for the simple reason that it had been rejected in America. He was then thirty-nine, adding in his deep New England voice that success had always come slow. In self-deprecating mood, he regretted that he had never been a real anything. Not much of a farmer, not much of a poet: he reckoned his output had been about ten pages a year over a period of sixty years. He was conscious of the formative influences of friendships with Edward Thomas, Lascelles

Abercrombie, Wilfrid Gibson and, in particular, Rupert Brooke. The fact that the Old Mill House was so close to the Old Vicarage of Grantchester and the orchard where there is still honey for tea, while in Trumpington village is the war memorial engraved by Eric Gill with the poet's name among the fallen, was sufficient to unleash a flood of memories.

Frost reminisced in a rich baritone voice about life in general and the early days, all unaffected, conversational, spiced with ironic humour, and seasoned with a few simple home truths. The informality made it hard to realize that here was not only a great American poet who had influenced the work of young American poets and critics, but he was also a great American institution. One thing puzzled him. As a poet he always despised fashion, yet he had become fashionable. He wrote poems and about poetry in the plainest terms, yet critics discussed his work in terms of the greatest complexity. He had never consciously played any literary tricks. Looking down at his big, black boots, he said that maybe recognition had come from craftsmanship and integrity – at least he hoped so.

During his stay in England, Frost took the opportunity to give a few lectures. He read some of his poems and talked. The effect at times was spell-binding. It showed why he was revered on both sides of the Atlantic, a vivid chronicler of life and people against the background of his native New England. He argued that poetry for its effect relied not on alliteration, assonance and rich vowels, but on a contrapuntal rhythm which played on a basic metric theme and no matter the length of the line or the number of accents, the base had to exist for the poem to succeed. The free verse movement in poetry received short shrift. 'I'd as soon write free verse as play tennis with the net down!'

Listening to Frost speaking and reading his poems with many a light aside was like witnessing a living, New England puritan tradition. In a hall of the University of London, his sallies received spontaneous acclaim, and T. S. Eliot, sitting in the fourth row, showed how a poet of a very different stamp, could warm to the old man's repartee. He was highly amused when Frost recalled receiving a card from Ezra Pound bearing his name, a number in Church Walk, and scrawled across the words, 'At home some-times'. As an invitation Frost was not over-impressed with it, but he eventually found himself in Kensington, remembered the card and tried his luck. Pound was at home and the meeting proved more than fruitful.

Robert Frost answered a student's question as to how he went about writing poetry. The line he took was typical. 'I begin with some unaccountable feeling. I describe it like a hanker, something that you want like sugar or candy or a drink or companionship, and you don't know quite what it is. And when you start the poem you make a few mistakes and say this isn't what I'm hankering for, and then suddenly you get going.' Such was the recipe. The principal ingredient was its very simplicity.

T. S. Eliot OM

T. S. Eliot was very much a dual personality. The private face and public mask were clearly defined. To the world he presented a profoundly sensitive exterior made complex by a chilling repression. He reminded me of a quince, a hard astringent fruit, concentrated in flavour and somewhat restricted in appeal. He was a solitary, and a lonely man is like a well. If you drop a stone into it, you cannot get it out again. It is always tempting to look for the cause of a complex personality. In Eliot's case, it could have been due to the fact that he was a congenital intellectual. From childhood he was hedged about with austere, academic relations, a factor that is not necessarily a drawback, for an intellectual aristocracy often outlasts other forms of exclusiveness. Artistically the result can be gratifying, though it can encourage a reputation for aloofness which many people find distasteful.

Such was Eliot's public mask. The private side was quite different. He hated the wrong type of publicity and resented the intrusion by the popular Press into his private life. The two were kept scrupulously apart. Only a few knew the relaxed mood when Eliot could be enormous fun. On those occasions there was no trace of disillusion, no hint of aloofness. His anecdotes were heightened by his habit of reaching the pay-off line with a dead-pan gravity. He was anything but big-headed – quite the contrary – and often laughingly said that he hadn't read and certainly did not always understand everything that was written about him.

Eliot's career was a rich tapestry of many colours. I once asked him what were the principal events that had shaped his life, particularly incidents that had changed its course. Harvard, 1906, undoubtedly made a big impact. Irving Babbitt's classes left a deep impression, sufficient to inspire an attack on his humanism in a strong essay some twenty years later. The next event of consequence was his stay at the Sorbonne and the introduction to literary Paris. It also marked the writing of *The Love Song of J. Alfred Prufrock*. Then came the return to Harvard and the award of the Sheldon Travelling Fellowship. On the eve of the First World War, he was in Marburg, Germany, and when hostilities began, Eliot went to Merton College, Oxford, where he prepared a thesis on F. H. Bradley. He regarded this period as particularly fruitful for in London his close friendship with Ezra Pound began and it was in his Notting Hill Gate flat that he met Wyndham Lewis. Both men exercised considerable influence on Eliot's views and outlook.

After leaving Oxford in 1915, Eliot married Vivienne Haigh and became a master at Highgate Junior School where John Betjeman was a pupil. He spoke about his next job with an air of resignation. He found himself in the foreign department of Lloyds Bank. That occupation ended after the Armistice. A holiday in France proved eventful. His companion was Wyndham Lewis and in Paris they met James Joyce. It was a meeting of kindred spirits. Eliot recalled the pleasure when in 1922 he became editor of the influential critical quarterly, *The Criterion*, and how in that year Ezra Pound persuaded him to cut by half *The Waste Land*. Three years later Eliot joined the publishing house of Faber and Gwyer, now Faber and Faber, eventually becoming a director. Then in 1927 he took an important decision. He became a British subject and to the horror of many in the literary world, described himself as 'a classicist in literature, a royalist in politics and an Anglo-Catholic in religion'.

Eliot's first full-length play, *Murder in the Cathedral*, brought about a sensational change in his position. He resolved under the inspiration of the Christian faith – for he had been received into the Church of England in 1927 – that he would write a play which could be performed in church and understood by ordinary churchgoers. It was not an easy play though some critics believed it to be the best he wrote, but it had one effect. Almost overnight Eliot ceased to be the jealously guarded property of the *avant garde* and became the laureate of High Anglicanism. In their eyes the play was the product of ascetic scholarship and an astringent intellectual exercise.

Eliot's reputation was established. Many critics maintained that his poetry was the richest yeast we had. For Eliot it was part of a home-coming. In 1627, Andrew Eliot, a cordwainer, was born. He left the Somerset village of East Coker in middle age to go to America. In 1940 T. S. Eliot returned to the same place. The poem *East Coker* begins with the words, 'In my beginning is my end'. It ends 'In my end is my beginning'. In between were generations in

Boston, though Eliot himself was born in St Louis, Missouri. In between came this man who made such an impact on society and especially literary society, yet an assessment of Eliot's greatness is not easy. So much of the general appreciation of his work has been paradoxical. The significance of his pen outstripped the understanding of the general reader. Eliot received uncritical reverence from disciples who lacked the technical erudition necessary to interpret the art on which they conferred lip-service.

That Eliot was accepted in academic circles went without saying. Scholars and critics were agreed in their admiration. He was named by some as the greatest modern poet, critic and belletrist, as well as being an outstanding playwright. The award of the Nobel Prize for Literature in 1948 and the Order of Merit in the same year gave official confirmation of that ranking. Scholarship added the credit of so changing the format of British and American poetry that its techniques were improved. In the light of such an approved reputation it was hardly surprising that the man in the street accepted Eliot as the greatest living man of letters. A state of ecstasy is to be reckoned among the more generous lapses, an error on the magnificent side, but enthusiasm ran wild when Eliot was elevated to such heights.

The best thing is to examine some of Eliot's works. For many people his reputation as a poet rested on the poem *The Waste Land*. At the time it was written, in 1922, it became a symbol of post-war disillusionment, an expression of apprehension, a dark glass through which his life was viewed with unusual clarity against a monochrome background. His poetry had an odd power of expression, whether in quatrains, in free rhymed verse, or in the blank verse of *Gerontion*. Words were used sparingly. Connecting phrases were omitted. Concentration on condensation was marked. Many of those early lines were striking. His sentences cut like broken glass. They had a splintered sharpness. It was terse poetry with hidden, fragmentary meaning. Take three graphic examples: 'a pair of ragged claws/Scuttling across the floors of silent seas', 'the yellow fog that rubs its back upon the window-panes', and 'I have measured out my life with coffee spoons'. It is true to say that the 1917 series of *Prufrock* poems enriched our poetic tradition, while it is possible to pick out isolated phrases from his early poems and several sentences from his early prose, like this one taken from the anthology of Ezra Pound in 1928: 'No vers is libre for the man who wants to do a good job', or a 1934 line in this metaphor, 'The minor poet who hitches his skiff astern of the great galleon has a better chance of survival than the minor poet who chooses to paddle by himself.'

Four Quartets are difficult to understand. As the title indicates, each poem is structurally a poetic equivalent of the classical symphony or quartet or sonata, as distinct from the suite. The structure becomes clear when all four poems are read, as they are intended to be, together. Essentially they are of the same structure as *The Waste Land*, but they are far too obscure for the general reader. Eliot felt this difficulty himself. He evaded the issue by saying that he was occupied with frontiers of consciousness beyond which words fail, though meanings still exist.

There are times when I feel that Eliot's ambition was to do for verse what James Joyce did for prose. The polysemantic verbalism of Joyce involved the distortion of an original word so that several different meanings were suggested almost simultaneously. Eliot resorted to allusions, quotations and symbolism. No doubt *Ulysses* is now more or less understandable, though I question whether *Finnigans Wake* can be tackled as confidently. Joyce had a private language. No one can be certain that he knows what he meant. The individual has to recreate each work afresh for himself. Eliot tried in similar fashion with *The Waste Land*, though without the ability of Joyce to show the workings and free-wheelings of his mind.

Eliot introduced a new poetic tradition in the theatre. *Murder in the Cathedral* – the title was not Eliot's invention – had impressive choruses. *The Family Reunion* and *The Cocktail Party* had conversational verse. He claimed he had turned poetry into a flexible medium for current expression, though at times it was difficult to distinguish the words from the prose, and very ordinary prose at that, especially when it was heard rather than seen. Many in the audiences failed to realize the form and took it for granted that the play was in prose; it was claimed the effect of the verse-rhythms worked upon them at a deeper level than that of conscious realization. *The Cocktail Party* divided audiences and critics alike, polemical discussion centring round questions of interpretation.

As to the value and significance of these plays, judgement is still reserved. It is partly through their influence that we had such an appalling welter of so-called verse attempting to imitate Eliot. Critics summed up *The Cocktail Party* by saying it was mental stimulation and made audiences think on a serious note. No doubt that was all to the good, but it would have been more constructive if these gentlemen had discussed in more detail what Eliot had to say in these plays and poems. The author took refuge behind a favourite quotation: 'It is never what a poem says that matters, but what it is.' In short, we were asked to accept Eliot as an outstanding writer without analysing what he was saying in print.

In *The Confidential Clerk* – the product of four years' work – Eliot wrote a play with a light touch containing the inner message that men should keep faith with the best that is in them. I attended the world première in Edinburgh in the company of the author and later over dinner heard his reactions. He anticipated that the critics would find different meanings to the play, and critics were never wrong, but the fact remained, it meant just what it said. If anything else had been intended, he would have said so. He argued that if a playwright wanted to say something serious it would be better to do so in comedy rather than in tragedy. Reactions both during the performance and afterwards were incisive. This simplest and most deep-felt play since *Murder in the Cathedral* was about the physical problems of three illegitimates and had moments of touching pathos and drama in this family thicket. Eliot felt that Alan Webb as Eggerson played one of those delightful old men we all feel we have known. Denholm Elliott's sensitive interpretation of Colby was in sympathy with his verse, while Margaret Leighton's moving scene with Colby in the second act produced the superb, emotional crescendo he wanted. *The Confidential Clerk* was a comedy that bordered upon drama, even religious drama. Eliot was disappointed over one small point. After *The Cocktail Party* première no critic spotted the parallel with Euripides' *Alcestis*, but after *The Confidential Clerk* everyone nailed the parallel with Euripides' *Ion*.

The change in Eliot was by then total. As a young man he was the private property of a wildly enthusiastic *avant-garde*. His early poems and the contemporary poems of his friend Ezra Pound, had transformed the imagination of every poetry reader whose imagination was capable of transformation. He used to say how he enjoyed that early notoriety. He joined in the fun and admitted that he wrote outrageously about his elders, an *enfant terrible* behind the prim mask of an American bank clerk. Eventually came the sensational transformation, though to many the severe ecclesiasticism of Eliot's Christianity was profoundly unsympathetic. At one stage he appeared more interested in the propagation of points of view than in pure literature. His *Notes towards the Definition of Culture* in 1949 was sociological. This preoccupation with social and cultural speculation tended to make him primarily a propagandist rather than a man of letters. It is permissible to wonder whether at times Eliot was taken too seriously. External factors undoubtedly helped his reputation. Writing in a restricted medium meant few rivals and assured attention. The same applied to his poetry, while competition in poetic drama was negligible.

On the other hand Eliot will always be a particular delight to those who cherish dignity and fastidiousness in contemporary criticism. His influence was not so much technical or even literary, as purely aesthetic. In 1963 the *Collected Poems, 1909–1962* were published to celebrate his seventy-fifth birthday. It contained 'A Dedication to My Wife', a tribute to Valerie who brought him such joy in the closing years. The flame of ecstasy burns a spiritual oil. There was always something of the will-o'-the-wisp about the ecstatic candle of T. S. Eliot.

George Macaulay Trevelyan OM

Trevelyan did not like company or society, nor was he at all convivial. He had no small talk, preferred isolation, tempered by a few congenial contacts. One of his great joys was to return to his home in Northumberland and the tremendous pleasure he gained there from walking. I recall how once he said that every Cantab and Oxonian ought to walk to Marble Arch from their respective colleges, adding as an afterthought that the wisdom of our ancestors, surely not by accident, had fixed these two sites of learning at the same distance from London. He worked it out that the Cambridge student should start at five o'clock, encouraged by the prospect of a second breakfast waiting to be eaten in Royston at eight o'clock. Another suggestion was an ever stiffer test, namely that a man should walk the eighty miles from St Mary, Oxon to St Mary, Cantab in twenty-four hours, but as Trevelyan added, there is no orthodoxy in walking. It is a land of many paths and no-paths, where everyone goes his own way and is right.

That also applied to shooting-parties at Hallington, where once being missed, he was found reading Homer behind a hedge. His home in Cambridge reflected his interests. Even when widowed (his wife died in 1956) and almost blind, he would entertain invited visitors, young and old, with that combination of a sharp tongue and a kind heart which, we are told, makes the finest company in the world.

But, wherever he was, George Macaulay Trevelyan was an impressive figure. In an age in which scholars are plentiful and artists rare, he occupied a unique place in the history of English letters. Although Gibbon, Macaulay and Clarendon were his superiors as stylists, while some ranked R. H. Tawney above him on the same score, Trevelyan stood out as the poet of English history. Innumerable passages of lyrical beauty in his books reflect the workings of a poet's mind. His imagination pursued facts, and being that rare phenomenon, a natural story-teller, he focused them with exquisite feeling. Had he wished, Trevelyan could have used this gift of imagination in poetry rather than in history. That he did not do so may well have been due to the richness of his inherited tradition, for his great-uncle was Lord Macaulay, who, with Gibbon, reigns supreme in English historical writing, while his father, Sir Otto Trevelyan, was an eminent historian. It was not surprising to find that his sense of duty as historian was highly developed. He roamed over all centuries with equal ease and zest, from Garibaldi to Wyclif, from Queen Anne to Sir Edward Grey, and never failed to bring the past to life. He was a historian in the Whig tradition.

But there were signs that other influences were at work. His preoccupation with Time was a recurring theme. Here it is tempting to make a comparison with a poet like Wordsworth, who was intensely concerned with the feeling of loss inherent in the very nature of Time, an aspect strongly emphasized in the study of history. In his *Autobiography* Trevelyan wrote:

> More generally, I take delight in history, even its most prosaic details, because they become poetical as they recede into the past. The poetry of history lies in the quasi-miraculous fact that once, on this earth, once on this familiar spot of ground, walked other men and women, as actual as we are today, thinking their own thoughts, swayed by their own passions, but now all gone, one generation vanishing after another, gone as utterly as we ourselves shall shortly be gone like ghosts at cock-crow.

Here are sentiments that Proust as well as Wordsworth would have understood, though perhaps not so deeply as this historian who was unable to accept the tenet of personal immortality. It may be that the circumstances of Trevelyan's life increased this attitude to the passing of time. The formative years of youth were spent in the Border lands where Roman walls, ruined abbeys, battlefields with their unknown dead, and peel-towers left their impress on his mind. His family background could be termed both aristocratic and upper middle class. His father knew intimately the leading figures of Victorian society, and his marriage with Caroline Philips, the daughter of a Manchester merchant, Free-trader, Unitarian, friend of Cobden and Gladstone, consolidated the family link with liberalism. Trevelyan grew up in a highly selective world of art and politics. The passing of that era whetted the edge of Trevelyan's preoccupation with history.

His education followed the lines of any rich young man of that day. Preparatory school in Berkshire, Harrow and Trinity College, Cambridge. At Harrow he was fortunate enough to have as history masters, Robert Somervell and George Townsend Warner, the former having a rich command of English. To his credit must go the teaching of such men as Winston Churchill and Trevelyan. At Cambridge, Trevelyan was influenced by Maitland, the English medieval and legal historian; by Cunningham, who was inaugurating the study of economic history; and by Lord Acton, the Catholic historian. He disliked Seeley, Acton's predecessor in the Regius Chair of History, who was an advocate of scientific history and continually denounced Macaulay and Carlyle. For friends Trevelyan chose such young man as Bertrand Russell, G. E. Moore and Desmond MacCarthy, contacts that strengthened the liberal attitude to life which he had inherited from his family, an attitude primarily protestant, infused with a scepticism of all doctrinaire beliefs either in politics or religion.

Historical research turned Trevelyan's mind to a historical movement bound up with belief in individual freedom. He was attracted by the Lollards, by the Peasants' Revolt, by the stirring of national consciousness in England. The work was published in 1899 entitled *England in the Age of Wycliffe*. It was well written and had considerable success, was reprinted fourteen times, bore the distinctive Trevelyan style, and gained him the Fellowship at Trinity. Then followed the elementary stages in the making of a don, but, finding the critical academic scholasticism too stultifying and restricting, he decided to leave Cambridge to write literary history. It was a revolt against the existing attitude to the subject.

At that time history was no longer written for the general reader. It was treated as a science. Techniques, evidence and statistics were the only things that mattered. If the results were unintelligible to the public, it could not be helped. It was of secondary importance. History was a specialist occupation by professionals for professionals, and had no connection with literature. Trevelyan opposed this doctrine. Merely to concentrate on constitutional, economic and diplomatic fields of research was unsatisfying to his temperament. He wanted the human influence in history.

Trevelyan described his marriage to Janet Penrose, a daughter of Mrs Humphrey Ward, the novelist and social worker, as the most important and fortunate event of his life. Amongst the wedding presents was a collection of books on Italian history, including Garibaldi's *Memoirs* and Belluzzi's *Ritirata di Garibaldi nel 1849*. The story of Garibaldi appealed to Trevelyan's creative genius. He turned his pen to the subject with such success that the resulting trilogy has been given a permanent place in the historical literature of the world.

It is impossible to comment on each of Trevelyan's works, but I must mention *History of England*, which took three years to write. His own comment was unnecessarily modest,

> In April 1926 my *History of England* came out. It has been, as regards sales, the most successful of my books, except the *Social History*, because it treated so necessary a subject as the history of England at the length, and to some extent in the manner, which suited a large public, including schools and Universities. Some day, very soon perhaps, it will be replaced, but it will have served its generation.

The wish was an understatement. Its social value has been incalculable. Millions of Englishmen garnered from this book the little history they will ever know. Well over 200,000 copies were sold, but in schools copies were used innumerable times, while many schoolmasters based their courses on it. Before the last war Trevelyan was working on a social history of England to serve as a companion volume to his *History of England*, which mainly dealt with war and politics. In 1940 he decided to omit the early part of the work and begin with Chaucer. It was published in 1944 under the title of *English Social History*. The sales were remarkable. In seven years more than 400,000 copies were sold – a record among history books.

It is impossible to do full justice to Trevelyan's literary craftsmanship. He was true to his early environment and his family outlook. He was a historian in the Whig tradition. Much of his writing was covered by the work of his great-uncle, but he managed to escape from the shadow of his kinsman, and endowed his work with a personal quality. Historic episodes that were infused with dramatic action inspired some of his finest writing. Many tributes have been paid to his genius, but the last and greatest distinction of his academic life gave considerable joy. The Mastership of Trinity College, Cambridge, is a Crown appointment, and when the vacancy was created in 1940 by the death of J. J. Thomson, Winston Churchill must have derived a measure of personal pleasure in conferring it on a school contemporary and, in one sense, a rival historian, for Churchill's *Life of Marlborough* was published about the same time as *England under Queen Anne*. Trevelyan's feeling for his College was deep. When his appointment was made, he recorded that it had made his life as happy as anyone's could be during the fall of European civilization.

History for Trevelyan had a literary and moral purpose. He was absorbed by the mystery of time, by the mutability of all things, by the succession of the ages and generations. He maintained that the present only takes us by surprise because we do not sufficiently know and consider the past. With Treveylan as our guide the story of man became far more wonderful than the wonders of physical science. It also provided an insight into the historian's thinking, cast light on many aspects of his personal beliefs. As he once said, the proper study of mankind becomes man.

Cambridge Women

Cambridge has a fascination peculiar to itself, the intimacy of a community farthest from work-a-day life, civilized, cultured, perhaps a trifle spoilt, but withal of the world. A weakness is that the system is male orientated. Sexual equality is claimed, but makes little impact. Female success is not news unless the media picks up a story. A contributory cause might be that Cambridge women are not publicity conscious. Oversell is frowned upon. That can be left to the men. The Archer set-up in the Old Vicarage in Grantchester is a good example. The distaff side is a distinguished academic at Newnham College. She does not need to compare the field of scholarship with the outpourings of a facile pen. The public that matters can pass judgement on comparative values. Not being recognized in public is almost a bonus to the likes of Mrs Archer. The attitude is common. Many women of distinction remain unnoticed and unknown to the general public.

One such used to scrub floors as a VAD in a military convalescent home on the Gog Magogs and later worked as a land-girl on Station Farm before cycling home to Great Shelford for tea. That girl was Rose Macaulay. The best-selling novel *The Thorn Birds* was written in a small Cambridge flat by Colleen McCullough, while she worked as a typist at Pyes, but in spite of media attention, recognition is slow. Sylvia Plath read English at Newnham, met Edward James Hughes whom she married, lived in a Newnham flat which she described as a 'dusty, gloomy, coal-bin of a house' made bearable by its closeness to Grantchester Meadows. Sylvia won American recognition with *The Hawk in the Rain*, enjoyed five years of success, but was still not recognized in Cambridge. Unhappily the marriage failed and the slender, talented Bostonian girl committed suicide.

Still in Newnham, a woman buys household goods every week in the corner shop, looking like any preoccupied, slightly weary housewife. Few people realize she is Lady Fuchs, wife of Sir Vivian of Antarctic fame. I once asked whether she had ambitions to be on that expedition. That suggestion had been made to her husband. The reply had been that if she could carry 80 lbs on her back every day for four months and be able to trek 1,800 miles, the application would be considered. She decided to concentrate on gardening in Cambridge, but it was not always the case. Her honeymoon with 'Bunny' Fuchs was spent climbing in the Dolomites, while she accompanied him on an expedition to the Great Rift Valley in Africa. Altogether Joyce Fuchs is a remarkable woman, but reserved and happy in anonymity. On the other hand, some women thrive on publicity like Lady Trumpington, a prominent figure in every sense of the word in the House of Lords. Before elevation, this redoubtable lady took her duties with equal zest as wife to Alan Barker, headmaster of the Leys School. They made a first-class team. When she was around there was never a dull moment as she is unpredictable, immensely popular and a complete extrovert.

Quite different was Joan Robinson, known as the rice-bowl economist of Cambridge, who had the rare academic distinction of being elected to a Professorship in Economics through succeeding her husband, becoming one of the brightest figures in the Economics Faculty. Joan was a brilliant theoretician who pressed her case forcibly. Inevitably controversy followed for these views in practice were on the far left of international and national politics. She denied being a Marxist, preferring the left wing of the Labour Party, but at times the dividing-line was wafer thin. Argument was in her blood. Her great-grandfather, Frederick Denison Maurice, the Christian Socialist, lost a Chair of Theology because of his beliefs, while her father, Major-General Sir Frederick Maurice, sacrificed his army career on a point of principle. After graduating, Joan married and went to India with her husband, Austin, who took the post of tutor to the Maharajah of Gwalior. It was then that she developed her fondness for the East. A natural protestant rather than a conformer, her views on morality at times were somewhat unconventional, but she was always stimulating company with a compelling voice. Her room in Sidgwick Avenue reflected varied interests with modern Chinese paintings, a Ben Nicholson, and a lithograph from Leningrad. Few people realized that this silver-haired lady dressed in oriental clothes was an academic of such eminence.

The same might be said about a short, dumpy woman often seen walking along All Saints' Passage, nothing special about her features, nondescript appearance, indifferent make-up, and a pronounced Russian accent. She was Lydia Lopokova, the celebrated Russian ballerina, whose performances in the Diaghilev Ballet were unsurpassed for delicious gaiety and wit with a rare knack of holding audiences in the hollow of her small hand. In private life she was Lady Keynes, a strange marriage in the light of Keynes's homosexual activities. Even so, after leaving the stage Lydia devotedly looked after her husband who was in delicate health, and accompanied him on economic missions abroad. Cambridge taught Keynes arrogance, superiority to others, the repudiation of general rules and the implications of an antinomian philosophy, but it was this squat little woman who showed Maynard that wisdom about human affairs depends on humility and sympathy. She deserved better reward for her loyalty, but public recognition of artistic skills mattered little.

Should any Cambridge woman feel aggrieved about this apparent lack of public awareness of feminine achievement, a shrewd campaigner on their behalf has returned to their midst in Germaine Greer, who received part of her university education by the Granta. She has moved into a country house just outside the city, ostensibly to indulge in gardening and rural pursuits, though maybe planning a sequel to the *Female Eunuch* that dramatized women's imagined misuse by men. A naturally aggressive supporter of women's lib, Germaine has shown signs of mellowing with the years, but the fire is still there should it be needed.

I have left to the last an unusual woman. During the closing years of her life, it was a common sight to see on the footpath by the Granta a wheelchair with its occupant wrapped in a dark rug, enveloped by a black shawl, with a black, wide-brimmed clerical shovel hat jammed on her head. Fixed to the arm of the chair was a small easel. Hour after hour she would paint, whatever the weather. No attention was paid to the occasional passer-by. Some were curious, others sympathetic, even dropping money on the table, and occasionally someone would ask if she minded them looking at what she was painting. The reply would be a gentle rebuke, 'No, no more than if you were reading my private correspondence.'

That sad figure was Gwen Raverat, daughter of George Darwin, Professor of Astronomy and granddaughter of the evolutionist. A severe stroke had paralysed her left side and made walking impossible. Fortunately her brain was not affected. Wood-engraving and line-drawing were out of the question, but she could still paint, a blessing that eased the frustrations of helplessness. Her book *Period Piece* won international acclaim. It is a classic of its type, an insight into the domestic life of the upper-class academic scene with graphic pen-portraits recalling penny farthings and horse-trams, chaperons, lamplighters and beggars, evocative of a Cambridge long gone. Gwen Raverat was physically unknown to the general public, but she ranks high in the line of distinguished Cambridge women.

Krishna Menon

Krishna Menon had the habit of backing into the limelight like a carnivorous dove. He was a peripatetic one-man delegation, a mysterious figure with full Cabinet rank, but no Cabinet seat. He was unique in the conventional run of politics, and certainly one of the most mobile figures in the business of statesmanship.

Pin-point a trouble spot in any part of the world, and before long Menon appeared like an intermediary between the Almighty and the human race. His movements covered all the Chancelleries and Foreign Offices. Activities such as these invited comment. What sort of a man was Krishna Menon? Was he a Communist? What were his motives?

I met Menon on many occasions in different parts of the world, and though his circumstances altered, the impression never changed. His features were unforgettable: the eyebrows, the aquiline nose, the voluble hands, the brooding demeanour, the mephistophelean smile. To me he symbolized the new Asia. He was the world's most European Oriental. I recall Menon when he lived in a humble one-roomed flatlet in Camden Town. Then he was not immaculate. He wore a threadbare overcoat and shabby flannel trousers. But he was a dedicated man, dedicated to the struggle for the freedom of India. As to whether he was a Communist, it is difficult to say. He was certainly a Marxist. He allied himself with all types of fellow-travellers. But I feel he was far too individualistic to have been a satisfactory Communist. He was a Socialist agitator and the most militant of pacifists.

The diversity of uses to which Menon put his intelligence and energy was remarkable. He began his career as a nationalist under the influence of Annie Besant, developed his Socialist faith as a pupil and friend of Harold Laski and for many of his twenty-eight years in London was the chief spokesman and lobbyist for the Indian Congress cause. Working for sixteen hours a day, he combined this with reading for the Bar, took first-class honours at the London School of Economics and practised political oratory, as he once said, 'at practically every street corner in London'. He was an industrious member of the St Pancras Borough Council and a courageous air-raid warden in blitzed North London. He was also the first editor of Pelican Books.

Menon's friendship with Pandit Nehru was extraordinary. The two men were from completely dissimilar backgrounds. Nehru came from an aristocratic Brahmin family of Northern India: Menon from a working-class home in Malabar. Nehru went to Harrow and Cambridge. Menon studied at LSE. Yet Menon was probably the only man who could interpret and explain Nehru's foreign policy. The paradoxical position of India in world affairs during those first dozen years of her independent existence – a position of influence unsupported by power – was the achievement of these two men, Jawaharlal Nehru and Vengalil Krishnan Krishna Menon, but ironically Menon, as Indian Defence Minister, virtually nullified all that had been achieved by Menon the tireless and brilliant negotiator.

He was a complex character, dual-faced in some of his dealings. He fell from power when political enemies in New Delhi accused him, as Defence Minister, of failing to equip the army to meet Chinese aggression, but countered by saying he had been thwarted by the Finance Ministry when he asked for a foreign exchange allocation of 137 million rupees to buy automatic weapons and other military hardware. Such is the lot of Defence Ministers in many countries. He also had strong differences of opinion with several of his generals whom he treated like newly commissioned subalterns. But in spite of personal dislikes, he was an able administrator. On an everyday basis, I recall several idiosyncrasies. He frowned on smoking and alcohol, and never seemed to eat. At dinner his plate was invariably untouched. His only frailty was an endless chain of cups of tea.

To the Western World, Krishna Menon was a gaunt enigma of independent India, a Machiavelli of international politics.

The Grimaldis

Monte Carlo is essentially the setting for strong personalities. One of these is Prince Rainier, shrewd, single-minded and practical. He leads a life of rigidly limited obligations, the majority with cold-cash reasons. By temperament and in practice he is a realist, though his definition of realism would be far from rigid. In his private life he is a man of infinite variety of interests. In a button-down age, he is completely self-contained though it may be a measure of the time's repressiveness that a man who is simply himself should come to seem something of an eccentric. Since the death of his wife, Prince Rainier has shown the honesty of a person living each moment as it happens. Against his native background, he is complete. Even a brief visit emphasizes the degree of informality surrounding his life outside public gaze.

An unobtrusive private entrance is hidden in a corner of the castle's ornate façade. An elderly servant opens the door of a small old-fashioned lift, a relation of the ones that lasted for so many years in the Ritz of London. It wheezes upwards, shudders to a halt, and the door opens into the Prince's study, a comfortable room that looks lived in. Prominent on a stand are powerful naval binoculars trained on the harbour.

It would be no exaggeration to say that few Monaco happenings escape his attention. He has a finger on the pulse of the place and is concerned in sensible fashion with the control of all its activities. Expansion is possibly uppermost in his concerns. Apart from reclaiming more land from the Mediterranean, the only avenue is upwards, and overdevelopment could destroy Monaco's character, already sadly scarred by the rash of skyscraper buildings. He is conscious of having to restrain this tendency before it gets completely out of hand.

Part of the Prince's education was in England, but the memories of Stowe School are hardly flattering and he has nightmare recollections of trying to play rugby football in seas of mud. His involvement in every aspect of the Monaco Grand Prix is total. His comments on the drivers are pertinent while the engineering complexities of the cars are appreciated with knowledge. One of his ideas, which I wish could become a reality, is that of staging a Formula Libre race over the circuit. The result would be more than hairy.

The affairs of Monaco have been controlled by the Grimaldi family since the twelfth century. In the hands of His Serene Highness Prince Rainier III they are safeguarded in twentieth-century fashion.

The career of Grace Patricia Kelly was one of the real-life fairy stories of this century. It centres round the fortress-castle rebuilt by the Genoese in 1215. Grace was the product of a wealthy and famous family. Her father, John Kelly, built a multi-million-dollar construction business and was 1920 Olympic single and double sculls champion. Her brother Jack won the Henley Diamond Sculls in 1947 and 1949. Together they shared one characteristic. They were needling perfectionists who knew exactly what to choose from the stuff of the times to give themselves the look of the times, while remaining absolutely themselves.

Grace Kelly's stage debut took place in *The Father* on Broadway in 1949 with Raymond Massey; her first great screen impact was the Zinnemann picture *High Noon* with Gary Cooper; Alfred Hitchcock added the dimensions of worldliness and humour in *Rear Window*. Her role in *The Country Girl* with Bing Crosby won an Oscar, though possibly the film she enjoyed most was *To Catch a Thief* with Cary Grant. Years later there was speculation about a film come-back that was sensibly turned down. Having made the decision to quit at the top, what was there to prove, what could she have become – only an older actress, not a better one.

The man who altered the course of her life was Pierre Galante, editor of *Paris Match*. He introduced her to Prince Rainier. In her role as Princess Grace of Monaco she carried out her public duties in a manner that won the hearts of everyone. Her charm and loveliness were as fresh as a gentle breeze. Alfred Hitchcock once described her as a delicious combination of passion masked by coolness. She was a woman of classic, at times radiant beauty.

Her special interests in Monaco were the Red Cross, the Garden Club which she founded, and the Princess Grace Memorial Hospital. This concern for medical matters was genuine. During an official inspection of the Mobile Hospital she displayed an extensive knowledge of equipment and treatments. She was clear and didactic and on such occasions her voice tended to become metallically hard. It was this icy manner on formal occasions that caused those who did not know her to say it was the result of repression rather than good breeding. Nothing could have been further from the truth. On official engagements she conducted herself in a manner that conformed with Monegasque protocol. Only when it was over did she relax and become herself.

The death of Princess Grace was a tragedy. It devastated her husband and children, robbed Monte Carlo of much of its magic, and left a gap that can never be completely filled.

Somerset Maugham

Much of Somerset Maugham's work will survive the test of time. His attitude towards the unfolding human scene was once symbolized by somebody as one vast shrug of the shoulders in human shape. The description was unfair. No one, let alone a writer of Somerset Maugham's sensibilities, could possibly be indifferent in his heart, whatever mask he might assume, to the mystery of our being. 'Life', said Maugham, 'is the novelist's business', and he proceeded to reveal to us something of our low cunning and bestiality as well as our sublimity.

Whenever I met Maugham, be it in London or the South of France, it was difficult to realize that his span of life reached back to a period that was a bygone page in history. The world he entered lit itself by gas and paraffin lamps, looked upon a bathroom as a luxury out of reach of all but the wealthy. His descriptions were graphic: how the well-to-do drove in broughams and landaus, lesser folk in hansoms and four-wheelers popularly known as growlers, and lesser folk still in buses drawn by stout horses. German bands and organ-grinders wandered about the streets of London, while on Sundays the muffin man made his rounds, ringing a bell. It was a very different world when Maugham entered St Thomas's Hospital. He took a couple of furnished rooms in Vincent Square for 18s. a week. His landlady provided a good breakfast and high tea when he came back from the hospital at 6.30 p.m. The two meals cost 12s. a week. For 4d. he lunched at St Thomas's on a buttered scone and a glass of milk.

So much has been written since he died about his success, financial and otherwise, that it is forgotten how he had to struggle for ten years to make a living. His mother died when he was eight, his father two years later. He spent five years at St Thomas's, but was an unsatisfactory student. His heart was never in his work. He wanted to be a writer. He wrote a novel called *Liza of Lambeth* and sent it to a publisher. It was accepted and published during his last year in hospital. Sales were encouraging. On the strength of its modest success, he quitted medicine and made writing his profession. The next ten years were tough. Maugham said he only averaged £100 a year in earnings.

The book which mirrored Maugham's personality was *Of Human Bondage*. It is long and discursive. He wrote it to rid his mind of certain obsessions. The first draft was made in 1897–8. It was rejected by several publishers. The author put it aside for several years, during which time he became a well-known dramatist. He then spent two years rewriting the book. It was published in 1915, gradually became popular, and today is one of the major novels of modern literature.

What of Maugham the man? The mordant fluid of his satire splashed on his pages. When you met him, you became aware of an elusive quality, a hardness that was terrifying in its cold asceticism. Usually it directed its blades at self-indulgence, at the hypocrisy that attempted to palm off self-interests as altruism. I remember him saying that five years spent at St Thomas's were not wasted. They taught him almost all he knew about human nature for in hospital you saw it in the raw. People in pain, people in fear of death, do not try to hide anything from their doctor. If they do he can generally guess what they are hiding.

There have been many descriptions of Maugham's nature and personality. This novelist and dramatist, who stood between the generations, and was contemporary with Wells, Galsworthy and Bennett, has been termed complicated and enigmatic. Others saw him as thoughtful, tolerant, kind to the point of being sentimental. Judged only by his writing, there was no doubt about Maugham's savage irony, corrosive satire and cruel exposure of the weaknesses of the flesh. Yet none of this was apparent when one met him. Derogatory epigrams about human nature were few. I recall a remark made after lunching with him in the Dorchester Hotel in London. It was that November must have been exceptionally mild because from his window he had watched young people continually making love in the exposed greenery of Hyde Park.

Somerset Maugham was then in his eighties. It was difficult to believe for he walked, talked and acted like a man twenty years younger. His only acknowledgement of the fact was this remark: 'This morning I went to bed at three a.m., I got up as usual at nine a.m., and I did not feel quite as fresh as usual. That is one of the signs of approaching old age'!

Somerset Maugham symbolised one vast shrug-of-the-shoulders in human shape

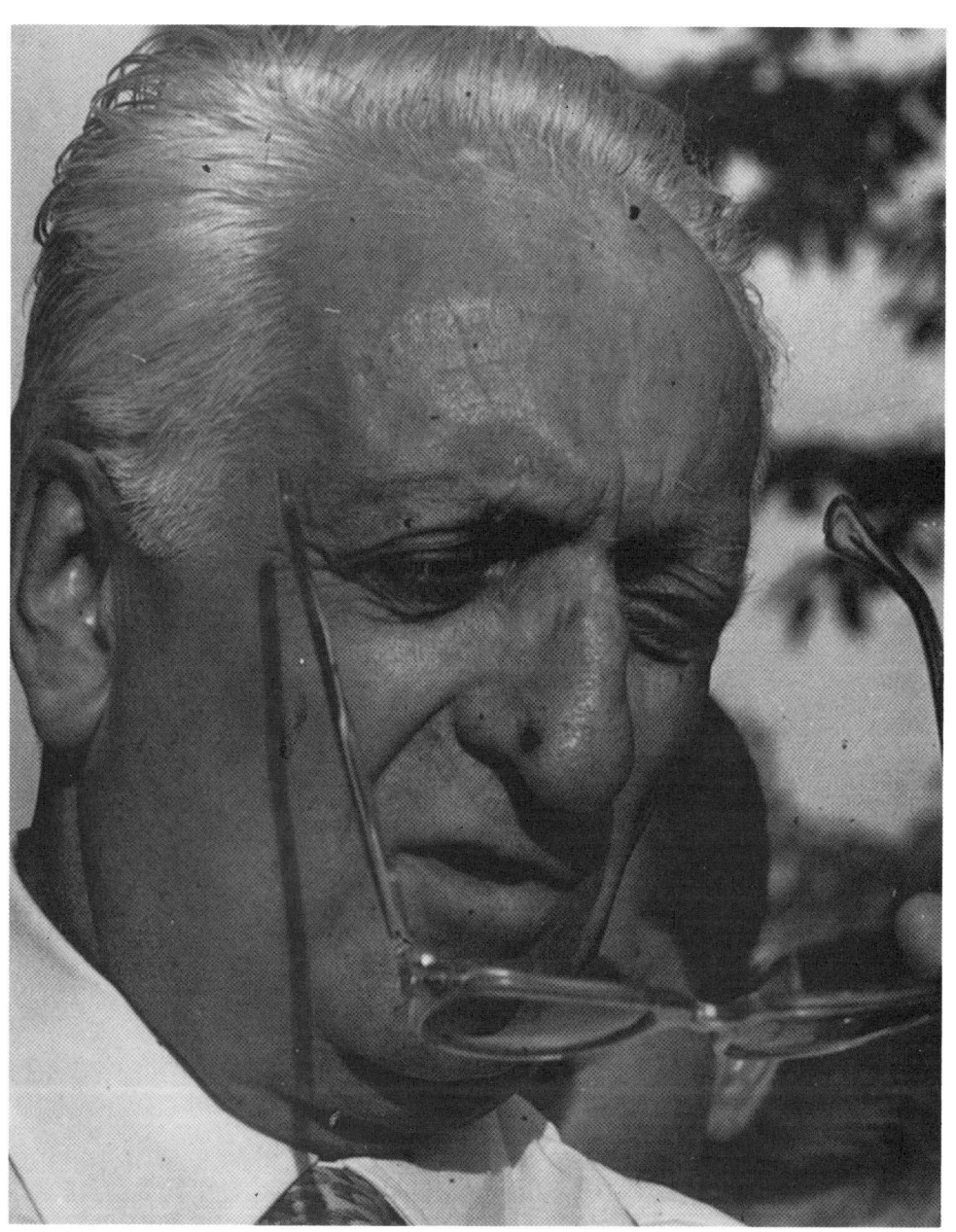

Enzo Ferrari is a law unto himself

Jacob Epstein was synonymous with controversy

F.R. Leavis, the problem figure of Cambridge University

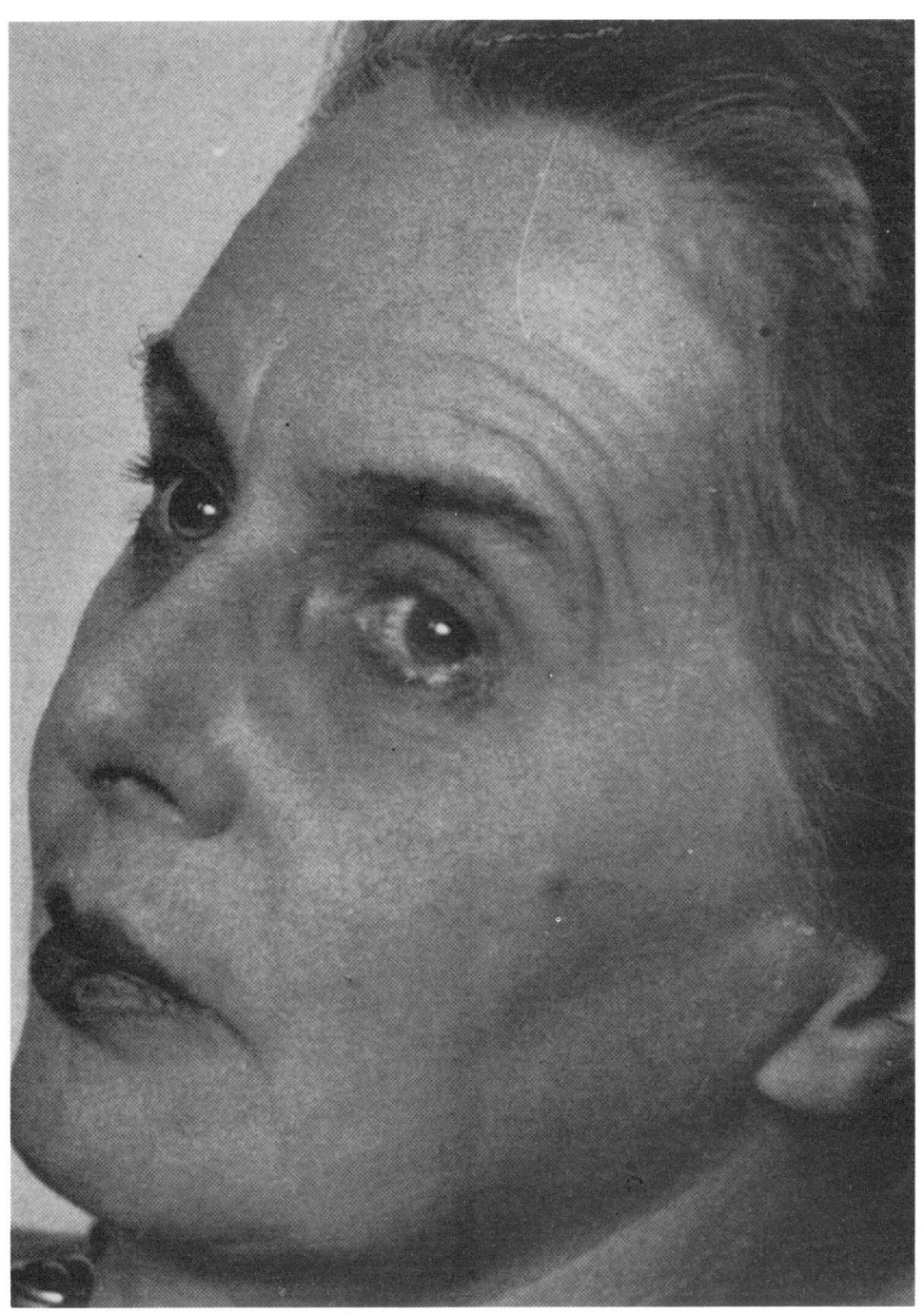

Dame Ninette de Valois had that intangible quality we call genius

G.M. Trevelyan was absorbed by the mystery of time

Princess Grace was a woman of classic beauty

Sir Julian Huxley mistakenly resembled the
fictional image of an astringent professor

Krishna Menon, the machiavel of international
politics

Viscount Samuel was a statesman of rare
intellectual distinction

A layman found it difficult to appreciate the
range of Lord Adrian's research

Enzo Ferrari

The Ferrari saga is remarkable. The Commendatore is a law unto himself. A man of mercurial moods, of sudden generosity and equally sudden temper, at times unemotional, it never does to underestimate his capability or determination to get his own way. To understand Enzo Ferrari it is necessary to know something of what has gone before.

In Italy the name has a definite but indefinable aura. To the average Italian it identifies the designer and manufacturer of one of the most successful racing cars, yet ironically the internal combustion engine which has conferred on Enzo a fortune and supremacy in his profession has also brought him absolute grief. A tragedy occurred in 1956 when his only son, Dino, was killed in a car crash. Other men have lost their sons but have survived emotionally, but with Enzo it affected normal human responses in himself and blocked his awareness of them in others.

Some insist that the Commendatore believes in nothing. That is not true. Nothing can stem his unremitting compulsion to turn out the fastest, most competitive racing cars in the world. Such is still the target of this octogenarian, whose ambition is never satisfied whatever the cost. Here you encounter a typical Italian approach to life. In Italy you are much more respected if you get the better of someone else than if he gets the better of you and no one is very critical about the way this may have been accomplished.

Like the Irish and the Jews, Italians are the victims of short-range optimism and long-range pessimism. And yet, because the Italian character is so inconstant and unpredictable, it presents a challenge. In that sense Enzo Ferrari is a true son of Italy. What lives in his imagination is real. His Maranello kingdom is a kingdom indeed. He is not manacled or chained. Broadly speaking he does what he likes. His decisions are sometimes eccentric, but his sense of purpose has never failed him. He is that most intimidating of creatures, the totally unaffected egomaniac. He is

131

always right and never afraid. He never wonders. He never doubts. His ego is very secure.

One of his executives, an engineer with many years' service at Maranello, is alleged to have said:

'I wish the Pope would make you a Cardinal, Enzo.'

'Why a Cardinal?'

'Because then we'd only have to kiss your ring.'

It maybe apocryphal, but it certainly is apt about this autocratic doyen of motor-racing. I have always found him a formidable opponent, persistent, at times unscrupulous and not always ethical, but single-minded in endeavour. Even though his heir died, he must find consolation in the knowledge that the name of Ferrari will always be remembered and respected, not only in Italy, but throughout the automobile world.

Sir Jacob Epstein

The man in the street regarded the very name of Jacob Epstein as synonymous with controversy. He saw him as an untamed man systematically destroying all that was traditional in art. Certainly no sculptor of the twentieth century in this country aroused so much interest as Epstein, but eccentricity alone would not produce such a reaction. His work imprinted itself vividly on the imagination. It was disturbing. It caused the artistically lazy to readjust their values, a process that was resented, for the modern cult tended to atrophy the sense of beauty by the banal.

It is significant that there are so few sculptors today compared with painters. The reason is mainly economic. A painter can complete a painting within weeks, maybe days: a sculptor may take months, perhaps years to complete a work that has involved heavy outlay in materials without any guarantee of a ready sale. A consequence of this situation is that little is known about sculpture. Critics with more or less sound judgement in painting often express opinions on sculpture that are not worth reading. This ignorance is largely due to the paucity of opportunity for study. Methods of mechanical reproduction make it possible to study pictures, but photographs of sculpture are seldom satisfactory.

Epstein drove a wedge into the art world. One either liked his work or hated it. Neutrality was out of the question. A comparison between the sculpture room at the Royal Academy and an exhibition of Epstein's work brought out this point. The bronzes, plaster casts and marbles in the former resemble motiveless echoes of other echoes virtually nullified by unfortunate juxtaposition. By comparison the dark bronzes of Epstein are disconcertingly alive with dynamic intensity and vigorous weight. Epstein was a sculptor in the complete sense of the word, as were the great sculptors of antiquity and the Renaissance. He knew how to tackle metal. He could hew granite, carve marble: a skilful workman handling a variety of materials with nimbleness and knowledge. He possessed the tireless energy and vigour the work demanded.

But what of the man himself? What were his reactions to the savage attacks on his work over many years? For a man who had such a robust exterior, he was surprisingly sensitive. He felt he had been reproved and morally condemned by his inferiors. It all began in 1908 with the unexpected outcry against his first public commission, the eighteen over-life-size carvings placed on the British Medical Association building in the Strand. He was only twenty-eight years old and the scandal had a profound effect on his future attitude. He resented the carvings being attacked as immoral, arguing that they were never criticized as sculpture. It marked the beginning of a crusade against philistinism. There was no shortage of targets with censure coming from many quarters, men like Belloc, Conan Doyle, and three Presidents of the Royal Academy, Dicksee, Llewellyn and Munnings. The condemnations wounded almost beyond healing.

Only once did Epstein refer in depth to those bitter years. It was in his studio surrounded with clay, stone and marble with finished bronzes and casts, everything dominated by the massive, almost completed, figure of Field-Marshal Smuts that now stands in Parliament Square. Next to it was an unfinished shrouded figure. A bust of George Bernard Shaw gave the illusion of being in heroic size. A striking contrast was provided by a female bust, the embodiment of youth, with sharp shoulder blades and finely modelled neck. The floor was pale with dust from hours of carving. It was only necessary to look around to realize something of his astonishing versatility.

In one sense the battle had been won. Persistence had been rewarded. No longer was it necessary to protect women and children from what had been described as monstrous blasphemies and obscenities. The public now went overboard with admiration. Thousands flocked to pay homage at a national exhibition of his work. And yet the insults lingered like festering wounds. He believed it was symptomatic not only of a hatred of art but a hatred of Jews. On that subject he was almost paranoiac, an attitude probably affected by his early background. Born in 1880, of Russian–Polish parents, he grew up in New York, and it was there that the earliest formative influences made themselves felt on his art. He attended the School of Students League, and did modelling in the evening. His first work was a book dealing with Jewish types in New York. The money he made from royalties and from the sale of other drawings enabled him to go to Paris. He went as a sculptor, not a painter, and enrolled as a student at the Ecole des Beaux-Arts. His first big commission, obtained through the recommendation of Muirhead Bone, was the sculpture for the BMA buildings. He was given fourteen months to do eighteen colossal figures. This was the first time that his work was described as dangerous and immoral. The statue representing *Maternity* came in for severe criticism. Father Bernard Vaughan was particularly virulent. 'The sacred subject of maternity', he said, 'has been treated a thousand times with idealistic beauty, but the Strand mother suggests merely brutal commonplace.'

The Oscar Wilde Memorial at Père la Chaise, Paris, was the next difficult task, for cemetery sculpture imposes severe restrictions. Epstein worked in England on a twenty-ton block of Hopton Wood stone, and conceived a vast winged figure, a messenger swiftly moving with vertical wings, giving the feeling of forward flight. Though it was purely symbolical, people tried to read into it a portrait of Oscar Wilde. This work has an extraordinarily potent appeal, but at the outset the police took offence and covered it up. The Hudson Bird Sanctuary panel in Hyde Park likewise roused a storm of controversy, though today it is difficult to see what the critics saw wrong with *Rima*. The storm of abuse died away and the strangely elusive beauty of this small panel blends perfectly in its green sanctuary. *Night* and *Day* likewise set the critics baying. The entire work merged easily into the horizontal courses of St James's Park station. They were not meant to be seen in isolation. Divorced from their context and viewed at a wrong angle, it was natural for them to appear distorted. *Night* came in for major criticism through the popular naturalistic conception that Epstein should have portrayed it by an attractive lady with a sad face and dressed in flowing black drapery. *Genesis* flooded the art world with comment. The statue, carved in a block of Seravezza marble, portrayed the symbolic truth of the eternal primeval feminine, the mother of the race. It was another facet of the same idea that prompted the earlier study of *Visitation*, though the latter had muted accents in keeping with the more intimate demands of the theme. A storm of protest rose from women who complained that their sex had been insulted. It was tantamount, as Epstein commented, to saying that art should be clad in the demure habiliments of a Mother Superior. To have refused Epstein the right to create *Genesis* in the way he did would have denied sculpture the right to exist. In elementary terms, according to Epstein, sculpture is the form given to a thought – the sculptor's thought, not that of the moralist or the art critic.

Bitter attacks were made on Epstein's statue of Christ on the grounds that it was distorted and oriental. People did not want to accept its stark realism, for Christ is shown accusing, pointing in reproach to his wounded hands. Few sculptors have handled a religious subject more reverently or with more poignant realism. He accepted that any attempt to intrude on the province of those artists whose innocuous work had gained the sanction of the ecclesiastical authorities would be greeted with a storm of abuse from that quarter. Artists no longer depict Christ as they feel him, such as the Christ of Fra Angelico in San Marco in Florence, which shows the joyous Christ of the resurrection. What the public expected was a conventional Christ, not an artist's sincere conception, but a third-hand rendering, a realistic study of a model who belonged to the late Renaissance. Epstein ignored that formula and embodied his own conception of Christ in sharp, unveiled austerity. This statue alone would be sufficient to name Epstein as one of the greatest of sculptors.

Epstein took from the metal – without doing any violence to its nature – a portrayal of character, built, in large measure, on the achievement of a subtle interplay of light and shade. Critics have said that he brought out all the worst qualities in his portraits, that he aimed consciously at ugliness. That is ridiculous. No artist aims consciously at ugliness. It is questionable whether an artist aims consciously at producing beauty either. He endeavours to express the character of what he is depicting. Technical dexterity is only half the battle, but is should be remembered that Epstein was limited by the restriction of his medium. He could not make the bronze look like flesh. The rough surface of his bronzes often upset people, but this uneven finish gives both character and likeness to the face which is never entirely round and smooth. Noting where the innumerable small planes begin and end, as well as their direction, makes the individual head. An entirely smooth surface would produce far greater distortion.

Any attempt to gauge the full value of Epstein's art forces us to realize how imperfect a vehicle of expression is language when it attempts to explain the significance of another art-medium. This much can be said. Epstein introduced a new creative intelligence into sculptural vision. Although he died some years ago he is still too near to be adequately assessed. Instead I prefer to sum up with one of his own quotations: 'I rest silent in my work' – words superb in finality.

Alfred Noyes

The signs of tradition and loving discrimination exercised over many years in conditions of security, soothed and delighted the visitor to Lisle Combe, in the Isle of Wight. It was the perfect shell for a poet's sensibility. The grounds blended into the sub-tropical undercliff, well away from Farringford, but very close to the landscape of Tennyson's poetry. There, in our kitchen-midden world, Alfred Noyes lived with the immunity of a mystic. By that I do not mean that his art had no relation to the world about him, that he was, as we inelegantly say, an *escapist*. He was perhaps the least mystical of poets who concerned themselves with the inner life. Mysticism would have shattered his world; it was not the mystical world that attracted him, but a very different thing, the mysterious – that is to say, whatever in life fascinated by being hidden, ambiguous, illusive and hard to understand.

Noyes was born with a love of words. He was one of the most distinguished survivors of a generation formed in the nineties or earlier, and came to maturity before 1914. At the beginning of this century English poetry was in a state of ebb. Browning and Tennyson had gone: Swinburne and Meredith had reached that veteran stage from which poetry rarely finds great expression. Edward Thomas and Rupert Brooke were, in one sense, made by the First World War, whilst Yeats survived as a reconstituted post-war poet. The names that stand out as the greatest representatives of the specifically English tradition of that period are Thomas Hardy, Walter de la Mare and Alfred Noyes.

I think it was because Noyes had seen so many things in human nature and the world that he did not wish to be forgotten, or to forget, that, to our gain, he became a poet and writer. He created his own world dyed through with his imagination. He blew great comprehensive iridescent bubbles, in which the human beings he described, though they had, of course, a recognizable resemblance to real people, only attained in that world their full reality. They existed in a medium which was not the atmosphere we ordinarily breathe. When we speak of the reality of such worlds, we only mean that we have been successfully beguiled. We are really paying homage to the shaping imagination of their creator. Noyes's work was full of delicately observed actualities. He had the faculty of analysing his impressions, of going into them not only far, but as they say in Norse fairy-tales, 'far and farther than far'.

The appeal of poetry – of pure poetry – is direct. I might even say it is magical. It impinges on the senses through the immediate impact of visual and auditory images. The visual images are literally seen, if only by the inward eye; the auditory images, embroidered in words, are literally heard, like notes of music. Those who value poetry as an expression of life found richness in the poems of Alfred Noyes. They are easy and diffuse, not tightly knit. Graceful and vivid, their charm lies with the close relation to spontaneous emotion, and the ease with which that moment of emotion finds an outlet in fluent, dignified English. So it happens that without committing his verses to memory as poetic treasures, lines that Noyes wrote recur to one as the simplest vehicle of some thought or sentiment. The sheer joy of life bursts through the closing stanzas of *The Swimmers' Race*:

> Now to their feet they leap and, with a shout,
>> Plunge through the glittering breakers without fear,
> Breast the green-arching billows, and still out,
>> As if each dreamed the arms of Hero near;
> Now like three sunbeams on an emerald crest,
>> Now like three foam-flakes melting out of sight;
>>> They are blent with all the glory of all the sea;
>> One with the golden West;
> Merged in a myriad waves of mystic light
>> As life is lost in immortality.

Noyes personified the difference between a creatively imaginative work and work which is the product of intelligence. Intelligence is a modest selective faculty; it borrows and envies 'this man's skill and that man's scope'; it can achieve wonders, but it cannot do one thing – it cannot create that unity of apprehension which is the life-breath of an inspired poem, it can never create supreme moments of poetry, inspired in every syllable and accent, such as can be found in the deeply suggestive lines of the *Aphrodite of Melos*, in which, as Edward Thomas said, the 'physical and spiritual are perfectly mingled in significance'.

Eternal Beauty, even on earth revealed,
>Above Time's girdling mists thou still
>>canst show
This radiant prophecy of the great new dawn,
The sculptured breasts, each like a soft
>>white shield,
>And the firm body like a slope of snow
>>Out of the slipping dream-stuff half
>>>withdrawn.

The words are remarkable for revealing delicacy. Noyes harnessed winged horses to the heavy car of prose. Every line he wrote, whether you like it or not, showed a love of his craft you had to respect. On occasions critics said that much of Noyes's work was limited. Others found the range of his work exceptionally varied and referred to *Drake*, his longest single poem, marked perhaps with a certain floridity; or put forward the simpler dignity of his completed trilogy, *The Torch-Bearers*. But there were moments when the scale was miniature. It was the lyric, not the epic, Chopin not Wagner. Those who demur should remember that the greatest truth is ever spoken in a still small voice.

There were times when Noyes was the most masculine of our poets, when his style and rhythms laid stress on the naked thew and sinew of the English language as in the imagined horrors of *Lucifer's Feast*, and the grimly realistic pictures like *In a Railway Carriage* and *An East End Coffee Stall*. Occasionally a note crept in suggestive of Hardy's coarse homespun; then Noyes would switch to the land of faery, that realm of the fourth dimension lying all about us, yet unexplored except by the poet.

How true it is that a stormy age is incomplete without at least one poet who sits by himself and cares only for his craft. It is a thought which in our time we reserved for the poet of Tennyson's isle. William James once said that the great use of a life is to spend it for something that outlasts it. Alfred Noyes lived that faith.

Mario Borelli

Father Mario Borelli is unlikely to be noticed in a crowd. Peasant-type priests are common in any Italian slum, but Borelli is a man apart, a man who has proved that miracles can be made to happen in a dreary setting. Naples is a palimpsest, a blending of overtones of extremes. The contrast between luxury and heart-rending poverty is comparable to the ostentatious villas and luxury flats of Johannesburg and its non-white townships, though in one sense Naples is worse. It has human refuse dumps beside the harbour that absorb the very poorest of the Naples poor. A hundred yards from the Via Roma is a world of squalor and degradation. In the *baracche* or shanty town are shacks made from scraps of lino, egg boxes, and corrugated cardboard and tin, built on the foundations of bombed buildings, rat infested and without sanitation. Water has to be carried by a pail from a pump, disease is prevalent, and typhoid not unknown. Illegitimacy and incest, thieving and prostitution are common. Gutters run with filth. In these sleazy alleys roamed the dead-end kids of Europe, unwanted and unloved – that was until Father Mario Borelli obtained permission from the Archbishop of Naples to lay aside temporarily his cassock and live in the streets with the *scugnizzi* as one of them. He lived among them for seven months, eating and sleeping as they did, finally becoming accepted as a leader of a gang. His own background helped for he had been born in the slums and was one of a family of ten. From this experiment came the Casa dello Scugnizzo, the House of the Urchins.

Borelli acquired a small, abandoned church that became the home of six boys. Chalk marks drawn across the floor summarily separated the area into a dormitory, a dining-room, a schoolroom, and a play area, if a few square feet of red tile can be called by such prosperous-sounding titles. An anteroom whose ceiling had collapsed was cleared, a piece of corrugated iron took the place of the roof, an iron pot or two were found lying around, and there was the kitchen. It would be difficult to find a more unpromising beginning with success threatened by poverty. Only Borelli's tireless efforts and imagination produced the answer.

He laid down almost no rules. The House of Urchins is run with the freedom of mutual trust. Everything is on a voluntary basis. The boys are free to leave whenever they will. They do not choose to do so. I saw them sitting down to their evening meal, once abandoned children, as mischievous as only Italian youngsters can be. When they reach fourteen they go out to work, if they can get it in this city of so many unemployed, and they divide their wages into three. One-third goes to pay for their keep, one-third is put by as savings for later on, and one-third is kept to spend as they like. Father Borelli's trust is complete. In his shanty town shack, the door is never locked. Inside was a bookcase, empty of books, which serves as a dispensary. Medicine and drugs in full view, yet nothing had ever been stolen.

Sceptics have said that the House of Urchins is a poverty-stricken, patched-up ruin of a building. Borelli's answer was that it is exactly as it should be. These boys were not in a show-case. They were not in a Home. They were at home. Home to them used to mean the streets. It still means the streets – plus a rough shelter and abundant affection. If this disused church were too clean, they would feel strangers and dirty. As Borelli emphasized if you build a smart house, you become an institution. An institution must have rules. People who live there become inmates. They are bound to be regimented. Children in an institution do not yawn, stretch themselves, and say, 'Well, I'm for bed.' They are for bed when the bell rings. Then they are assembled for night prayers and marched in silence to a dormitory. That must never happen to the Borelli children. In the House of Urchins boys behave as any boys do at home. They don't draw on walls and smash windows. When they go out to play they usually remember to come back in time for meals. The big boys come and go as they please. Little boys are given the same supervision as parents give to lads of that age. They are all part of a family. Borelli's work has prospered. Hundreds of abandoned children are no longer dead-end kids of the most desperate dead-end city of Europe. The experiment based on freedom and mutual trust has worked. The Neapolitan priest has quietly succeeded where others have failed.

Donald Campbell

Sir Malcolm Campbell and his son, Donald, made headline news for over forty-two years, a span of remarkable achievements. Donald I knew better than his father for as a family we were responsible for the design and build of both Bluebird I and II, as well as contributing to their financing, in the quest for the world land-speed record. Both men were different in many ways. It was understandable. Each had individual marks of style and personal traits, but shared in common both skill and courage. I have known both types in the motor-racing world where speed is the essence and several told me that there were times when they had been frightened. Donald felt the same. I doubt whether there is anyone in controlling tremendous speeds who does not sometimes feel fear.

One or two drivers find racing purgatory and contrive a mask of indifference in the hope that it will be mistaken for imperturbability, but, as the start-time draws near, self-control wears thin and moods become the language of strain. Courage is will power and no man has an unlimited stock. When it is used up, he is finished as a driver, though he does not always know it. Recovery from injury is not everything. A man may return to racing although his spirit has gone, and instead of being in contention, he circulates like a mobile chicane, a menace to others and himself. These signs must be recognized and the driver advised to retire as the alternative can be tragic. This is where a firm line must be taken. This worry did occur after Donald's horrific crash in Utah, but he made an incredible recovery. The after-effects of a deaccelerating G-force from 400 mph to zero in a matter of seconds had no lasting symptoms apart from one that caused both amusement and a touch of embarrassment. He found that without warning one eyelid would drop so that a serious conversation with a woman could be interrupted by an involuntary lascivious wink. On another occasion in Australia Donald had another precautionary medical check-up by a regular RAAF doctor flown to

Muloorina who pronounced him physically fit and in fine condition.

Donald was very superstitious and firmly believed he was in contact with his father. Nothing could shake that conviction and in a way it was a source of strength and comfort. On one occasion everything was set for a test run. He was given the thumbs-up sign, but nothing happened. Finally he indicated that the run was off. He had been in touch with his father who advised him not to drive that day. Everybody played ball. Nobody pooh-poohed the story. I am sure we were right for who were we to pontificate on another man's private views.

Success did not come easy. Many people in England became restless about the protracted testing without positive results. Such criticisms did not take into account the conditions under which the record-breaking attempts had to be made. The fault was in part due to the paucity of information that reached the British media. Donald kept a detailed diary that has never been published. He gave me a copy and this extract casts fresh light on the project at Lake Eyre:

The Bluebird project returned to Muloorina with all associated personnel. Four days of continuous high winds frustrated the endeavour. On Monday the 13th I flew to Adelaide to effect a change of timekeepers who were on a rota system. On the night of the 13th, heavy rain fell in the Lake Eyre region; the southern extremity of the course was flooded for some two miles and the northern end was also affected. However, the centre 8 miles escaped.

On July 15th a test run at 300 mph was made to evaluate the surface. To everyone's astonishment, the track stood up well.

Friday, July 17th dawned calm and fine. The first run was made at 7.23 a.m. At 350 mph the tyres lost adhesion and power had to be reduced. This loss of adhesion induced some instability as the vehicle fish-tailed across the course. There is little doubt that, had it not been for the tail fin and the locked differentials, we would have repeated Utah's performance. Bluebird cleared the end of the measured mile still accelerating at a speed calculated by the official timekeepers at 430 mph. This approximately corresponded with the cockpit instruments.

The return run was commenced at approximately 8.10 a.m. Three miles south of the measured mile the vehicle broke through the surface of the salt, cutting ruts up to an inch and a half deep. This acted as a very effective brake and was accompanied by very high frequency vibration of relatively low amplitude. It was immediately clear that the course had been severely damaged and there was, therefore, no alternative but to apply 110 per cent rated power. Subject to official confirmation, Bluebird established a new record of 403.1 mph.

The Bluebird functioned faultlessly and it was a great pity that the speed achieved did not truly reflect the performance of this magnificent vehicle . . . The condition of the track is perhaps most graphically illustrated by the fact that the plume of flying salt behind the vehicle was so dense that it triggered the official photo-electric timing mechanism on each occasion that the car passed through the traps. The time interval between the system being initially activated by the nose of the car breaking the beam and the plume triggering it for the second time, was approximately two-tenths of a second.

In conclusion, on Saturday 25th July, the Bluebird and all the support vehicles drove in procession down King William Street, Adelaide, to be greeted by the Lord Mayor and City Council at the Town Hall. The procession was given the most tumultuous reception by some 250,000 people – a crowd estimated by the police department to have been the largest ever seen in the history of the city. To those of us concerned, this was the deeply touching climax to the endeavour.

Donald's physical and moral courage were of a kind that not only represented a triumph of will, but a constitutional indifference to danger. Somehow we have lost this breed, maybe because there are fewer peaks to be climbed. The Campbells record is an inspiration. Sir Malcolm claimed the land-speed record nine times raising it from 146 mph to 301 mph between 1924 and 1935. Donald broke the land- and water-speed records before he was killed trying to go even faster on Coniston Water. No trace of him was found, only a helmet and his teddy bear mascot, Mr Woppit.

He once told me that he was not afraid of dying. He meant what he said. Donald enjoyed life to the full and the manner of his death was somehow appropriate. The challenge claimed his life. I am sure that he lived more in the time that he had than most men who live many years longer. The Campbell tradition for pioneering zeal now rests on the slender shoulders of his daughter, Tina. She was very special in his eyes. By current standards, he was strict, almost old-fashioned. Make-up was not encouraged, neither was lipstick. I remember after dinner with him in his home at Horley that he told Tina to go to bed early because she was taking her driving-test the following morning. He adored her and the feeling was mutual.

Today Tina, like her father and grandfather, is reaching out for her ultimate frontier. In October 1984 her boat was destroyed in an almost carbon copy of the crash that killed her father. Like him, she is proudly independent and possessed by the same determination – to reach out to fresh peaks.

Elizabeth Taylor

Another film star who defies age, and at times weight, is Elizabeth Taylor. On one occasion Jean and I were invited to lunch by Walter and Elizabeth Hayes, one of the most delightful couples on the Grand Prix scene. Walter, as Vice-President of Ford in Europe, was responsible for Ford's success in European racing. It was therefore appropriate that Cristina Ford, wife of Henry, should be at the table. Next to me sat Elizabeth Taylor. The two women faced each other with thoughts they almost kept to themselves. Elizabeth Taylor is proof that a woman can be big and still be sexy, a point that Richard Burton never tired of making, but added it was a pity her bottom was not underslung. Comments of that kind were common but Elizabeth could more than hold her own and accused the ageing star of being contentedly enslaved by what Ben Jonson called 'the fury of his gullet and groin'.

Since eight years of age Elizabeth Taylor has only had an identity as an actress or, more accurately, a public personality. For good or evil her entire life has been devoted to living a dream peculiar to her time and place, a compound of legend and unreality, an inextricable tangle of the real and the unreal which she, least of all, seems capable of sorting out. She is a survivor. The tally of near-disaster reads like a black catalogue: slipped disc, tachycarditis, pneumonia, tracheotomy scar on her neck, meningism, plus more than twenty operations. Add to this an impressive roster of husbands which suggests that she believes that marriage is a kind of emotional surrender with divorce the realization of the surrender value. The Burton–Taylor saga showed it could be mutual. He gave her a twin-jet Hawker Siddeley executive aircraft christened 'The Elizabeth' at a cost of one million dollars, and fabulous diamonds that included the 33.19-carat Krupp diamond as a birthday present – flamboyant gestures reminiscent of the reaction to Mae West's rocks, 'Goodness, what beautiful diamonds!' 'Goodness', came the reply, 'had nothing to do with it, dearie.' Not to be outdone, Elizabeth reciprocated with a present of a helicopter valued at more than £200,000.

Such was the measure of the woman opposite Cristina Ford. With her background there was no question of being intimidated. She did not have to earn money, just spend it. And there is a world of difference. Trivialities were discussed with earnest insincerity. Everyone within earshot was meant to hear what the two women had to say with all the sophisticated venom of the over-forties. Nothing is more off-putting than to see a woman trying to be the artist consummate in coquetry, aping the Maupassant gamine, but forgetting she has left it thirty years too late. Here was the glass of fashion and the mould of expanding form ranging between the superbly explicit and the low-falutin, for Elizabeth delights in calling a spade a fucking shovel.

This interlude had little to do with racing, though that was why we were there. Occasionally the subject would crop up. Cristina played a one-upmanship card by telling Walter that this was the race they had to win because all the cars had Ford engines. There was a measure of satisfaction in pointing out her mistake though clearly she intended to stick to the story even though Walter added his deft correction. Elizabeth Taylor regarded the Monaco Grand Prix as a personal promotion appearance that could never receive the privileges given to Princess Grace and she petulantly reminded me of a previous occasion when with Burton they were refused permission to land from their yacht just before the race unless they had the necessary armbands. A messenger had been sent to the BRM pit asking for badges, but with so much happening with the cars, I developed a Nelson eye.

After lunch Cristina announced that she was going to inspect the cars in the pits. This she did. Unfortunately nobody recognized her so Elizabeth had the last laugh.

F. R. Leavis

Dr Frank Leavis was the problem figure of Cambridge University, equally disliked and praised, and the centre of a controversy that continued for years in the Common Rooms. He split the English Faculty into two camps like civil war in the world of literary criticism. According to some academics, Leavis was an anathema and a damn nuisance: to other members of the Faculty and generations of students, he could do no wrong. For them he was the leading critic of his age, the greatest since Matthew Arnold. Only on one point did both sides agree: Leavis would never run away from controversy, retreat was out of the question. This was highlighted in the famous attack on C. P. Snow that created the biggest upset in English literature since the eighteenth century.

In action Leavis was abrasive. His intellect had the cutting edge of a razor. He revelled in the glare of publicity, yet in private life the image was quite different. There was no hint of basking in the reflected aura of an international reputation. The public mask and private face were totally different. In appearance Leavis never varied. He disliked ties and always wore an open-necked shirt. In warm weather a frayed pair of khaki shorts were resurrected. Sandals were preferred to shoes. Lean, sinewy, and sun-tanned in summer, he carried books and papers in a knapsack slung over his shoulder. His mode of transport was a creaking bicycle with suspect brakes. It was a familiar sight to see him making heavy weather of the slight incline in Trumpington Road, spurning the luxury of a three-speed gear, pedalling away and giving a helpful shove to one of his children who cycled slightly ahead. A favourite habit when he called was to sink into an armchair sideways so that his legs rested across the arm. Our youngsters were at the age when knees had to be scrubbed. It was difficult to insist when the knees of this eccentric don had avoided the use of soap. He had another quirk that must have been a nuisance at home, but even more tiresome for a host. He declined to eat anything after lunch with the result that whoever sat next to him at dinner became conscious of eating whilst he stared at an empty plate.

In many ways Frank Leavis was a typical product of East Anglian stock, somewhat puritanical in outlook and deficient in humour. His father was a tradesman in Cambridge and sold musical instruments in a shop near Parker's Piece; his grandfather had been a piano-tuner at Denver; his great-grandfather a basket-maker, while Uncle Frederick was landlord of the Six Bells off Mill Road. After the First World War in which he served as a stretcher-bearer, he went to Emmanuel College on a scholarship, read history, but only scraped an indifferent 2nd in the first part of the Tripos, switched to English under Richards, and finished with a 1st. His ambition was to be a teacher. Little did he think that years ahead he would make Downing College world famous for its English studies.

The feud between Sir Charles Snow and Dr Leavis had been brewing for some time. If conversation lagged, it was only necessary to mention Snow's name to get things moving. In his eyes Snow represented the superficial culture and introverted snobbery of High Table complacency. It came to a head when in his Rede Lecture entitled *The Two Cultures and the Scientific Revolution*, Snow attacked the universities and the educational system for not placing sufficient emphasis on the new scientific cultures. Leavis interpreted the comparison as a rejection of literary and historical traditions. The lecture received tremendous publicity and went through innumerable editions, building up in the process Snow's reputation, particularly in American universities where a college in the University of Buffalo had been named after him.

The counterblast was planned with care. Leavis chose the Richmond Lecture, founded during the Second World War by Sir Herbert Richmond, Master of Downing, and delivered it in the hall of the college under the title *Two Cultures – The Significance of C. P. Snow*. No punches were pulled. The opening set the tone: 'If confidence in oneself as a mastermind, qualified by capacity, insight and knowledge to pronounce authoritatively on the frightening problems of our civilization, is genius, then there can be no doubt about Sir Charles Snow's.' Leavis went on to attack the *Two Cultures* theory. He referred to its utter lack of intellectual distinction and embarrassing vulgarity of style, calling it a document for the study of the cliché. Of Snow's authoritative tone on science and literature, while only a genius could justify it, one could not imagine a genius adopting it, and Snow was not a genius.

His superficial literary culture was something which people who loved literature could only regard with contempt. As a novelist Snow was without a glimpse of what creative literature was or why it mattered. There was no more significance in his completed books than there was drama or life. The thinking was representative of a shallow materialistic philosophy. The 'literary intellectuals' were merely *New Statesman* scribblers and Sunday newspaper reviewers. Snow was as intellectually negligible as it was possible to be. To call his argument a movement of thought was to flatter it. The comparisons between scientific and literary values were meaningless. Worst of all, Snow's insistence that material progress was the world's first priority was a pernicious untruth. There were higher values at stake.

When the smoke cleared, little of Sir Charles or his theories had survived the broadside. He was badly shaken, but decided not to reply. He believed that the adverse publicity that followed killed any chance of a Nobel Prize. He accepted the Downing undergraduates' offer to deliver the following year's Richmond Lecture, but made no reference in it to Leavis.

A great deal has been written about Leavis's criticism, his dogmatism, roughness in controversy and puritanism, but it nevertheless established him as one of the greatest of literary critics, reinforced by the output of some twenty books, though at times it was a pity that the dogmatism and an uncompromising style were over emphasized; but that was Leavis and a leopard cannot change its spots.

His principal weapon was a periodical called *Scrutiny*, the most remarkable critical quarterly in the history of English letters. It began in 1931 when a group of research students founded it in the Leavises' house. Contributors and staff were unpaid. In the thirties it printed 750 copies and its circulation at the end of its life in 1953 only totalled 1,500. Leavis was its principal editor throughout. Its influence was immense because he used it as a sounding-board for a wide range of cultural issues. He was never afraid of stepping out of line and making controversial statements, but on one occasion he ran into unexpected trouble. He wanted to quote from *Ulysses* in his lectures. As it was a banned book he wrote to the Home Office for permission to import a copy. Shortly afterwards he was summoned to see the Vice-Chancellor, who showed him a letter from the Public Prosecutor saying that the Cambridge police had been monitoring his lectures. It concluded with the recommendation that Leavis should be suitably and firmly dealt with. So much for the good old days.

After he retired I asked Leavis whether he had many regrets when looking back on his academic career. There was only one discordant note. He was still bitter about the manipulations of some members of the Board, who disliking his attitude to literature and criticism, had persistently blocked his progress in the English Faculty. On a personal note, he admitted disappointment that, after being nominated for the Chair of Poetry at Oxford, the election went in favour of Robert Graves. Had he been successful the experience might have had a mellowing effect. However, it made no such impact on Graves.

Viscount Samuel

It was difficult to realize that Lord Samuel's span of life reached back to a period that was a bygone page in history. His childhood was spent in a London that knew no motor cars or motor buses, taxis or tube railways: there were no bicycles, except the high 'penny farthings', no electric light or telephones, no cinemas or broadcasting. Instead there was a continuous dull roar of horse-drawn traffic. His own memories were graphic: how in the afternoon he used to go shopping with his mother in a brougham, or in summer for a drive in Hyde Park in an open barouche, with its roomy shallow body, and lofty box for the coachman and footman; how occasionally a couple of mounted police would appear trotting down the middle of the road, waving to the coachmen to draw to the sides. Then, in an open-pair horse-carriage, Queen Victoria would drive by, at her side the Princess of Wales, and perhaps two or three grandchildren opposite. On the rumble at the back of the carriage would be two attendants in Highland dress, their arms folded. All the people in the lined-up carriages would stand, the ladies drop curtsies, and the few gentlemen raise their tall top-hats, as the Queen and Princess passed through, bowing to each side.

Such were the earliest recollections of a statesman who brought to the service of his country an intellect of rare distinction. After he entered Parliament in 1902, Lord Samuel's political life was indeed rich. He served in three Cabinets; as leader of the Liberal Party, he formed, with Ramsay MacDonald and Baldwin, the three-party National Government; occupied the post of Home Secretary with marked ability; played a prominent part in the ending of the General Strike; and could claim among his chiefs and colleagues such men as Campbell-Bannerman, Asquith, Lloyd George, Grey and Churchill. But a statesman's place in history ultimately depends upon the fate of the policies and institutions with which he has been identified. I once asked him to select what he considered to be the most important of the many constructive achievements in his long career. He named the part he played in a movement of historic importance. As a Jew he was profoundly concerned for his people, and he was one of the first to win the attention of the Cabinet for the policy of establishing a Jewish National Home in Palestine. In 1920, after the Mandate had been conferred on Great Britain, he was called to be the first High Commissioner for Palestine and Transjordan.

Lord Samuel was that rare type of statesman, a politician doubled with a philosopher. It was a toss-up whether he devoted himself to a life of thought or politics. The life of thought never lost attraction or importance for him, and there were moments in his career when it was apparently with relief that he felt again beneath him the firm ground of abstraction. His speculative interests were keenest at those points where philosophy influences men's beliefs most directly. He described how, during the years when he was host at Government House in Jerusalem, Einstein was a guest. He walked along the ridge of the Mount of Olives. During the conversation Einstein said that he thought the trouble of the world had come through science advancing faster than morals; that only when morals caught up with science would the troubles be ended. Today the state of human affairs highlights the need for philosophy, science and religion to draw closer together, a theme that filled Lord Samuel's mind.

He was essentially a man of action, yet his intellectual integrity at times prevented him from touching some of those levers which circumstances may compel a man of action to pull. He could not make an unfair appeal. The change from the Asquith to the Lloyd George regime was a change to an appeal to the subconscious and usually the baser side of it, both in the public and in those actively concerned in carrying on the war administratively. Lord Samuel knew all about such appeals, but could not bring himself to make them. He was out of touch with what is instinctive and emotional in human nature, which is so much to the fore at such times. When the split in the coalition came, he went out with Asquith and was outside the government for fifteen years. It is interesting to recall the vicissitudes of the National Government Cabinet and the reasons for the withdrawal of the Liberal leader and his colleagues. According to Lord Samuel, the greatest crisis in which he was concerned was in 1914, in the days that preceded the outbreak of the First World War. He had then been a member of the Cabinet for five years. As to the right course to take in that critical moment, they were at first divided in their views. For Lord Samuel's part, he was quite clear on one point, which seemed to him to govern the whole situation. It was that nations have a duty to honour their treaty obligations. Unless that rule was regarded as absolute, the world would become an anarchy, the scene of continually recurring conflicts. That was a point which seemed to him quite obvious.

All of us possess memories which, at the touch of some association of ideas, return vividly with every detail. I recall a day when Lord Samuel, who was one of my sponsors for the Royal Institute of International Affairs, lunched with me in Oxford. His talk had the merits of order, brevity, clearness and good manners. It excluded trivial egotism. To brush aside the insignificant was instinctive. He praised, I remember, Mr Gladstone, an admiration that might have been anticipated. He recalled something of the sense of national loss when it was heard that he was dead, and described the scene in the Abbey when he saw the old statesman lowered into the grave in the presence of the leaders of the nation, and the moment after the ceremony when the Prince of Wales, who had been the chief pall-bearer, stooped to kiss the hand of the little bent figure of Gladstone's wife, who was shrouded in black from head to foot.

He commented on Gladstone's untiring attention to detail, even in extreme old age. When he stood for Parliament at the election of 1895, Gladstone had sent him a personal letter of support. Two years later Lord Samuel ventured to ask him for a similar letter on behalf of the Liberal candidate at an important by-election then taking place. He received a reply, on one of the familiar postcards. Although his eyesight was failing, the eighty-seven-year-old statesman took the trouble to write with his own hand to this young supporter with whom he was hardly acquainted. Some weeks later Lord Samuel showed me the original card. It read:

My Dear Sir,
Notwithstanding the numerous attractions of the request that you are good enough to make, there is one preliminary objection of a conclusive nature, namely, that the duty proposed is one for the actual leaders of Parties and not for a wholly retired politician. My wishes, however, are all with you.
Yours very faithful [sic],
W. E. Gladstone,
Jan. 26. '97.

Today when Liberalism is attempting to recapture its one-time authority, Lord Samuel used to stand out as the embodiment of its former authority in the somewhat detached atmosphere of the House of Lords. Whether or not he thought of himself as a great man, I could never discover. He would probably have said that the term was an exceedingly vague one, and would certainly not have trusted the reports of introspection on such a point. Certainly, few men have been able to gather as fine a vintage from life's vineyard. The choicest was kept for the private side of his life.

Dame Ninette de Valois

Ninette de Valois, founder and creator of the Royal Ballet, is a mixture of extremes. Completely selfless in her pursuit for perfection in others, her authority in that role was total. Young dancers were fearful of her displeasure. What *Madam* said was final. There was no arguing, but though a disciplinarian, she has the genuine affection of hundreds of dancers who owe their success to the exacting training. Ninette has retired as Director, handing over to Sir Frederick Ashton. In a way it was a natural sequence. After being with the Diaghilev Company which she joined following training with Cecchiti, the great Italian teacher, Ninette de Valois founded her Academy of Choreographic Art, later to become the Royal Ballet School; then became a choreographer and created seventeen of the Company's first twenty-two ballets; talked Lilian Baylis into giving her the Sadler's Wells Theatre; engaged Constant Lambert as musical director, and persuaded Frederick Ashton to leave the Marie Rambert group. Out of this emerged the Royal Ballet and an unmistakable English style developed after lacking any balletic tradition.

There is every reason to be proud of such an achievement and to show it, but here is the contradiction. Ninette de Valois has always shunned any personal limelight. She is genuinely shy and reserved when it comes to self-publicity, although in private a relaxed conversationalist. I recall an occasion at the Opera House when preparations were in progress for an evening performance of *Le Lac des Cygnes*. The rehearsal was in full swing when I arrived with Ninette de Valois. It was an interesting experience. I wandered in the castle grounds devised by Leslie Hurry. Somewhere in the background a carpenter was at work. I could hear feet pattering on stone steps. A pianist thumped out the strains of the mazurka. A slender, sylph-like girl unbuttoned her skirt, shook it off, and joined several other faun-like creatures who danced as if they had been blown together by the music. At the evening performance, a bell summoned us. Stalls and boxes filled. Every tier of the amphitheatre was packed. Lights faded like dying glow-worms. Applause greeted the conductor. He bowed, tapped the stand with his baton, and the theatre welled to the music of Tchaikovsky – familiar chords – then slowly the huge curtains parted, and delicate wraiths of grace floated across the stage. It was a visual interpretation of a musical emotion. Music and ballet fused in an inarticulate, unfathomable speech leading us to the edge of the infinite.

Ballet had become the ectoplasm of music. We followed the romance of Odette and Siegfried until the final voyage through the waters of the lake to the world of eternal happiness. All the time in a box by the stage, Ninette de Valois was observing with a critical eye.

Madam has that intangible quality which we call genius. Her enthusiasm has never waned. Her methods have not dated. By cutting herself off from her time, she has rendered herself timeless, a priceless legend.

Salvador Dali

At the time of writing Salvador Dali lies in a clinic almost next to his museum in Figuéras, a sick old man waiting for death – a sad final act for this artist and professional genius, who has been likened to an excited prawn with his long, twitching moustache and black button eyes. The description was a fair pen-portrait of this exhibitionist. He played the role so often that it became second nature. I recall a television discussion when Dali arrived in the sombre black of an undertaker, high white collar, black string tie, pallid face, over-blacked hair, arched eye-lines, and clutching the inevitable gold-topped cane. The programme began with Dali assuring me that his outrageous days were over. He no longer slept in a black open coffin, instead he had become the first atomic artist. He drew inspiration from the heavens through the end of his moustaches and demonstrated by moving his arms vigorously up and down to suggest a pulling-down action. The chairman commented that the action seemed vaguely familiar, while Sir Gerald Kelly, who sat next to me, growled 'absolute balls', a remark that regrettably was not picked up by the microphone.

A more private occasion was in Madrid. At our dinner-party, François Cervert, the French Grand Prix racing driver, brought as partner an exquisite creature with eyes made up to look like clotted dog-daisies. François exuded the gaiety of a youth who had just learned the facts of life and found them hilarious, but even he had his social set-backs. We had decided to watch a performance by one of Spain's finest flamenco dancers, not in a strip-joint with acres of goose-flesh, but in one of Spain's best-known restaurants. All the ingredients were there for an interesting evening as other guests included Salvador Dali. He lived up to his reputation of being something of an enigma. He painted dreams, fantasies and the jumbled disorder of the human conscience and enjoyed playing out some of the incongruities he discovered in his own complicated personality in public happenings. Dali was one of the earliest 'happening' artists. Invariably something happened, but you were never sure what it would be. That night was no exception.

He began by describing to Cervert his scheme for Helena Rubinstein's New York apartment, which included a fountain spouting from a grand piano hanging from the ceiling, adding that it would never be played. The design was turned down. Not so the enormous stuffed bear with drawers in its stomach which he had offered to Else Schiaparelli. He then recalled giving a lecture on a scorching summer afternoon dressed in a diver's suit, carrying a billiard-cue, dagger in belt, and a pair of Russian wolfhounds in tow.

By that time François was beginning to look glazed. He woke up when a sultry-looking girl with half-closed eyes took the floor while guitars thrummed in the background. People around began to clap and stamp their feet in tune to the music. Still the girl remained motionless. Then suddenly up went her arms, click went the castanets, and the music rushed after her as she moved into a dance. She had style, elegance, passion. There was hardly a sound as she danced, only the guitars and the rapping of her high heels. There were moments when her body was stationary except for a slight tapping of her heels, but her arms and hands were still dancing, weaving slow patterns in the air. Then she would plunge into her corybantic frenzy again, bending, shuddering, turning and glancing over her shoulder. All the time, above her hair, at her waist, in the air around her, like cicadas on a summer day, was the sharp rattle of what the poet Martial called the *Poetica crusmata*. Then, when least expected, the guitars broke off and the girl stood as still as coloured marble, hardly breathing, to be rewarded by a volley of 'Olé's'. The spell was broken. It had clearly aroused Dali as he rose to his feet, smiled at each of us, beckoned to François' partner and together they disappeared into the night.

The Frenchman's expression registered disbelief. He was saddled with Dali's companion, a woman of uncertain age, with a green, drowned-looking face, weirdly scissored hair and tight black dress. All French gestures are variants of the shrug. His night had vaporized into a mist. He reacted as if nothing out of the ordinary had happened. I suppose from Dali's point of view, it hadn't.

C. B. Fry

At a time when interesting sporting personalities were rare, C. B. Fry stood head and shoulders above the figures of several decades. As a cricketer he was the stylist of the Golden Age with fluent rhythm and delicate touch. In retrospect he should be judged as anyone must be on the merits of his best performance and there were many. The ideal way to sift these out was to get the man himself to make the selection. That opportunity presented itself at Buckler's Hard by the Hamble on Southampton Water, where Fry spent so many years on the training-ship *Mercury*. It was towards the end of his life, but memory and comments were as pertinent as ever.

He admitted that the choice was wide, particularly in cricket. To isolate one innings was not easy when the total of runs in first-class games had been over 30,000, that included eighteen Tests for England against Australia and eight with South Africa. He recalled in detail the 232 not out in 1903 for the Gentlemen against the Players at Lord's, while two seasons earlier there had been eighteen centuries with an aggregate of 3,146 runs including six consecutive centuries. But the one that gave lasting satisfaction was when as Oxford captain he scored 100 not out in the University match. He also reminded me that cricket writers forget his prowess as a fast bowler. Against Cambridge in 1895 he claimed six wickets in an innings and also had a hat trick against the MCC.

In other sports Fry recalled how in soccer he played for England and was full-back for Southampton against Sheffield United in the 1902 FA Cup Final. In rugby he played for Blackheath and the Barbarians, but missed a Blue through injury. In athletics he had concentrated on sprinting and jumping, both high and long, and described how at Iffley Road, Oxford, his long jump of 23 ft 6½in stood as a world record for twenty-one years. Other achievements apart from sport were recalled with equal gusto. He emphasized that when he went from Repton to Oxford in 1891, money was tight. An £80 scholarship at Wadham had to be eked out with spending money of about thirty shillings. It meant hard work to justify his place. He made the grade and took 1st Class Honours in Classical Mods and could still feel satisfaction at finishing ahead of F. E. Smith and Lord Simon. On the other hand, there had been several disappointments.

Before the Second World War he met Hitler and regretted not being able to change the Führer's militaristic indoctrination of youth movements. He had no joy in converting Russians to cricket, but in those days there was no Mikhail Gorbachov. Another frustrated ambition were the attempts to become a Member of Parliament. Liberal supporters in Brighton, Banbury and Oxford City had not been numerous enough to win the day, while Tories and Socialists had not been swayed by his rhetoric. Then there was the Albanian affair. During the League of Nations period, England was extremely popular politically in Albania. Fry was in Geneva with Ranjitsinhji on the Indian delegation and served on the Finance Committee. The leading Albanian delegate, a bearded bishop, had been empowered to find an English country gentleman with an expendable income of £10,000 a year, the price-tag for the vacant throne. The bishop felt that Fry would be an admirable choice. Unfortunately that kind of money was not available. On reflection Fry believed that Ranji, a man of great wealth, would have underwritten the venture, but it would have meant severing their relationship, but he sometimes wondered how his life-style might have been affected in such a role. The last disappointment was never being elected to serve on the MCC Committee. He felt that was because of his being something of a rebel and an unguarded remark to the effect that some of the members did not know the difference between an off-break and an off-licence.

I was surprised that the years on the *Mercury* were not included. Fry disagreed. That work had been his life to the exclusion of other interests and temptations and, as such, was part of him. It is impossible to place Fry in one category. There were so many facets – scholar, politician, sportsman, writer, and inspirer of youth. He went through life with a casual air that concealed a shrewd brain and a probing eye through his monocle. In public he could display that kind of diffidence that conceals and often protects an enormous private egotism, but externally he was the perfectionist as smooth and as hard as Perspex, yet a more selfless or generous person it would have been hard to find.

Sir Julian Huxley

Sir Julian Huxley resembled the fictional image of an astringent professor who only came to life in a laboratory or lecture-room, yet nothing could have been further from the truth. The label became less a libel when he was part of the Joad–Huxley act on the 'Brains Trust', but even then he seemed cold and clinical. Alongside his brother, Aldous, he missed out on publicity. Not for him *Brave New World* or the controversial *Heaven and Hell* and *The Doors of Perception*, books that some felt induced youngsters to experiment with psychedelic drugs. It was not his line. He did not indulge in fantasy. That did not mean he was strait-laced. In his home at Hampstead he was witty and uninhibited. Topics could switch from embryology to Africa, the behaviour of ants or cancer, even the courtship of herons. The subject was unpredictable. He was interested in anything to do with the conservation of wild life in Africa, the place of man in nature, the control of world population, and, like Sir Martin Ryle though from a different angle, he had deep concern about the future of man and his role in the universal cosmic process.

Julian Huxley was brilliant in so many spheres. It was sad that the public rarely saw the warm side of his nature.

Ingrid Bergman

Ingrid Bergman was a brilliant interpretative actress whose real life oustripped in drama content the roles she played on screen and stage. Her childhood in Sweden and her marriages including the controversial elopement with Roberto Rossellini are described by Alan Burgess in *Ingrid Bergman My Story* in eloquent phrase and detail. The pages confirm that Ingrid was a complex personality impossible to contain in a fixed mould. For someone who had starred with Humphrey Bogart in *Casablanca*, Ernest Hemingway and Gary Cooper in *For Whom the Bell Tolls*, and was a friend of such men as Howard Hughes, David Selznick and George Bernard Shaw, it was surprising to find how vulnerable she was to criticism. Yet in adversity Ingrid's courage was remarkable, especially her stoical acceptance of double operations for breast cancer and the unpleasant effects of radiation treatment. That chapter of her life remains an object-lesson and example for all those who have to cope with this dreaded disease.

It was the little things that hurt, particularly when critics were unnecessarily vicious as happened when *Joan of Arc at the Stake* was produced and directed by Roberto Rossellini at the Stoll, the oratorio by Arthur Honegger and written by Paul Claudel. Some critics were fascinated if confused, others were just bitchy. I took the opposite view and a long time later Ingrid told me that the wording of my phrases had meant a lot to her at the time. They epitomized what she had attempted to portray. I am glad that Burgess included these lines in the Bergman *Story*. I repeat them in memory of one of the loveliest of actresses: 'In the engulfing darkness and piercing shafts of light at the *Stoll* she suggests the spiritual statuesque calm of one who has climbed to the summit high above the gross world. She evokes the sadness of things supremely well . . . The quality she possesses is more than beauty: it is strangeness in beauty.'

In more ways than one it is a poignant epitaph of her life.

Lord Adrian OM

It has been said that there is no institution in the world like Trinity College, Cambridge, where so many young men of promise – very often not always fulfilled – have passed the formative years of life, and made their friendships and undergone the influences that set their feet on the ladder of life, to say nothing of the innumerable men of learning and science and College administration who have grown old working within its walls. For more than four hundred continuous years men have hoped and planned, worked and played, liked and disliked one another, formed and altered their opinions in a thousand different ways now utterly forgotten, from the time when the supreme issue in balance was whether England – and therewith Trinity – should be Roman Catholic or Protestant, down to the present day.

Sometimes Trinity men have been in opposition on a crucial issue, as when Lord Chancellor Francis Bacon opposed Chief Justice Coke on the question of King's prerogative. Sometimes they were in conjunction, as when Earl Grey passed the great Reform Bill, with Lord Althorp as his principal lieutenant. Sometimes they have touched the same issue at successive stages; for instance, the conception of self-government in the British Dominions owed much to Charles Buller, its extension to Campbell-Bannerman, who conceded self-government to the Boers, and its definition to Earl Balfour. But whether they are of men who have agreed or disagreed, helped one another or hindered, the Trinity names are reasonably numerous; indeed, the College has helped in educating two kings of England, six Prime Ministers, and all those Cabinet Ministers, bishops, judges and other notabilities who look down from their engravings massed on the walls of the Fellows' Parlour in neglected profusion.

In October 1908 a student entered Trinity as a Westminister Exhibitioner and a Major Entrance Scholar in natural science. That undergraduate was Edgar Douglas Adrian. His student days were exceptionally brilliant, and he was elected to a Fellowship in

1913. He had pursued natural science as a student of medicine, completed the clinical part of this training at St Bartholomew's Hospital, and taken his MD degree. During the First World War he was mainly occupied in the treatment of cases of shell-shock, first at Queen's Square in London, and then at Farnborough. At the latter place he was associated with a number of distinguished men, such as G. I. Taylor, F. W. Aston and Lord Cherwell.

Though Adrian could have been a most able and successful physician, his predominant interests were in teaching and in scientific research on the physiology of the brain and nervous system. After the war he accepted the invitation of the College to return to Trinity as a College lecturer. He came back to the staircase E Great Court, on which he had lived as an undergraduate, merely ascending one flight from E 1 to Newton's room in E 4. In 1929 Adrian became Foulerton Research Professor of the Royal Society, and relinquished his College lectureship. He held this post until 1937, when he became Professor of Physiology in the University and a professorial Fellow of the College. Members of Trinity received with utmost satisfaction the news that the Crown had appointed Adrian to the Mastership of the College upon the retirement of G. M. Trevelyan in 1951. It would be tedious to enumerate the many honours that were showered upon the Master. He was elected Fellow of the Royal Society in 1923, became President in 1950, but it was the two greatest – the Nobel Prize in 1932 and the Order of Merit in 1942 – that endorsed his reputation as one of the greatest of scientists.

For a layman it is difficult to appreciate the range of Adrian's researches. I recall an occasion when he tried to fill in the background against which to survey his work. He was both patient and lucid. He pointed out that apart from some cases of gross mental defect, few neurologists would claim that they could tell from an examination of the brain structure whether it was that of a very stupid or a very clever man, a man who had been thoroughly schooled or allowed to run wild, a fact that was not so much a reflection on our methods of examining brain structure as a tribute to the immense range of intelligent behaviour.

His survey of past methods was interesting. He referred to the writings of the French physiologist Xavier Bichat in 1799, who, when dealing with the supply of arterial blood to the brain pointed out that men with long necks were often slow and hesitant and men with short necks energetic and decided, ascribing the difference to the greater distance between heart and brain in the long-necked. Adrian next touched on the science of physiognomy developed by Gall and popularized in this country by his pupil Spurzheim describing their naïve method of trying to correlate the shape of the head and face with the known character of the subject. Unfortunately Gall's work was taken too seriously and went too far, the science of physiognomy being changed to that of phrenology.

Adrian came next to Lombroso's famous book on *Criminal Man* published in 1876, which began by regarding all criminals as distinct anthropological types with definite structural peculiarities pointing to atavism or degeneracy. He found peculiarities in their skulls, in the convolutions of their brains and in their general build. He said that these views never won general acceptance, final disproof coming in 1913, when Dr Charles Goring examined a large number of prisoners and found that Lombroso's physical criteria were no commoner among them than among the general population.

Professor Adrian stressed that the fate of these theories showed how easy it was to jump to false conclusions when we looked for correlations between particular habits of body and particular habits of mind. The difficulty was largely one of measurement, of reducing the data to numerical form; and it must always be present when we were dealing with such intractable material as the shape of the head or the honesty of its owner. He said that ideas about brain physiology in relation to behaviour faced the same difficulty and some conclusions could be equally rash, but he was confident we now had a method which told us something about the general pattern of activity in the brain.

Some twenty years earlier Dr Matthews had investigated with him the claims that Hans Berger had made about what he called the electroencephalogram – how by applying two electrodes to the surface of the head and connecting them with a string galvanometer, it was possible to detect a regular current fluctuation with a frequency of about 10 cycles a second. Berger gave evidence to show that these currents were generated by the brain, and he supposed that they represented its basic activity. The rhythm ceased if the attention was aroused and it could not always be found, but it was there so often that Berger felt justified in naming it the rhythm. Adrian and Matthews had no difficulty in finding the rhythm in the record from the surface of the head and in satisfying themselves that Berger was right in supposing it to come from the brain.

Adrian then went on to say that it was a well-established fact that there were considerable variations in the electrical records of brain activity in different individuals. The difference was as characteristic as differences in the shape of the head or in handwriting. The subject in his original experiments showed a fairly persistent rhythm over a period of years, and various of his colleagues had remained true to their particular type for the same length of time. The most striking difference was in the rhythm. In most people the waves appeared when the eyes were closed and the attention relaxed, but they did not then continue indefinitely, usually varying in size and in mode of onset, and the sequence was broken by frequent gaps. At either end of the scale there were two extreme types, a small percentage of subjects with an extremely constant rhythm, and a small percentage with none at all.

He described how there were other features of the electro-encephalogram which appeared less often. The waves could be faster or slower than usual, they could be irregular in size and frequency and there could be occasional isolated spikes. He found such records were often associated with definite evidence of clinical abnormality, epilepsy or some kind of nervous instability.

Adrian then talked of a method which aimed at adjusting a disturbed balance of the different parts of the brain mechanism. No one knew much about the way in which such a balance was achieved in the normal brain, but it was found that deliberate injury to the frontal lobes would diminish the forces which led to anxiety and criticism of self and others and would produce at all events a more tractable patient who was not necessarily the worse for the permanent loss of some of his brain. He pointed out that we produce much the same effect temporarily on our brains by some of the drugs we take to escape from our troubles, though alcohol and morphia and aspirin may all adjust the balance in different ways. The surgical treatment was, of course, irrevocable and no one would want to use it without very good cause, but he believed that before long surgeons would have a much better under-standing of what they were doing and would be able to pick out those parts which caused mental imbalance. It was significant to note that the balancing factors were not necessarily confined to the brain. An overactive thyroid could disturb behaviour and the disturbance could be corrected by removing it surgically or controlling it by drugs.

I recall the warning that Adrian issued, that if our behaviour was under the control of our brains and if our brains could be altered by the neurosurgeon to make our behaviour conform to the standard pattern, we should be watchful of the frightening implications of such a power; but he pointed out that there was no reason to single out the medical profession in general and the brain surgeons in particular for such heart-searchings: those who had to do with the training of the young, who implanted moral principles, or, if we preferred it, established the conditioned reflexes, had more responsibility for mankind than those who dealt with the structure of the brain.

His closing words were clear. The physicist has the same dangers to face when he finds new ways of splitting the atom as the chemist when he makes a new insecticide and the pathologist when he extracts a bacterial toxin. The advances of scientific knowledge can be harmful if put to the wrong uses. In taking more responsibility for the brain we had to make sure that we left some responsibility to the individual. We were not all so well balanced that we should reject this chance of mending our ways.

One further honour was conferred on Lord Adrian when he became Chancellor of Cambridge University. After his death the tradition has been carried on by his son who inherited the title. He is internationally renowned as a biophysicist whose work on the electrical charges affecting muscle fibre and reactions is at the forefront of current cell physiology research. The pattern is familiar. Not only is he Master of Pembroke College but in 1985 he became Vice-Chancellor of the University. The Adrian link with Cambridge is safe.

Richard Dimbleby

Television creates a myth of its own. As a medium it eats people, is no respecter of persons, builds its employees into images that pander to the tastes of viewers, and acts as a seismographic record of world affairs, ideas and individual behaviour. Personalities are encouraged to reflect the tastes of the day. Viewers have come to accept, indeed expect the sounding-off of Robin Day, the best square on the screen; the archness of reinstated Angela Rippon; uninhibited Les Dawson; the bored weariness of Michael Parkinson; prissy Jan Leming; tactful Ludovic Kennedy; ill-tempered Peter Snow and the wish-to-God-we-were-out-of-hereness of the 'Newsnight' team; suave Alastair Burnett with City-slick accent; Russell Harty for ever identifying himself understandably with the lower-middle classes; Kenneth Baker, the answer to insomnia; the inanities of Terry Wogan, and so on. At the moment all are credible figures of entertainment and edification, but let their appeal wear thin, the images are smashed and someone else takes over. Media popularity rarely lasts.

There has been one exception. Richard Dimbleby was in a class apart. Over a period of nearly thirty years he established a relationship with viewers that was akin to a warm-hearted friendship. His reassuring natural talents endeared him to millions. That unruffled manner was real. Naturally polite and considerate, though maybe not an intellectual giant, he was a remarkable pioneer with endless 'firsts' to his credit. He was the first BBC War Correspondent: the first BBC News Observer: took part in the first live television relays across the Channel and over the Atlantic via Telstar; he described the lying-in-state of King George VI from the Great Hall of Westminister; he was the first television commentator at the Coronation of a British Sovereign, a marathon that meant seventeen hours in Westminister Abbey; the first BBC War Correspondent to enter Berlin with the Allied Troops and broadcast from Hitler's chair in the bombed study; the commentator at the funeral of Sir Winston Churchill and at numerous Royal events and State occasions – there were so many memorable moments that set standards of performance and conduct in broadcasting that never varied.

To the public Richard was a symbol of stability, part of the fireside, a welcome visitor. Such was this acceptance that it became difficult to imagine what he was like away from the camera and microphone. In the non-cathode ray tube life Richard was a sort of 3D wide-screen, coloured version of what he was like on television. Characteristics were the same – immensely friendly, unruffled and reassuring, a family man at the head of a family business, not in the City but a busy little street in suburban Richmond. The post was managing director of the *Richmond and Twickenham Times* and a couple of other small Thames Valley papers. One afternoon I enjoyed a personally conducted tour of the premises. Clearly Richard was immensely proud of the paper that had been founded nearly a century earlier by his grandfather. It was owned by a family trust, all the directors were Dimblebys and between them they owned all the shares. It was a genuine family concern. Richard was very knowledgeable about local affairs and many leaders from his pen reflected sound common sense. In everyday life Richard was neither a man of the world nor pompous in outlook. He was just himself.

Of the occasions when we came into contact, none stands out more vividly than our final meeting. It was on a plane from New York. The weather was foul. Thick fog meant landing at Shannon. It became obvious that we would have to spend the night in Ireland. Hotel rooms were full, so the only alternative was camping out on none-too-comfortable airport chairs. Richard staked his claim, but doubted whether there would be much sleep. His assignment in New York had been the visit of Pope Paul VI to the United States, the first time a Pope had met an American President in America. During the conversation I asked how it compared with other 'firsts'. He agreed it had been a landmark on a minor key, but the memory would not last like one that never ceased to haunt him even though it was as long ago as 1943. He had been in the first party to go through the pine-woods to the concentration camp at Belsen. What he saw was frozen in his brain: the piles of corpses, dying people who were living skeletons, the filth and decay of agonizing death. The stench had been terrible. It was the ultimate degradation of evil men.

As Richard talked, an airport official came across and told us he had been able to secure a hotel room for my wife and myself. We met the following morning. Richard looked very tired. For once his cheeks looked grey. He said he had not been too well in New York and probably eaten something that had disagreed, but all would be well as soon as he got home. Unfortunately that was not to be. Shortly afterwards, he entered St Thomas's Hospital. Two days later, after an operation for cancer, he died at the age of fifty-two. For millions there was a sense of personal loss. He had become part of daily life. I still wish that if only I had known the extent of his illness, he would have had that room and been spared a night of painful discomfort.

Richard Dimbleby was a truly great professional and an incredibly brave man. We are fortunate that the family tradition has been carried on with distinction by David and Jonathan.

Henry Moore OM

Common responses to art are abuse and flattery. On the one hand, hell knows no fury like a man confronted with a work of art he cannot understand. On the other, no revivalist meeting yields excesses of praise more wild than those of the art lover oozing over a favourite painting or sculpture. Reactions to Henry Moore make a textbook case. In his time he had been at the receiving end of both reactions. In a broadcast speech at the first Royal Academy dinner held after the war, the then president, Sir Alfred Munnings, made an attack unprecedented in the history of that institution on three artists: a Frenchman, a Spaniard and an Englishman. He identified the modern school of painting with Matisse and Picasso, but an English sculptor, Henry Moore, was the main target for Sir Alfred's attack. He did not mince words. Referring to Moore's *Reclining Figure* at the South Bank Exhibition, he maintained it was an outrage, fit for the dumping-ground and nothing else. Strong criticism to hurl against the only British artist to have won the 500,000-lire award at the Venice Biennial Exhibition and the only one to be given a whole floor for a show at the New York Museum of Modern Art.

At the time Moore refused to comment. He excused himself on the grounds that he had not heard the broadcast, but Sir Philip Hendy, the Director of the National Gallery, added a pertinent postscript: 'Sir Alfred Munnings has informed the British public that Moore exists. The rest of the world has known it for a long time.'

With such thoughts in mind, I met the sculptor in the seclusion of his sixteenth-century cottage at Perry Green, a hamlet in Hertfordshire. It is a commonplace to ruminate on the astonishing similarity between little men and great men – a thought which occurs frequently in the political arena – but in Moore was a man entirely unlike what might have been expected; no sheltered artist who had always lived on the margin of life, no arty poseur, but a quietly spoken Yorkshireman, with many of the homely qualities of that county. Life was not always easy for this son of a coalminer whose childhood ambition was to be a sculptor. Scholarships to the Leeds School of Art and the Royal College of Art in London showed that he was not mistaking appetite for ability, though in both places he found the normal academic training in sculpture unsatisfying. The formative influences came from outside sources. Roger Fry's *Vision and Design* opened Moore's eyes to the range of African Negro and Mexican sculpture. The foundation of much of his later work was based on the full three-dimensional realization of and truth to material which are the characteristics of African Negro sculpture.

Moore talked of his initial reaction to the British Museum galleries: and the monumental impressiveness of Egyptian sculpture, the magnificent Etruscan sarcophagus figures, and the Sumerian sculptures. A Royal College of Art travelling scholarship had taken him to Italy for six months. There he had avoided the Renaissance influence and sought the simple, monumental forms of life, finding what he wanted in the chapel of Santa Maria del Carmine at Florence – the solemn solid figures grouped on the walls by Masaccio. Several artists influenced Henry Moore, such as Blake, Giotto, Picasso and Turner; the palaeolithic cave-paintings in Spain left their mark; but nothing equalled the impact of those Masaccio paintings, reinforced by the solemnity of Mexican sculpture. Moore was interested in the rounded, solid shapes into which life builds itself. The trend was self-evident when you looked round his studios. Walking from one figure to another, and the disordered groups, varying from hand-size to life-size, it was obvious that here were no pure abstractions. Each piece, in its own individual way, was deeply involved in humanity; each was an expression of the significance of life. These were no fag-ends of the set form-values of Renaissance Europe. Moore's sculpture takes us back to the simple rounded forms of life.

It was interesting to find out how Moore approached his subject-matter. It was by no means an aribitrary or stiffly intellectual approach. He sometimes began by drawing with no preconceived problem to solve, with only the desire to use pencil on paper, and made lines, tones and shapes with no conscious aim, but as his mind took in what was so produced, a point arrived where some idea became conscious and crystallized, and then a control and ordering began to take place. Or sometimes he started with a set subject; or, solved, in a block of stone of known dimensions, a sculptural problem he had given himself, and consciously attempted to build an order-relationship of forms which would express his idea. But if the work had to be more than just a sculptural exercise, unexplainable jumps in the process of thought occurred and the imagination played its part. His concern had never been with individual human beings, but – like Giacometti – with archetypes. His major contribution to the art of our time is the vision he possessed of these archetypal men and women, kings and warriors, being related to images more massive and more permanent than man himself. Moore's metaphors have ennobled man by relating him to forms that are timeless and tangible – rocks, trees, armour, blades, shells. At a dinner-party in Cambridge one of my guests was Noel Odell who, on an Everest expedition, was the last to see Mallory and Irvine as they left the penultimate camp and almost reached the summit when a storm blotted them out. Moore was fascinated by the account of the event, but was particularly interested in the primeval shapes of rock formations at that height.

One of Moore's well-known pieces is called *Kings and Queens*. It consists of two figures in bronze, somewhat over life-size, seated side by side. I was curious to find out the significance of this group. Moore explained that it has nothing to do with present-day kings and queens, but is more connected with the archaic or primitive idea of a king. The clue to the group is perhaps the head of the king, which is a head and crown, face and beard combined into one form and in Moore's mind has some slightly Pan-like suggestion, almost animal, and yet, he thought, something kingly. How the group came about he did not know, unless it might be that he had read stories to his daughter in which kings and queens had appeared a lot and might have made his mind open to such a subject. The formal relationship between mother and child is another that had a continuing appeal to Moore as a sculptor.

Moore's respect for material was impressive. When he carved wood, it was frequently in a shape which preserved its quality of growth and movement. Sculpture in wood usually has an upward and vertical movement like the tree from which it came. On the other hand, when his work was in stone, the shape was always more concentrated. He discovered within the block forms that symbolized the life he found in them. It was as if he had become aware that these figures were always in the block and had merely stripped away the concealing shell to reveal them in their stoniness. He was a superb carver. He could make the grain of wood and the curve of stone clothe his ideas with a marvellous richness of texture. Sculptures grew from tiny maquettes often no more than a few inches long which were kept in a workshop near the house, a sort of private Lilliput. A few of these miniatures would later be transformed into full-size bronzes. The rest would stay as ideas, and he recalled Sickert telling him that he would let his drawings sit in a drawer for a while. The question of output is difficult. It is possible to ask whether a healthy flow of Moore bronzes, all nicely textured and patinated, was quite a substitute for a smaller number of carvings in stone and wood, which he used to show us before he grew to international fame.

Henry Moore's art is a challenge: a challenge to lazy habits of thought, to complacency of vision. There are conventional ways of seeing, eating and talking, just as there is a conventional way of looking at nature. An artist is a man who views nature with clear-sighted vision. He is continually garnering material from his experience of things seen, but he knows that appearances do not necessarily correspond to reality. Graham Sutherland once observed, 'I found that I could express what I felt only by paraphrasing what I saw.' Because Moore's work does not aim at reproducing natural appearances, it is not therefore an escape from life, but may be a penetration into reality. The seated and reclining figures in the studios, whether immediately recognizable or not, seemed to reflect something of the vitality of their creator's aims. He often chose to hollow out the human figures, so that one sees them from more than one angle at once – looking through them as well as at them, sensing the contrast of rough and smooth, of rounded forms against sharp and thin.

His works may or may not appeal to the individual beholder. His women may be tortoise-headed or pin-headed – they certainly are not the heads of Madonnas or angels as we see them – but controversies concerning their aesthetic merits must not allow us to forget that Henry Moore is the only English sculptor to have really found new contents and new forms for the human figure. Formally, and in his exploitation of his material, he moved on lines first explored by Barlach. I question whether Moore liked working closely with architects. Such an association all too often ends with an unsatisfactory compromise. In that sense architecture is no longer the mother of the arts. The best it can offer is a position where sculpture can be appreciated for its own sake and also enhance the buildings. A good example is the Lincoln Centre in New York where in the centre of a pool is one of Moore's largest bronze sculptures. It is in the series of *Reclining Figures*. He chose bronze because it would stand up to the extremes of the New York climate better than stone. In any case, to transport a stone carving of this size would have been a task for Hercules. It is 24 ft long, 16 ft high, and was completed under a massive greenhouse, specially built at the end of his garden in Hertfordshire. It was Moore's idea to have it in the pool itself. For some time he had been interested in the idea of a sculpture whose hidden features could be revealed by reflection in water. Reflection provides an extra viewpoint, making it possible for sculpture to be seen, not only from buildings above and at eye level, but from underneath as well. He tried it out by means of a working model and a small garden bathing-pool.

It is a flat country where Henry Moore lived. Hardly a low hill for forty miles to the North Sea and anything a few inches above sea-level is silhouetted against the sky, with no background to belittle it. That is the way Moore liked his sculpture to be seen, only by the imagination and by the sky.

Unemotional and Nerveless

Few spectators realize the intensity of nerve strain in sport. Golf is near the top when it comes to this form of cold-blooded torture. I have watched many championships in this country and America and in almost every instance those with any chance of winning were tensed to near breaking-point in the last round. The signs are individualistic, finger-prints under stress. Henry Cotton was a good example. He had one ambition – to become the greatest golfer the game has known. To achieve such fame, shot-making had to reach a pitch of automatic perfection. No golfer has come so close to complete co-ordination of mind and muscle. The theory of the game was analysed in every detail. He has fixed ideas how a golf ball should be hit. They may not tally with other theories, but such is the Cotton creed.

Only one thing was missing. The ability to eliminate error. It was here that Cotton came up against a ruthless opponent – his own temperament. Back-breaking, hand-blistering hours spent practising and experimenting meant nothing when his temperament resisted automation. In every championship, Cotton had two opponents, the course and himself. To master both meant eliminating as far as possible outside interference and interruption. Anyone who has experienced the hurly-burly of an Open Championship – and crowds were less controlled in his heyday – will realize the impossibility of being allowed to play in lonely isolation. Seclusion could only be of his own making. That was what happened. On the first tee, he retired to his own ivory tower.

Spectators milled around in their thousands. Photographers clicked their cameras. Autograph hunters trailed behind. Through it all strode a golfer with pale, strained features, outwardly unseeing, completely impervious and oblivious to distractions. Henry Cotton maintained his concentration, but only at a price. A lesser man would have broken down. That inner struggle thrashes about in the brain of every man who aspires to win the Open Championship. Pounds will be lost in weight. Solid food is often out of the question on the last day. A glass of milk is sufficient. Players may go to bed early, but few sleep. Statistics show that in golf more top-line professionals suffer from duodenal ulcers than in any other sport. If the strain is great here, it is twice as fierce in the United States where stake-money is fantastically high and competition cut-throat. Over the years a new breed has come to the fore, men who conceal emotion and only let the public catch glimpses of their true selves, though there were significant exceptions among the older generation.

Never have fairways seen such an extrovert as Walter Hagen. His showmanship made the antics of players like Jimmy Demaret, Brian Barnes and Lee Trevino look funereal. He was a born jester, but he brought to the game more than a nimble wit and a taste for clashing colours. He blended the timing of Danny Kaye with the skill of Jack Nicklaus. It never paid to underestimate Hagen. He sauntered through a key match with a casual indifference that disarmed and deceived. The insouciance was a shrewd veneer. In a split second the frivolous mask disappeared. In its place came ice-cold concentration. He was the Jekyll and Hyde of the links, the most calculating strategist seen in championship golf. Few have matched his analytical approach to an opponent. Bobby Jones rated him as the ideal match-player. Hagen was the first of the giants of machine-like precision. He set such a hot pace that contemporaries had to work at their game, otherwise they would have never touched the stake-money.

One of these was Gene Sarazen, the pocket Hercules whose smile was likened to that of a Cheshire cat. This stocky, olive-skinned little man, son of an emigrant Italian carpenter, began life as a caddie at Apawanis. He hit the headlines in 1922 for the first time when he won the American Open Championship, having entered from the obscure club of Titusville. Both names were new to the golfing world, but Sarazen never looked back. He went through life with a casual air that concealed a shrewd brain.

Some fifty years ago Bobby Jones realized an ambition that will probably never be repeated. In one season he won the Open Championship at Hoylake, the United States Open Championship at Interlachen, the British Amateur Championship at St Andrews and the American Amateur Championship at Merion, a clear thirteen-stroke victory in an Open Professional Tournament at Augusta, and his 36-hole Walker Cup match at Sandwich. He played top competitive golf on both sides of the Atlantic from April to September and never finished below first place. In

Henry Moore's art is a challenge to lazy habits of thought

Alfred Noyes was born with a love of words

Joan Collins is an ageless fantasist

Ingrid Bergman's real life outstripped in drama her screen and stage roles

Bertrand Russell, one of the most brilliant mathematicians of the century

Dame Laura Knight was animated by an electric vitality

Graham Hill was immensely popular

Sir George Thomson, physicist, with the portrait of his brilliant father, J.J. Thomson, reproduced on a Swedish postage stamp

Sir Martin Ryle, Astronomer-Royal, who believed our cleverness had grown prodigiously, but not our wisdom

Pope Paul VI seemed intent on martyrdom

temperament, Jones was a curious mixture. Highly strung, the strain of competing exacted a toll on health and weight. Often during a championship, he was unable to eat and became physically sick, yet no sign of this inner struggle was apparent on the course. He personified unruffled calm. His shot-making style was a joy to watch. In contrast to the flamboyant flourishes of Hagen, the lazy rhythm of Jones's swing was almost effortless, yet the amateur still subjected his game to microscopic analysis. His withdrawal from the competition scene was regrettable, but the timing was faultless. How few champions end their careers at the peak.

Among counterparts in later generations of outstanding professionals, the phlegmatic approach continues. The strains are greater, but only occasionally become evident. Poker-faced golf is the order of the day. Sam Snead was such a man. He won every major championship, except ironically the United States Open, being runner-up five times and third once. He is the epitome of the true West Virginian, though his understating humour is almost English. It moves between sharply defined monosyllables and shrewdly placed silences. He is never oleaginous. Whoever heard of a West Virginian being smug, smooth or smarmy? He is not even urbane. On the contrary, Snead is an accomplished hand in the acerbity business.

Peter Thomson dominated the Open Championship to such an extent that for eight years speculation centred on who would be runner-up. Only on three occasions did the Australian occupy that place; the other five saw him crowned as Open Champion. Here was not the usual rough-tongued Australian, but a quiet, good-humoured fellow who played as if he enjoyed every minute of it. Fred Daly similarly made golf seem a happy affair. This breezy Ulster golfer was one of the most popular on the circuit. He admitted that when he won the Open title at Hoylake, the nervous tension was killing, yet outwardly unruffled, he whistled his way round the course to victory. Similarly nobody could realize the inner turmoil of Bobby Locke, as this somewhat portly South African, wearing the inevitable plus-fours, white cap and white shoes, strode majestically down the last fairway of the Old Course, St Andrews to win the Open title again. Gary Player was quite different temperamentally. The stamina of this little golfer is remarkable. 5 ft 7 ins in height and weighing about 150 pounds, he outdrives opponents far more powerful. This ability to retain the peak of physical fitness is due to a rigid training schedule. His aggressive approach to shot-making and refusal to admit defeat has become legendary. He never quits. This aggressiveness is left behind on the fairways. At home just outside Johannesburg, I found him completely relaxed with his wife and family.

Arnold Palmer is in a class of his own. Golfing skill is his instinctive nature. He neither refuses nor insists on showing off. It just happens. His imagination, free from the shackles of ordinary work-a-day citizens, moves in a golfing world where 'Arnie's Army' sweeps across the fairways in support of their man. Palmer has no private personality. Everything about him is public and he is open daily.

Through the exposure of television, the skill of Jack Nicklaus is known to millions. Close-up shots by the camera have frozen tense moments when pressure was immense. No other golfer reflects so truly the tremendous concentration needed in the closing stages of a championship. This sense of awareness comes across sharply. Nicklaus is seen as a man of real power, unafraid of the big gestures, physically in enviable trim, muscular in build and full of bristling energy. That attitude is constant in public and private life.

Tom Watson has a perpetual youthfulness that never ages. The reflexes of this freckle-faced professional are more predictable. He registers anxiety and disillusionment far more than his poker-faced colleagues. Watson is brilliant, but pleasantly anonymous. Completely different is the swashbuckling Severiano Ballesteros, whose confidence makes anything possible. Without question the Spaniard is the most colourful figure on the world circuit. He burst on the scene in D'Artagnan fashion, a style not seen since the days of Walter Hagen. At the outset his temperament was troublesome. Set-backs had a lingering effect, but then the Latin temperament is a law unto itself.

To narrow the choice to one professional whose public and private images are extremes, my nomination would be Ben Hogan. Here is a golfer who attained a peak of perfection in mastery of shot-making that has not been surpassed. In 1948 he won eleven tournaments including the United States Open Championship with an all-time low of 276 and a second PGA title. Everything was set fair for total domination of the golfing scene, when a near-fatal head-on crash with a bus in the fog threatened to terminate his playing career in 1949. Recovery was near miraculous. Later that year Hogan came to England as non-playing captain of the American Ryder Cup team. I was responsible for the planning arrangements. When we arrived at Southampton a convoy of Rolls Royce cars was waiting to take us to the Savoy Hotel. I was in the leading car, but after a few miles it was clear that Hogan was far from happy. Accustomed to the flow of traffic on a different side of the road, he was continually tensed at what appeared to be a potential collision with each approaching car. The best thing was to drop behind at the tail of the convoy. The following day the journey by road continued with coffee with the dons of Christ Church College in Oxford, followed by an official lunch at Stratford-on-Avon, finally arriving in a somewhat weary state at the Grand Hotel in Scarborough. Hogan was far from fit. In constant pain with a tight rubber suit under his clothes, he was under stress even by walking, yet never once did the galleries know of the handicap.

Grim determination worked wonders. Instead of watching from a wheelchair, Hogan came back to the tournament scene. There were no token appearances. He won three national championships in 1953, finished first in the five events he entered, including his second Masters Tournament at Augusta, his fourth United States Open title, and the Open Championship in Carnoustie at his first attempt, plus his third PGA title. Seldom has a patient had such a recovery. Yet it is not in victory that the clearest picture remains of this remarkable golfer. The occasion was the United States Open Championship at the Olympic Golf Club at Lakeside, a course laid out by the Pacific. Hogan's admitted ambition was to be the first man to win five US National Open Championships. He played so brilliantly that the title looked booked. Certainly the vast crowd surrounding the home green had no doubts. Sarazen rushed forward with a hand microphone. In the interview beamed across the States, Hogan was congratulated on achieving the near-impossible. Hogan responded by holding up an outspread right hand, the splayed five fingers symbolizing the feat.

Then the news seeped through that a 1000-to-1 outsider had a remote chance of tying. Jack Fleck was roughly two hours behind Hogan, playing a lonely round without any spectators. Figures kept coming through that confirmed it was still possible. At last Fleck stood on the last tee. A hooked drive found the rough. That was that. A wonderful effort, but it was sure that Hogan had it in the bag. We reckoned without this unknown pro. Very calmly he played a magnificent recovery that just reached the huge green. I asked him afterwards what were his inner reactions to the situation. His recollection was vague except that one thought kept running through his mind: he had to swing the club without forcing. No finer shot has been played under pressure. The putt – about 30 ft – must have looked a mile. Without any sign of nerves, Fleck studied the line, then struck the putt as casually as if only a dollar was at stake. It dropped into the tin. The scene that followed would have done justice to a Cup Final goal. Fleck raised both arms in excitement, then swayed, and looked as if he would collapse. Police escorted him to the official tent. Then occurred one of those little acts that few know anything about, but in reality so frequently happen behind the scenes.

Fleck was literally speechless at his feat. He had played himself out on his feet. Reaction set in quickly. The first to appreciate the situation was the defending champion, Ed Furgol, the man who had just seen his title disappear. He took Fleck under his care, led him off to the locker-room, saw that he rested, went with him to the Press room, and gave the answers that were wanted. Furgol's only comment was that he had been in a similar position himself the year before and knew something of Fleck's mental whirl. And finally, Ben Hogan came and offered congratulations on a fine performance, a genuine gesture even though his own triumph had been frustrated.

The play-off was expected to be one-sided. I thought Hogan would turn on the pressure and win by five or six shots. The prediction was way out. Fleck shot a 69, one under par. Hogan shot 72. The end came at the eighteenth. Hogan pulled his tee-shot into the hillside rough. Fleck played safely down the middle with his spoon. Hogan was ankle-deep. He swung, scythe-like, but only the lush grass came up. He swung again. The ball shifted a couple of feet. The green was only 130 yards away, but still Hogan had to aim for safety with a sideways shot. This time he made it. Fleck was on in 2. Hogan was 40 ft away in 5. To his credit Hogan sank a 40-footer for his 6. Fleck played the putt near enough to make the next one a formality. It gave him his first tournament victory and the national crown. Fleck was in a daze. Later we met in the St Francis Hotel. Because the United Nations was meeting, the President was in San Francisco, and the sixth floor had become the equivalent of the White House. Fleck said that the day before, he was nobody, just an unknown professional. Now he was American Open Champion, and he had just been congratulated by the President. No man had known such a day. It was a fairy tale come true.

But what of Ben Hogan? His bid to stand alone in the record books had failed. Later that night I dined at Trader Vic's in San

Francisco with Ben and Valerie Hogan and Bing Crosby with his wife. No man had ever put so much into the preliminary preparations for a golf title, yet his praise for Fleck was unstinted. It was sincere recognition of the fighting qualities he possessed. And in later weeks he went out of his way to help in Fleck's readjustment to the new role. This gesture from a man who is utterly unemotional was rare.

Ben Hogan has that intangible quality which we call genius. His enthusiasm for the game did not wane. His methods were not dated. By cutting himself off from his time he rendered himself timeless. The Spanish have a word *duende*. It has no exact English equivalent, but it denotes the quality without which no flamenco singer or bullfighter can conquer the summit of his art. The ability to transmit a profoundly felt emotion to an audience or gallery of strangers with the minimum of fuss and the maximum of restraint. That is as near as our language can come to the full meaning of *duende*. Ben Hogan has it in rich measure.

Three Scientists

Sir J. J. Thomson OM

When the Cavendish Laboratory was formally opened in Cambridge on 18 July 1874 by the donor, William Cavendish, 7th Duke of Devonshire and Chancellor of Cambridge University, few of those present could have imagined that the laboratories would be indirectly responsible for horrors like Hiroshima and Nagasaki, and the threat of world extinction. Such thoughts would have been dismissed as fictional pessimism, frivolous and morbid. Pure science was a thing apart, but even in such rarefied atmosphere, there was time for donnish humour. At the entrance to the Cavendish Museum is a marble bust by Boehm of James Clerk-Maxwell, the first occupant of the Chair of Experimental Physics. It is inscribed dp/dt, the differential coefficient being Maxwell's favourite pun on his initials. In the second law of thermodynamics $dp/dt = JCM$.

The initial period of theorizing soon gave way to solid achievement in the field of research. Anti-nuclear supporters today condemn many of these pioneering scientists as enemies of society, men without social conscience or moral integrity. The absurdity of such accusations came from the men themselves who contributed richly to man's knowledge of himself and the mystery of the universe. Censure lies not with them, but should be directed against politicians and industrialists who have misapplied the fruits of their discoveries. The dividing-line between positive and negative uses is often narrow and moral issues can quickly be ignored through political and national ambition.

The scientists themselves are a race apart. One such figure was Sir J. J. Thomson, physicist, Master of Trinity College, Cambridge, and a significant influence in world history through his discovery of the *electron*. When he isolated an atom of pure electricity, he set in motion the theory of nuclear as well as atomic structure. Under his guidance the Cavendish became the leading research school in experimental physics. The reward for this revolutionary finding was the Nobel Prize for Physics, honorary degrees from twenty-three universities, a knighthood, and the Order of Merit. Achievements and honours on this scale conjure up a mental picture of an international scientist conscious of status and overbearing in manner, if not conceit. Nothing could have been farther from fact. 'J. J.' was brilliant, but he was always approachable and helpful to those who worked for him. I only knew him in the last year of his life, so it is not possible to assess what he was like during his prime, but stories abound about him, many from his wife, Rose Elizabeth, the daughter of Sir George Paget and a first-class mathematician in her own right. They created a composite word-portrait of a kindly family man with many idiosyncrasies and a tendency to be absent-minded.

Her favourite was of an evening when 'J. J.' changed for a dinner in Queens' College. After he left, she went into the bedroom and found his trousers lying on the bed. Fearing the worst she rang the porter's lodge to enquire if they had seen the Master leave. She was told he went past their windows fifteen minutes earlier. She next rang Queens' and asked the President's wife if her husband had arrived safely and was he looking all right. She was assured he seemed in good spirits, but with a slightly odd touch. He was dressed for dinner with black tie, but appeared to be wearing well-worn gardening trousers, no doubt a Trinity eccentricity. The absent-minded gaff was for long a source of family amusement.

Sir George Thomson

His son, Sir George Thomson, also a physicist and Master of Corpus Christi College, had his own fund of stories about the old man, but these light-hearted anecdotes could not detract from world effects of those early scientific discoveries. This was emphasized when I heard him deliver the Cherwell–Simon Lecture in Oxford on *Nuclear Energy in Britain during the Second World War*. He outlined how the breakthrough in physics had had such a startling effect on human life. He did his best to explain so as to make it intelligible to those who were not in physics the meaning of some terms. He described how atoms, of which all matter is composed, were largely empty space. In that respect they resembled the solar system. The nucleus corresponded to the sun and furnished practically nearly all the other properties, chemical, mechanical, and so on, with one important exception, radioactivity.

He outlined the major breakthrough when Sir James Chadwick discovered a particle which was in a sense both atom and nucleus and was electrically neutral – the *neutron*. This could approach an ordinary nucleus without any repulsion and reach it when moving quite slowly. Nuclear fission occurred when this happened to very heavy nuclei. The energy released in the process was enormous, millions of times that of an ordinary explosive or ordinary combustion weight for weight. The evidence in practical terms was shown at Hiroshima.

It was a sobering account, the chain begun by his father carried to its logical development and conclusion by Chadwick. The following day such thoughts did not weigh heavily on Thomson's mind. Over tea he produced a large portrait of his father in profile and asked if I had any idea how it was going to be used. It was a proof sent to him of the likeness of 'J. J.' intended to be reproduced on a Swedish postage stamp, a gesture that clearly he valued.

Sir James Chadwick

Physicist and, up to the time of his death, Master of Gonville and Caius College, Cambridge, here was another scientist whom anti-nuclear advocates damn. He was quite different from the Thomsons, father and son, worked with Rutherford on the nuclear theory of atomic structure, achieved a personal triumph in the discovery of the *neutron* and became involved in mastering the problem of nuclear fission. He led the British team of scientists who co-operated with the Americans on the Manhattan Project, finally determining the operational application of the bomb.

Chadwick was introspective. After Nagasaki he became even more aloof and inaccessible. Like Sir Martin Ryle, but in another branch of science, he discovered his social conscience. The civil application of atomic energy had positive values that he approved. As Chairman of the Committee dealing with such matters he was influential in establishing the pattern of the British nuclear power programme, but always haunting him was the memory of what atomic power can do in war. The recollection never left him, but there was no way of going back. If he hadn't discovered the *neutron*, some other physicist would have done so with the same result, but it was a heavy mental burden to carry.

The fact that much of his technical research was difficult for a layman to understand had its lighter moments. I shared a platform with him in Liverpool. Sitting beside me was Lord Leverhulme, who had hearing problems. To overcome the disability and maintain contact with what was being said, he had a box-like contraption that acted as a microphone, regulated for loudness by a dial, and listening ear-plug. After a time the struggle to comprehend was too much. He switched off and enjoyed the peace of silence with a quiet smile of contentment that was not missed by platform or audience. Afterwards I told Chadwick of the incident. He thought that many of the listeners must have been envious.

Graham Hill

On the night of 19 November 1976, a Piper Aztec plane approached Elstree aerodrome. Conditions were poor. A blanket of freezing fog covered most of the Home Counties. Three miles from touch-down, the plane was over Arkley golf course when it hit some trees, burst into flames and crashed on the damp, fog-bound links. All the occupants were killed. In such tragic fashion Graham Hill died, along with Tony Brise and four members of his team. The accident was hard to explain for Graham was a pilot of considerable experience. Never one to take risks, meticulous in pre-flight preparation, and a stickler for keeping to the book, he had landed at Elstree on scores of occasions. This time, returning from a test session at Paul Ricard, he had sent a telex from Marseilles to the control tower at Elstree stating that he hoped to land about 10.30 p.m. The airport stayed open specially and the plane was one hour ahead of schedule. Something must have happened outside Graham's control. It is conceivable that ice on the wings and fuselage caused the plane to lose height, or a fuel shortage on the lengthy flight from Marseilles might have forced an emergency crash-landing on fairways that Graham knew so well. Whatever the cause, the disaster robbed motor-racing not only of one of its rising stars in Tony Brise, but the sport's most dynamic personality.

Graham was universally popular and enjoyed every minute of adulation with a saucy wink. Television highlighted his under-stated humour as he paced life, like a race, to suit his mental tempo; yet, in spite of this extrovert image, few really knew Graham. In that sense I count myself fortunate for he was seven years with BRM, the formative years of his career as most of his Formula One victories were at the wheel of a BRM, including ten of his fourteen World Championship wins. The man who joined us in 1959 was not sophisticated. Instead he looked a clipped, well-scrubbed conformist with short-back-and-sides haircut and a no-nonsense moustache. His tactlessness was so authoritative that I remarked that he didn't know the difference between tongue-in-the-cheek and foot-in-mouth, but any possible offence was minimized by his open-eyed manner.

It would be misleading to say that Graham's career was rags to riches but it certainly began on a low note. After apprenticeship with Smith's Instruments and two years' National Service in the Navy, he went on the dole and then joined a Brands Hatch racing-school as an unpaid mechanic before joining Colin Chapman in a similar capacity. He was twenty-seven when he had his first drive for Team Lotus. Two years later came the Grand Prix début in a Lotus 16 at Monaco. The result hardly hit the headlines for a wheel fell off his car. In 1959 he joined the BRM team.

As a driver, Graham was not a natural, like Clark, Stewart or Senna, but with experience and success his approach to racing developed and became more polished and mature. He was very nearly a classic driver but his style did not always appeal to the purist. He compensated for his shortcomings with confidence and concentration and few could equal him in racecraft. He was the master of Grand Prix tactics. His calculated approach to pre-race preparation was an object-lesson. It was difficult to discern that wet conditions worried him and he masked his anxiety with indifference, but the symptoms were evident as starting-time drew near. He was given to moodiness which is the language of stress, his moustache twitched and his eyebrows knitted, but he never gave way to fear. In time the aversion was overcome.

Highlighting incidents, victories, set-backs and disappointments during Graham's long stay with BRM is not easy – there were so many. The most memorable was winning the World Championship with the title hinging on the South African Grand Prix; but for sheer drama few races equalled the last lap in the 1962 International Trophy at Silverstone. With a couple of laps to go Graham was 9 seconds behind Jim Clark on a rain-soaked track. The last lap began with a deficit of 5.5 seconds which against a driver of Clark's calibre seemed hopeless. Graham made a ferocious charge and drove to the limit until right on the edge of Wodecote Corner, he took the flag inches ahead of the astonished Lotus driver. That win ranks among the celebrated victories that have been snatched against all odds. Before he got out of the BRM, his first comment to us was typical, 'That was dangerous, mustn't do that again', a cautionary self-rebuke that was soon forgotten.

There were times when the dice rolled against him. I think in particular of the horrific crash in the American Grand Prix at Watkins Glen which he was fortunate to survive. The car flipped over after a tyre deflated, throwing him out. The impact smashed both legs. I recall speaking to him on the trolley outside the operating theatre. His one concern was that I should speak to Bette on the phone to tell her that he wouldn't be able to take her to the dance on Wednesday in London. There was no mention of the pain or the serious injuries, no fear of surgery, no hint of being sorry for himself, just a wisecrack and a smile. He was a rare man.

One of the most controversial incidents in which Graham was involved occurred in Mexico in 1964 during a race that rocked the Championship. Twice before the world title had depended on the result of the final round. Casablanca in 1958 saw the duel between Mike Hawthorn and Stirling Moss; the 1962 South African Grand Prix was the decider between Clark and Graham. Portugal in 1984 saw the Championship clinched by Lauda after a race-long duel with his team-mate, Alain Prost, and the narrowest of points margin. Mexico was more complicated due to the point-scoring system. Graham had 41 points, but could only count 39 as he had scored in seven races. Surtees had 34, Clark 30. If Graham won he would again be Champion. If Surtees won, his total of 43 points would give him the title even if Graham finished second, for then his total could only be 42 points as he would have to discard the lowest scores of 2 and 3 points. Clark's hopes depended on Hill not finishing, with Surtees finishing no higher than third. Clark would then have tied with Graham on the 39-mark, but with more wins.

The crunch came on lap 29. Clark was leading 14 seconds ahead of Gurney, who in turn was 16 seconds in front of Graham. The third place was the focal point and Bandini was the threat. Lap after lap the Italian tried to overtake at a point where it just wasn't possible. At least, that was the opinion of Jack Brabham who was behind. On film it was clear that something was going to happen. Shaking fists did not subdue the over-excited Ferrari driver. On lap 31 he clouted the BRM exhaust pipes, spinning the car into the guard-rail. Bandini was able to continue, but the BRM exhaust pipes had been crumpled over. Graham completed a bruised lap and came into the pits where mechanics levered off the damaged ends. Graham rejoined the race in thirteenth place, one lap light, but his Championship hopes had gone. The incident cost BRM the world title.

After the race accusations were slung around. Some said that

Bandini had deliberately crashed the BRM, as part of Ferrari tactics. I was reluctant to agree. By temperament Bandini was fiery and impulsive, a fearless driver but never guilty of doubtful tactics. To win, a driver has to be on the razor-edge that separates success from disaster. Before we left the circuit Dragoni, Ferrari team-manager, Forghieri, chief engineer, and Bandini came to the pit and apologized. Bandini was in tears. Everyone shook hands. As far as BRM was concerned, the incident was closed, though several months later the Grand Prix Drivers' Association attempted to revive the whole business. Their intentions were good, but it was foolish to stir up trouble after such a long interval. Dangerous driving does concern the Association but disciplinary action when needed should be meted out by the controlling body of the sport. President Baumgartner had been present in Mexico, but no enquiry was held, no film evidence was checked, nothing was done and so it stayed. Looking back I think of the admirable way in which Graham accepted the disappointment, likewise Colin Chapman's sporting reaction when victory was snatched away minutes from the end. It was a dramatic conclusion to the season with Surtees taking the title by others' default.

I have left to the last what I consider to be the finest race of Graham Hill's career, the 1962 German Grand Prix on the wooded Eifel mountain course of Nurburgring with its fast succession of corners, bends and gradients. The drama began on the practice round. It concerned Carel Godin de Beaufort who set off from the pits with a television camera mounted above the left rear wheel of his orange-painted four-cylinder Porsche. Coming into one of the most testing places of the entire circuit, the brackets on which the camera was mounted broke and the camera disintegrated on the road. Graham came up behind and entered the curve at well over 140 mph, found his line strewn with camera debris and had to plough through the pieces that ripped an oil line beneath the car. The BRM went out of control on its own oil, left the track, and plunged into a ditch, tearing off the right wheel as it went. Miraculously Hill stepped out of the wreck unharmed though badly shaken.

Later I went to the Hills' room at Loch Mouhle and found Graham soaking in the bath. Bette's remedy was the soothing effect of bubble foam, a cure of mind over matter, but it worked. He was subdued over dinner. The only sign of strain was the drooping of one eyelid that often happened when he was over-tired. The next day the fourteen-mile circuit was almost awash with torrential rain that flooded the track and caused several minor landslides. Everywhere was enveloped in a heavy grey mist, restricting visibility to under 100 yards. Teeming rain did not deter the crowd, estimated at over 350,000 spectators. The lights on the illuminated map on the side of the Dunlop tower gleamed brightly through the curtain of rain and the ruins of the Schloss Nurburg on the hill appeared spasmodically through the mist. Next to us in the Dunlop tower was Herr Josef Strauss, West German Defence Minister, who talked as if the race would be a Porsche benefit. At the outset it looked possible for the scoreboard showed that Gurney was leading Graham and Phil Hill. The gap between laps was approximately ten minutes with race progress giving the first six cars on the board. The Porsche still led some fifty yards ahead of BRM and Ferrari with Surtees's Lola, Bonnier's Porsche and McLaren's Cooper in pursuit. Strauss enquired if I had noticed that the German car was leading, but as they began the third circuit, the BRM overtook the Porsche as the two cars accelerated past the back of the pits. From that point Graham never lost the lead, but neither did the pressures lessen. In spite of the frightful conditions and incessant rain, there was no respite, no relaxing, an unrelenting battle with the margin between the first and third cars never more than five seconds. At the end of 212 miles Graham won by a fraction over two seconds from Surtees's Lola after two-and-a-half hours' hard racing. Gurney finished less than two seconds behind Surtees. Herr Strauss was the first to congratulate Graham after one of the finest races ever seen on this famous German circuit.

Graham Hill's racing career should have ended at the peak, but he found it difficult to retire from the big scene when the moment arrived. He felt he could still hold the gate against the younger generation, but confidence alone cannot win races. At the end of 1972 he set up his own team with sponsorship from W. D. & H. O. Wills's Embassy brand. Unfortunately he did not appreciate the economics of running a Formula One team and the venture was not a success. In three years of racing he scored only three points. Midway through the 1975 season, Graham decided to retire rather than see his grid positions slip further and further back. It was a sensible move, but there was sadness after the announcement was made at the British Grand Prix when the former World Champion drove a lap of honour in his car.

That same emotion was evident in the Abbey Church of St Albans when several thousand mourners stood and remembered his passing. Bishop Runcie, now Archbishop of Canterbury, paid an eloquent tribute from the pulpit, recalling the selfless and generous side of his nature, his readiness to give of himself at all times to worthy causes, how he enjoyed life and even in the last hours retained his passionate love for the sport.

As the procession slowly made its way out of the Abbey Church, followed by Bette, their children Damon, Brigitte and Samantha, and his parents, the sight of that distinctive helmet on the simple coffin was like watching a legend pass into history.

Pope Paul VI

Cardinal Montini, Archbishop of Milan, was one of the last men on earth to speak to Pope John when he brought the Pope's sister and three brothers to the bedside where the much-loved Pontiff lay dying. Two days later Pope John XXIII died. The conclave that followed was unlike any other in history. It was the largest ever, eighty Cardinals met in the Vatican's Sistine Chapel, only a third Italian, and half of them the creations of Pope John. Speculation as to the possible successor had short-listed such Cardinals as the liberal Lercano; the popular Agagianian; the Canon lawyer, Cardinal Roberti; the youthful Suenens; Marella, of the gift of tongues; Urbani, Pope John's successor at Venice; and Montini, who had spent almost his entire life, except for seven years as Archbishop of Milan, within the Vatican's corridors of power and was known as the Dauphin.

The Cardinals retired in conclave. Dark smoke rose from the improvised chimney of the Sistine Chapel only a few times indicating that the ballot papers had been burned before with surprising speed puffs of little white clouds indicated that the choice had been made. In the case of Pope John it took three full days and twenty-four ballots. This time only twenty-three hours were needed. Giovanni Battista Montini was elected as the 262nd successor to the Throne of St Peter, taking the name of Paul, unused for three centuries.

Some months later I was in a prosperous nineteenth-century house overlooking Wimbledon Common, the official residence of Archbishop Ignino Cardinale, the Apostolic Delegate. The title sounded impressive but, as the Cardinal said with a resigned smile, it was misleading. It meant that the British Government did not recognize his existence and the title carried no diplomatic standing. He was just the link-man between the Pope, whom the Government did not recognize, and the Roman Catholic Church in Britain that had no legal status. The historic breach with Rome by Henry VIII, constitutionalized by Elizabeth I, and rubbed home by Parliament in 1688 had seen to that. All that has now changed. In 1982 Britain and the Holy See established full relations, healing the 450-year breach. The Apostolic Delegate is now the Apostolic Pronuncio to Britain, recognized as a diplomat, with the privileges involved, including inviolability of the Wimbledon house, though still without any recognition of the Vatican as such. The lack of such recognition and privilege did not seem to worry the Archbishop unduly. Born in Italy, but brought up in America, he had acquired a transatlantic ease of manner that was refreshingly relaxed. Through his influence a private audience with Paul was arranged, but he reminded me that Vatican protocol was strict. I would have to observe the ruling and allow the Holy Father to guide the conversation. Direct questions would be frowned upon.

The road from Rome to the Pope's summer residence at Castel Gandolfo went past a ruined aqueduct, across the plain and into the Alban Hills, up a steep, narrow street into a piazza and the entrance to the huge Renaissance papal palace built by Maderna, the architect of the façade of St Peter's. I attended a service in a small chapel attended by a group of pilgrims from Yugoslavia. For a non-Catholic it was strange to hear continuous outbursts of cheering in a church, yet somehow the Pope, by the obvious sincerity of his manner, by the delicate beauty of his hands outstretched to bless, avoided any jarring note. One had the impression of the head of a large family, speaking to everyone *en masse*, yet addressing us individually at the same time. It was a *tour de force* I had never seen equalled by another prelate, politician or head of State.

Meeting the Pope was an arresting experience. Some years earlier I had spoken to him as Archbishop of Milan. On that occasion we had just won the Grand Prix of Italy. He said he felt a slight affinity because he was the only Cardinal to have been driven round the Monza Circuit in a high-powered sports car. But now he was different. Here was a man whose sacred office stretched back to the time of Imperial Rome. From the temporal point of view he was surrounded by ceremony almost inherited from the Caesars, yet without the material ambitions of an emperor. He was the Pope, the Father in God of some 550-million Catholics with some 420,000 priests. The Office had invested him with the air of authoritative holiness. As a type Pope Paul would have brought joy to the heart of El Greco. On canvas we would have seen an intellectual aristocrat of the Church with long, slender fingers and dark, penetrating Italian eyes.

The conversation was short, but left a deep impression. It revealed how thin is the wall that divides the churchman and the statesman. By his actions he showed in the future that the age of religious neutrality had ended, that religion was not a clerical specialization. He broke out of the self-imposed Vatican confines which restricted the previous Popes travelling to the Holy Land and became the first Pope since St Peter to do so. The fresh pattern for papal travels symbolized the changed attitude of the Vatican to the contemporary world and found further expression in the first visit of the head of the Roman Catholic Church to the United States of America. His address to the United Nations linked spiritual authority with the temporal authority.

There were those who differed from Pope Paul, but none could call in question his fearlessness. To credit any man with all the gifts and qualifications needed for the Throne of St Peter is not possible, but he never allowed himself to be inhibited by fear of making a mistake. He was a man to the times, who interpreted the Church to itself and the Church to the world. He kept a careful balance between reforming zealots and reactionary traditionalists. He saw the special task of his Pontificate was to establish the Papacy as a visible spiritual authority able to guide mankind through the perplexities of the closing decades of the century. Physically he was not strong. One diplomat accredited to the Holy See commented that he 'seemed intent on martyrdom'. And so it proved.

Bertrand Russell OM

At the time of his citation for the Nobel Prize for Literature, Bertrand Russell was described as 'one of the time's most brilliant spokesmen of rationality and humanity and a fearless champion of free speech and free thought in the West'. In another field he made greater original contributions to philosophy than any other writer in this country since Hume. And yet, his long life was marked by contradictions. It was remarkable that the man who sat in Brixton Prison at the end of the First World War should have received at the end of the Second World War the blue and crimson ribbon of the Order of Merit, the greatest honour that the monarch and government can bestow on a distinguished citizen.

It is easy to describe Russell as a great man but more difficult to explain why. He was one of the most brilliant mathematicians of the century. His *Principles of Mathematics* and *Principia Mathematica*, both published before the First World War, determined the direction in which modern philosophy was going to move, yet few people have read the *Principia* and of that number only a handful have understood it, for assessment of the contents needed the competence of Whitehead or Wittgenstein to pass a judgement. It was brilliance in a rarefield atmosphere, yet Russell's name was known and respected by a cross-section of ordinary people in Europe and America. He exercised a magnetic fascination for the most unlikely people and often did the most unlikely things. Not many men of eighty-eight are imprisoned for identifying themselves with a campaign of civil disobedience against a government's defence policy. At that age most people are unmoved about threats to the future of humanity.

Somehow incarnation and death never greatly bothered the third Earl Russell. He was the product of one of the strongest hereditary strains and most dominating traditions that have existed in Europe. He was an unmitigated Russell, an aristocrat and a Whig: his grandfather was Lord John Russell of the Reform Bill. He had a superb intellect and a passion for freedom, yet somehow he never wholly understood politics. None of his political writings could compare with those of his godfather, John Stuart Mill. His parents died when he was a child and he was brought up by his grandmother who had him educated privately at home and earmarked for politics. The prospect did not appeal to this shy and lonely boy who preferred mathematical and philosophical speculation. He used to say that he was ten years old before he met anyone who hadn't written a book. The habit was catching for over fifty learned books stand to his credit. He blossomed at Cambridge where he got a First in Mathematics, was elected a Fellow of Trinity College and became a leader of that brilliant circle of intellectual young men so disliked by D. H. Lawrence but approved by Maynard Keynes and described as pre-Freud as well as pre-Hitler.

That Russell sparkled in challenging company was emphasized at a small dinner-party when guests included Sir John Clapham, gentle of voice and of a strangely veiled shyness; Harold Laski, whose rasplike vitality reflected the incompatibility between his personality and character; the reserved Field-Marshal Lord Ironside, imbued with democratic convictions and an autocratic temperament; and the sensitive-minded Bishop Stephen Neill, who was denied the seat of Canterbury because of ill-health. Russell was in a serious mood. His critical penetration flashed intermittently, but touched the vital spots in any argument. Occasionally he wielded a different humour. He laid about him with the blade of good humour. He played Porthos to Laski's Aramis, who told him he was an intellectual gadfly on the rump of an affluent society, continually asking awkward questions, often giving the wrong answers, and continually changing his mind. Russell's retort was that any honest man had to adjust theories to events as in 1920 when a visit to Russia caused him to modify his views on socialism, having seen the corruption inherent in the communist system. He was always convinced as to the rightness of his theories and as such had to act on what he believed to be true. There was always a strong case for each position at the time.

Ironside raised a question he had long wanted to ask. What prompted Russell in 1914 to be a pacifist and supporter of conscientious objectors? In reply Russell said that he had resisted the war on intellectual grounds. He wanted to try the method of non-resistance to aggression in the belief that it would disorganize the Germans. Ironside commented that such a foolish theory showed that Russell was no realist and less of a psychologist than logician. Clapham said that Russell at times sustained opinions ludicrously incompatible, believing in the utmost freedom for every human being, at the same time demanding that the will of the individual should be subordinated to the good of the community. The sparring between Neill and Russell ended in stalemate. Russell was a firm atheist who believed there is no God and no life after death. He was interested in impersonal objective truth which was just as elusive as religious faith and felt it was better for Churchmen to preach the virtues of tolerance and denounce the vices of cruelty and bigotry rather than advocate the unprovable.

Ironside asked Russell to refresh his memory on the reason for his jail sentence. He replied that it was for writing an article in *The Tribunal* in which he was critical of the United States army and was able to read the actual wording from a well-thumbed note in his wallet. It read, 'The American garrison which will by that time be occupying England and France, whether or not they will prove efficient against the Germans, will no doubt be capable of intimidating strikers, an occupation to which the American Army is accustomed at home.' Laski commented that if such views were still accountable in law, the prisons would house many distinguished names. Russell said that imprisonment had its compensations. Whilst in jail he wrote his *Introduction to Mathematical Philosophy* as a semi-popular version of *Principia Mathematica*.

There was another side to Bertrand Russell, far more lighthearted. Physically he was small; Lytton Strachey used to say that he belonged to the dangerous class of great gnomes; but he was never overlooked. Women found him attractive. With four wives to his credit, it was clearly mutual. At any party he was always surrounded by the prettiest women fascinated by the charm of this white-haired man with birdlike head and laugh like the yaffle of a woodpecker. His talk was usually dry but passionate, voice slightly donnish and clipped, sparkling wit and gleams of malice as might be expected from an advocate of free love, the rights of women, trial marriages and new methods of education that included a personal experiment aiming to prove the value of the utmost freedom for every human being. With his wife they had a school for children who could do whatever they pleased. In an intellectual free-for-all conversation there were invariably flashes of Russell's dislike of parents, policemen, schoolmasters, judges and the English public school system, prefaced by a dry pleasant smile.

An interesting aspect about Bertrand Russell was that the

thought of death never seemed to bother him. Such was his mental and physical energy that age was ignored. Maybe this atheistic conviction made it seem irrelevant. There was no last-minute conversion. Even at ninety-six his views had not changed, if anything they had become hardened. He regarded all forms of religion as false and harmful. He did admit that the thought of dying loomed large when a plane in which he was travelling to Norway crashed and ditched him in an icy sea, but the indignation was caused at the thought of his demise at the early age of seventy-six. Towards the end he almost welcomed death as the final confirmation of his theories and the possibility of proving the bishops wrong, though a wistful aside hinted it would be comforting to make contact in a future state when possibly memories might survive. It was wishful thinking. Bertrand Russell's ivory tower was like a Norman keep or one of the towers at San Gimignano, built to keep enemies out, and perhaps with inadequate recognition of its power to keep the owner in, even against his will. He was content, like the young Newton, to wander through strange seas of thought, alone.

As regards his own self-evaluation, this was reflected in his own obituary which he wrote predicting it would appear in *The Times* of 1 June 1962. It is worth recording once more:

By the death of the Third Earl Russell (or Bertrand Russell, as he preferred to call himself) at the age of ninety, a link with a very distant past is severed.

Russell's grandfather, Lord John Russell, the Victorian Prime Minister, visited Napoleon in Elba; his maternal grandmother was a friend of the Young Pretender's widow. In his youth he did work of importance in mathematical logic, but his eccentric attitude during the First World War revealed a lack of balanced judgement which increasingly infected his later writings. Perhaps this is attributable, at least in part, to the fact that he did not enjoy the advantages of a public school education, but was taught at home by tutors until the age of eighteen, when he entered Trinity College, Cambridge, becoming 7th Wrangler in 1893 and a Fellow in 1895. During the fifteen years that followed, he produced the books upon which his reputation in the learned world was based: *The Foundations of Geometry*, *The Philosophy of Leibniz*, *The Principles of Mathematics* and (in collaboration with Dr A. N. Whitehead) *Principia Mathematica*. This last work, which was of great importance in its day, doubtless owed much of its superiority to Dr (afterwards Professor) Whitehead, a man who, as his subsequent writings showed, was possessed of that insight and spiritual depth so notably absent in Russell; for Russell's argumentation, ingenious and clever as it is, ignores those higher considerations that transcend mere logic.

This lack of spiritual depth became painfully evident during the First World War, when Russell, although (to do him justice) he never minimized the wrong done to Belgium, perversely maintained that, war being an evil, the aim of statesmanship should have been to bring the war to an end as soon as possible, which would have been achieved by British neutrality and a German victory. It must be supposed that mathematical studies had caused him to take a wrongly quantitative view which ignored the question of principle involved. Throughout the war, he continued to urge that it should be ended, on no matter what terms. Trinity College, very properly, deprived him of his lectureship, and for some months in 1918 he was in prison.

In 1920 he paid a brief visit to Russia, whose government did not impress him favourably, and a longer visit to China, where he enjoyed the rationalism of the traditional civilization, with its still surviving flavour of the eighteenth century. In subsequent years his energies were dissipated in writings advocating socialism, educational reform, and a less rigid code of morals as regards marriage. At times, however, he returned to less topical subjects. His historical writings, by their style and their wit, conceal from careless readers the superficiality of the antiquated rationalism which he professed to the end.

In the Second World War he took no public part, having escaped to a neutral country just before its outbreak. In private conversation he was wont to say that homicidal lunatics were well employed in killing each other, but that sensible men would keep out of their way while they were doing it. Fortunately this outlook, which is reminiscent of Bentham, has become rare in this age, which recognizes that heroism has a value independent of its utility. True, much of what was once called the civilized world lies in ruins; but no right-thinking person can admit that those who died for the right in the great struggle have died in vain.

His life, for all its waywardness, had a certain anachronistic consistency, reminiscent of that of the aristocratic rebels of the early nineteenth century. His principles were curious, but, such as they were, they governed his actions. In private life he showed none of the acerbity which marred his writings, but was a genial conversationalist and not devoid of human sympathy. He had many friends, but had survived almost all of them. Nevertheless, to those who remained he appeared, in extreme old age, full of enjoyment, no doubt owing, in large measure, to his invariable health, for politically, during his last years, he was as isolated as Milton after the Restoration. He was the last survivor of a dead epoch.

The Fenner's Tradition and Ted Dexter

The opening of the Cambridge cricket season at Fenner's is full of promise. Early days are exciting, form uncertain, new names, strange faces, freshmen unknown quantities, but everyone knowing that if talent is there it will be encouraged. Fenner's has always been a nursery for recruits to county and England status. Success there can be a passport to Test recognition, a short cut denied those who graduate by the usual route. Outstanding players moulded by this tradition include names like F. S. Jackson, Ranjitsinhji and his nephew Duleepsinhji, Gilbert Jessop, Hon. Ivo Bligh, Lord Hawke, 'Gubby' Allen, A. P. F. Chapman, Norman Yardley, and, more recently, Trevor Bailey, dour even as a student, John Warr, lover of cricket from top to toe, John Dewes and David Sheppard, who shared an opening partnership of 343 in 1950 against the West Indians, who retaliated with 730 for 3, the three days' play producing 1,324 runs for 7 wickets. No Fenner's roster would be complete without the likes of Mike Brearley, Robin Marler, Tony Lewis, Derek Pringle and Phil Edmonds, who played a significant role in regaining the Ashes in 1985.

Peter May is the perfect example of a cricketer whose early promise at Fenner's matured and is remembered by many elegant innings. He captained England for a record 41 Tests before early retirement at 31, but in that comparatively short space of time he scored 4,537 runs with 13 centuries. His peak was in 1951 when appearing both for Cambridge and Surrey, he scored 2,339 runs with an average of 68.79. Surrey could do with another such talented undergraduate for, while he was with that county, the Championship was won 7 years in succession and 8 times in 9 years. From 1953 until he went to Australia in 1959, Peter May never finished on the losing side in a Test series.

There is never shortage of talent at Fenner's. The panels in the pavilion bear the names of men who have represented the University, counties and England for over a hundred years. Apart from those already mentioned, I single out one of the most brilliant players, Ted Dexter. At Cambridge he was something of a temperamental engima. The trouble was that he had the potential to shine at so many things. As a cricketer he was a joy to watch, but his personal dilemma was summed up by Neville Cardus:

> Apparently Dexter is undecided at the age of 28 whether he is (a) a great batsman, (b) an unpredictable bowler, (c) a journalist, (d) a television star (in Australia), (e) a potential golfer, or (f) a future leader of the Tory Party . . . it is beyond me that Dexter, a young man with his talents as a great cricketer, should think for a moment of giving up any of his days or nights to Westminister and politics.

Years later Cardus might still have said that it was not clear how Dexter saw himself. It is sad that such rich promise was never fully developed, except in cricket. Dexter led England in 30 of his 62 Tests. At times his style of captaincy invited criticism, but nothing dimmed the reputation as a batsman. Ted Dexter was the most exciting discovery of the post-war era. Since retiring he has developed the habit of backing into the limelight like a peripatetic one-man cricket delegation. At times aspects of the current cricketing scene give him the bellyache. He is honest enough to feel it, to show it, and to express it. With such a temperament is it inevitable. When an obstinate man with ability to match becomes dogmatic, he is bound to collect critics on the way, but the point is made.

As a young man Dexter could be somewhat naïve. I remember a conversation in a London hotel when he asked if I could suggest a commercial outlet for his skills. When I asked if he had anything specific in mind, he replied that all he wanted was a job that would give him time to play cricket in summer and probably tour in winter. When I said that a would-be employer might not be overjoyed by the prospect, the reply was that the fellow would have the benefit of his name. Such is the optimism of youth.

On another occasion at a dinner-party, I sat him next to Barbara Thorpe. True to form Ted rattled on to a seemingly impressed female. During a lull in the performance, she enquired what was his subject. On being told he was at Jesus College reading modern languages and specializing in Italian, Barbara, as Professor of Italian, remarked that she had never seen him at any of her lectures, but no doubt could expect him in the future. The subject was quickly shelved.

From time to time Dexter enlivens the television scene with

authoritative appearances during Test commentaries. He is always good value and is a reminder of how he might have fared had he pursued the ambition to become a Member of Parliament. There is still time. After all, if Jeffrey Archer can make the grade, it ought to be a walk-over, for Ted has charisma as well as ability.

Dame Laura Knight

It has been said that a work of art, in addition to looking well, must also speak well and act well. That is an elementary way of expressing in a phrase the triple nature of an activity which we frequently regard as having only a single nature. Aesthetes may say that it is only necessary for art to look well, but their neglect of the other facets means that they are only seeking a third of the truth about art. Art is a language, a medium of communication of which there are many forms of expression. An artist like Henry Moore, who was preoccupied with shape as shape, thought always of the solid three-dimensional entity of things and gave to his paintings a plasticity which hitherto seemed impossible. Then there is the pseudo-Gothic strangeness of John Piper's work with his owl-hooted, bat-haunted landscapes. And there was Graham Sutherland, a figure of controversy and lover of a world of wiry lines and flat patterns. The strong imaginative impetus of painters such as these is a guarantee in itself against stagnation, but they are not everybody's taste. One man's meat is another man's poison.

It is sometimes safer and more comfortable to concentrate on the test formulated by Tolstoy, that to invoke in oneself a feeling one has once experienced and having evoked it in oneself then, by means of movements, lines, colours, sounds or other forms expressed in words, so to transmit that feeling that others may express the same feeling – that is the activity of art. Few artists put this belief into visible shape with such thoughtful earnestness as Dame Laura Knight.

This little woman, animated by an electric vitality, achieved in her painting at its best what every artist longs to do – express their own personality with spontaneous freedom without losing the dignity and definiteness of a conscious work of art. In her studio in St John's Wood, Laura Knight was always free from the commonest fault of artists – exaggeration and false emphasis. She personified reticence and minute fidelity, but it was always the reticence of a singularly thoughtful nature. She often talked of the early days when Laura Johnson, as she then was, a promising student of the Nottingham School of Art, had her first picture, *Mother and Child*, accepted for exhibition at the Royal Academy of 1903. It was the beginning of a career that ranged through various aspects and types of landscapes, depicting the life of the local people, in Yorkshire, in Holland, and in Cornwall, and the influence of the Newlyn School. Her early life was a colourful amalgam of extremes. After the poverty of Nottingham came a patchy French schooling and a bohemianism that lasted well beyond her student years and finally the migration to London. It was always difficult to associate this little woman of the soft, enticing voice with the sweating plough-horses working over clayland or pugilists in the boxing-ring. They did not match her fragile emotions, yet she captured the primeval force of such scenes. The circus was another subject that excited her with an extraordinary fecundity of effort and expression. It opened for her a new world of inspiration although she was not circus born or brought up to the raucous sounds of the fair, another fertile field for her touch.

Her marriage to Harold Knight was an early romance that matured into a beautifully unpossessive partnership that was only broken after fifty-seven years. One night at dinner Harold remarked with a smile that 'we were married and lived happy ever after'. It was true. The secret was that they were dependent on their own resources and that, more than anything, ensured a sound foundation for their marriage. There was a traumatic period during the First World War when Laura had to face public and private opprobrium roused by Harold Knight's conscientious objection to putting on a uniform, when former friends who, without other recognition, drew away from an offered hand, but those days passed and were soon forgotten. Not so the Nuremberg Trial which she attended as an official artist. The experience left its mark. The horrors of the evidence and the Nazi war criminals themselves haunted her for many years.

Her most lasting impression that survived the test of time was her first backstage experience during a Diaghilev ballet season at the Coliseum. It made the pencil speak a language of its own. Lydia Lopokova let her use her dressing-room as a studio on the understanding that she kept quiet. The appeal never left her. I remarked that the pictorial opportunities offered by ballet stirred her artistic vivacity more than any other scene. The remark prompted her to take down a bundle of drawings from a shelf.

'Here,' she said, 'are some sketches of Pavlova which the public has never seen. I had forgotten all about them and only recently came across the pile when I was clearing out some old rubbish and junk.' I went through them, one by one. It was remarkable how such an economy of line could capture such rhythmic movement and grace. Laura recalled memories of those far-off backstage ballet days in word-pictures.

Her admiration for Pavlova was profound. She maintained that her exceptionally long, full throat, small body, and tapering limbs were perfect for her art. Facially Pavlova was not beautiful if features were the sole test, but her eyes, fascinating and heavily lidded, contributed to a general impression of haunting beauty that would not be denied. Laura said that only a handful of people ever realized the exacting strain and physical effort imposed on Pavlova before she attained the peak of perfection. Few in the audience could visualize their ballerina clutching a curtain in the wings, struggling for breath, completely exhausted, with sweat streaming down her back. Laura managed once to paint such a scene. She worked on it over a period of years, but in the *Manuka* disaster off New Zealand, it was lost with the paintings of several other artists and unfortunately she had not even kept a photograph of it.

In the folio I came across a rare sketch of Enrico Cecchetti, the maestro whose personality and genius became legendary. Laura was conscious of her debt to Cecchetti. He had a marked effect on her work. His emphasis on the perfection of balance and line opened up for her the composition possibilities of the human body in movement. Sketching in his classes called for meticulous precision in detail. The position of the dancers had to be accurate, otherwise there was trouble when Cecchetti examined the sketches. He was tireless at work. Those in his classes were completely exhausted at the end of each session.

Laura's sketch was faithful in every respect. He sat in his chair before the stage whistling the tunes for the exercises, and beating time with a slender malacca cane. Another idiosyncrasy was his habit of wearing an English sports cap. It was all there in the drawing. His figure looked poised for action. Maybe he had just sprinkled the floor with a red watering-can in case the resin affected the dancer's throats. He was never above sprinkling someone's tights with a few drops, while the cane had a habit of cutting across the shins of any girl who failed to reach his standard of balance and line. Such was the inspiration that lay behind the familiar ballet studies that we associate with the name of Dame Laura Knight. The atmosphere of days long past steeped itself in her mind. I am sure from the way she talked that whenever she saw the immense folds of rich crimson curtains parted by a vague, indistinct figure as the artist acknowledged the theatre's applause, she saw in imagination the outline of Pavlova taking her call in a manner that only she could do.

Whenever I see the lights lowered in Covent Garden and the overture begins, I think of that folio of sketches in a studio in St John's Wood, where the memory of Pavlova's dancing lingered lighter and less substantial than a handful of swansdown. The reaction is understandable, for Laura's work was like language to the eye. She set out to say something to us. And she succeeded in saying something which cannot be expressed in words. With her acute senses, she felt what I call the spirit of a scene, or the personality of a human being, and these immaterial qualities she incorporated in the form and colour of her work.

Good art is something at once very simple and very profound. In the hands of Dame Laura Knight it was a language which could be understood in all places and at all times. This message came out in public and private. It was her life.

Sir Martin Ryle

Sir Martin Ryle's achievements in science and pioneer work in radio-astronomy were rewarded by the Establishment with all the honours in its gift. The list makes impressive reading. Fellow of the Royal Society, 1952; first chair of Radio-astronomy at Cambridge, 1959; Gold Medal of the Royal Astronomical Society, 1964; knighted, 1966. Then, when Sir Richard Woolley retired in 1972, Martin was made Astronomer Royal, the first time in the 300-year existence of this office that the honour had gone to someone not previously the director of the Royal Greenwich Observatory. Then in 1974 Martin was awarded the Nobel Prize for Physics, jointly with Anthony Hewish.

At that point such acceptance seemed to turn sour. Disillusionment set in. Martin began to rethink his priorities. Fellow scientists urged him not to waste his skills, to stop acting like an eccentric. They misjudged their man. Martin never did anything without careful thought and reasoning, particularly when so much was at stake. He felt deeply that his scientific researches had been misdirected. Failing health had made necessary an operation for lung cancer. In 1984 he died. His wife, Rowena, has given me permission to quote from a letter he wrote to Professor Chagas of the Vatican Academy of Sciences and some notes in his handwriting found in personal papers: 'I am left at the end of my life with the feeling that it would have been better to have become a farmer in 1946. One can of course argue that somebody else would have done it anyway and so we must face the most fundamental of questions, should fundamental science be stopped?'

Remarkable words from a man whose scientific researches had achieved so much. The reasons he put forward to explain his change of heart were quite specific. They were not just a personal cry of despair that morality and personal responsibility were being pushed aside. It was much deeper. But before outlining them it is helpful to recall his career, some of the scientific breakthroughs, and remember what sort of a man he was. He came from an academic background. His father was a physician to Guy's Hospital, then Regius Professor of Physic at Cambridge, later Professor of Social Medicine at Oxford. Martin went to Bradfield College, after Gladstone's preparatory school in Sloane Square, graduated at Oxford in 1939 with a first in Physics, then to the Cavendish Laboratory to work with J. A. Ratcliffe on radio-aerial design.

At the outbreak of war Martin went to the Air Ministry Research Establishment where he joined one of the world's finest teams of electronic scientists, concentrated on the radar systems in the RAF and became a specialist in radio countermeasures against German radar. The need for this was highlighted on 12 February 1942 when the German warships, *Scharnhorst* and *Gneisenau*, passed through the English Channel from Brest to Kiel undetected on the English coastal radar defence because of massive jamming by German transmitters on the French coast.

After the war he returned to the Cavendish Laboratory. It was about this time that I first came into contact with him through a mutual interest in design techniques. He was interested in our team of experts who designed, manufactured and built the BRM racing engines, one of the most complicated engineering exercises. Martin studied the drawing-office prints with considerable knowledge and occasionally went with us to Silverstone to watch the finished product roar into action. Sailing was another form of relaxing giving another opportunity for designing skill. It took the form of a 16-ft catamaran that he designed, built and exhibited at the International Boat Show. Sailing on the Solent in his 18-ft auxilary sloop gave him immense pleasure.

At the Cavendish Laboratory he began a scientific investigation that skirted physics and other sciences involving analysing radio waves emanating from astronomical objects outside the earth. His initial equipment was a receiving aerial covering a wide area much longer than the length of the waves. He used two large aerials several hundred yards apart, their combined outputs becoming a radio version of the Michelson interferometer. Simple and effective. Suggestions that he might install a huge parabolic reflector like the one at Jodrell Bank were rejected. Instead Martin developed a new method called aperture synthesis which used eight parabolic reflectors set along a five-kilometre stretch of old railway line that simulated exactly the performance of a reflector that would have been too large to be constructed. These results were recorded by signals from the reflectors in digital form fed into a digital computer. These computer-drawn images produced fine details of radio galaxies, work that earned a joint award with Hewish of the Nobel Prize for Physics.

The research of Martin and his team included many significant discoveries. The publication of the third Cambridge Catalogue of Radio Sources undoubtedly aided the development of radio-astronomy and the discovery of quasars. He put forward the theory that radio-astronomy could decide between the evolving universe and the continuous creation theories of cosmology. Martin favoured the former and became involved in heated controversy with Fred Hoyle and his supporters, the argument finally tipping in favour of the Ryle school. Then there was the occasion when the Ryle group tracked the first Soviet sputniks and Martin suggested that artificial satellites could be used as navigational aids.

When the awakening of a strong social conscience caused such a change of heart, it is pertinent to look for the reasons. His fears were voiced in his letter to Professor Chagas that some forty per cent of professional engineers and probably more physicists in the United Kingdom were engaged in devising new ways of killing people, and while there were plenty of posts available in these areas it was practically impossible for a young graduate or PhD to find a socially.useful job. The misuse of science for military purposes inevitably meant that physics graduates would be absorbed into the defence establishment. He raised doubts about the energy programme based on fast-breeder nuclear reactors, basing such fears on the danger of accidents and the refusal seriously to consider alternative energy sources like wind and wave-power. He used to say that Orwell's vision of 1984 might not be so wide of the mark, particularly in the light of government predilection for surveillance and phone-tapping, an obsession that cable television would assist with a cable in every home.

Martin had seen enough at first hand to draw us back from the edge of the nuclear holocaust. He believed time to be very short and that either through error or a first-strike decision a nuclear holocaust was likely within years rather than decades. A sentence scribbled in his handwriting among his papers says it all: 'Our world is one – yet evolution has now reached the stage where as a species we may soon die . . . we as scientists should be able to see this more clearly than most and must use our influence to change the too limited aspirations of governments.'

212

No one would disagree, but the question is how. This good man and prophet in his own time summed up the sickness: our cleverness has grown prodigiously, but not our wisdom.

Elizabeth Arden

The image of woman can change almost by whim. The fashion of
the moment moulds appearance, clothes, even deportment, in
fact, everything can be made to conform to a current idea of
beauty. Dr D. L. Dickenson went one better. He attempted with
American thoroughness to create the typical American girl by
checking the measurements of 15,000 American women over a
six-year period. The statistics were handed to a sculptor to
produce a composite statue of the contemporary American female.
The result compared with the Aphrodite of Cyrene showed that
the Greek woman had a more masculine body, fuller hips and
waist, with larger and more pointed breasts. A similar experiment
in Britain would probably have similar results, for while a
characteristic American face is in the process of evolution, there is
little to distinguish between beauty-conscious women, either in
public or private, on both sides of the Atlantic. Beauty is
disputable, but not arguable. Neither is it new.

It is fascinating to skim the centuries and see what men have
appreciated most in feminine beauty. In the 1930s the limestone
bust of Nefertiti, the serene-faced Egyptian queen with an ice-cold
mysterious gaze, suddenly became accepted as the norm of beauty.
Young women began to shape eyebrows, tilt their heads, accen-
tuate cheek-bones and model profiles on the beautiful royal lady
who walked the streets of Tell-el-Armarna some 3,000 years ago.
The urge was understandable for there is no doubt about the
beauty of Nefertiti. The modelling of this bust in the Berlin
Museum was the work of a talented sculptor. Nothing short of
genius could have moulded the line from the lower eyelid, skirting
the cheek, to the arc of the mouth with the sealed, full lips. The
flesh could still be warm, soft and pulsating. Any woman today
would envy those languorous eyes, the shapely nose, fastidious lips
and face of exquisite sensibility.

Somehow women have never been content with their personal
appearance. It matters not which century is named, there will

always be females who attempt to improve on nature. Could Nefertiti return today she would find little unfamiliar on her dressing-table. Her stibium pencil was very similar to the present eyebrow pencil, but she would have a smaller range of coloured creams. From contemporary pictures it is reasonable to assume that the complexions were of a pale yellow and that Egyptians were not a dark race. Women who were not obliged to work or subjected to exposure were all portrayed as yellow, the tint getting paler as they rose in the social scale. Eyes were dark, expressive and lovely. Eyelids were painted with a black substance known as kohl, which not only added expression and depth to the eyes, but served as a protective film against the heat, ophthalmia being very common in Egypt. Green paint was used on the underlid. Fingernails were long and painted, often stained with henna. Lips full and painted, nose and chin small and neat, eyebrows plucked, hair usually black, but ears were on the large side.

A composite female of medieval times would be blonde in colouring with hair bound by a gold circlet. She would have white, almost transparent skin, an oval face with broad high forehead, blue eyes, small mouth, full lips, elegant and shapely body, rounded arms, shoulders in proportion, small firm breasts and long limbs. By contrast, the women of the Renaissance, as seen in paintings and sculpture, looked cold, calm and sensuous without a spark of individuality. Any century that could produce the first Elizabethan era would have been outstanding, and the women matched the grandeur of the hour, though some continental fashions seem strange to our eyes. Pierre de l'Etoile refers to nuns strolling along with hair powdered and curled. The lily-bosomed women of Lely's voluptuous portraits are indicative of the type of beauty for which the Restoration Court was famed. The eighteenth-century in England was a period of high living among women of the more leisured classes, though it was said that the difference between English and French women of this period was that between a Chelsea bun and a chocolate eclair.

It was Dante Gabriel Rossetti who divined a distinctive type of nineteenth-century beauty. The brooding, mystical beauty of Elizabeth Siddal as she posed for *Beata Beatrix* became the painter-poet's ideal and a national vision of perfection. The opening years of the twentieth century saw fashion attempt to make women with a new shape. A torso-length corset with a rigidly straight front compressed the figure into a shape like the letter S. Added effect was given by high-boned collars and somewhat padded hair styles surmounted by huge hats. Edwardian beauties invented new fashions with leisured assurance.

Since then females have slavishly followed the dictates of fashion – a word so often synonymous with ugliness that it has to be altered every six months. Long ago we ceased to marvel at bizarre creations worn because Paris or Italy decreed the styles, a habit that will persist as long as there is a preponderance of women who are peacocks in everything but beauty. It is tempting to be cynical. Women as a sex have become sphinxes without secrets. Nothing is hidden and precious little is sacred. Public and private masks, like the shop windows, dispel all illusions. That healthy colour which freshens cheeks is seen in a range of dainty boxes. Milk-like complexions are assured by a bewildering range of jars decorated with delicate care. The purlieus of hairdressing salons display the art and guile of the *coiffeur*. Women change their contours to order. Brevity has become the soul of lingerie. Varnish-bottles for fingernails stand in rows. Everything is there for man to inspect. Virtually every aspect of a woman's life or habits is ventilated for the benefit of the public.

Even so, females laugh and get away with it, while we drab creatures stand on the sidelines with appreciative eye, knowing full well that women's styles and masks may change but their designs remain the same. The path of feminine elegance is indeed complex. As soon as a change has been made, women pour scorn and ridicule on the fashion of yesterday. The present is always more attractive, a delusion, yet so feminine.

There is another angle of approach. Without seeking to belittle the influence of designers, I can show that fashions and masks change, not according to whim but by psychological pressure of the public. Feminine clothes mirror the prevailing mood of the moment. The fairer sex last century took shelter behind crinolines, chaperones, convention, and swooning. Ostensibly on the retreat, these young women encouraged, if not aroused men by a fleeting glimpse of an ankle interspersed with vapours. Men assumed the natural role of pursuers. During the interim period between the two world wars, women of marriageable age found themselves in the majority. Roles became reversed. Emancipated, independent and unmarried, women became the hunters. Ankles were of slight appeal. The range of enticement was extended to an almost comprehensive degree, which, because of the very completeness, failed to achieve its object. Equality of opportunity made women more masculine. The short-haired, flat-chested, chain-smoking, cocktail-drinking girl tried everything in her power to beguile men, who became effeminate by reaction, a tendency halted by the war, when once again men were conceded masculine virility as women fell back upon the allure of longer skirts and femininity in taste. Since then we have passed through varying extremes. The ability to shock has become outmoded because every permutation in bad taste and sexual vulgarity has been tried, even to the extent of a well-known female designer announcing that she had shaved her pubic hair into a heart-shape, presumably with Valentine's Day in mind.

One thing is certain. Women depend upon women for their dress appeal. Fashionably dressed women are not interested in the appraisal of men. With microscopic carefulness their eyes are for ever upon other women. The procedure never varies. Feline evaluations for those whose appearance and dress fall below a self-appointed standard and undisguised satisfaction when approval is won from women of like taste and outlook. In theory women dress for men. In reality, women dress for women, and undress for men.

The difference between male and female shoppers is significant. Women are extrovert, men furtive. Our shops are not blatant. We change in some dark recess. The articles we require are stocked away in unobtrusive fashion. Females are the reverse. They become shameless in vanity. Enter one of their shops and an obsequious acolyte steps forward. Everything becomes a work of art: the dainty manicurist transforms a delicate shell-like nail into a shining shield of colour; in the salon elegant young women conjure up fresh complexions. People who have never met before discuss trivialities with earnest insincerity. In such an atmosphere women indulge in a Turkish bath of immodest sympathy. Everything is not known, but everything is said. In such an atmosphere man is made to feel like a stranger on a butterfly farm, more conscious than ever that woman will be the last thing civilized by man.

Such thoughts were much in mind when I met Elizabeth Arden over dinner in the Savoy Hotel in London. I half expected a Maupassant gamine, the personification of what the medievalists portrayed in stained glass and wood-carving as luxury. Instead I was greeted by someone petite, hardly 5ft 4ins, trim, attractive and not young. I was surprised to learn she opened her first salon as long ago as 1910. Her skin was gently wrinkled with laughter lines.

Success stories can be tedious, but the Arden saga is fascinating.

Elizabeth Arden was really Florence Nightingale Graham, daughter of a Scottish–Cornish marriage. Her parents emigrated to Canada and she was born in Toronto. With such a name, nursing was an obvious career, but she tired of both. She confessed that the name Florence was never popular. An opportunity came after reading *Elizabeth and her German Garden*. She was also fond of Tennyson's *Enoch Arden*. Doodling after lunch, she wrote Elizabeth Arden on an envelope, liked it, and so the name was born.

Her enthusiasm for horses was unmistakable. In 1947 she won the Kentucky Derby with Jet Pilot so it was hardly surprising that she called her perfume 'Blue Grass', because the light, fresh scent reminded her of the smell of early morning meadows in the Blue Grass country renowned for its training establishments. Hence the prancing horse trade-mark. The following day there was an interesting postscript. A package of male Arden toiletries arrived for me at the Dorchester Hotel, followed by a visit of an Arden executive from the Bond Street shop. Charmingly she enquired whether I had received prints of photographs taken during dinner the night before. When told that nothing had been sent, she asked if I would let her have any prints that were taken of Elizabeth Arden. As a personal reminder of the evening she had brought a studio portrait of the lady in question. I asked why the interest in these particular prints and was told it would be contrary to Company policy if photographs of their founder were in circulation if they showed signs of age and inevitable facial wrinkles. The photograph I was given had been taken some years earlier and had no lines, wrinkles or blemishes. The face was as smooth as a billiard ball. I declined the offer. When the Savoy photographs duly arrived, Elizabeth Arden looked far more attractive than the touched-up likeness. Her private mask was far superior to the public-relations version. The image of mature beauty is not determined by a pot of cream.

The Mask of Death

The Formula One Grand Prix world is a very small one. If a driver dies, it means the loss of a friend. When Wolfgang von Trips was killed at Monza during the Italian Grand Prix, the instinctive reflex was to quit a sport that could bring such senseless loss of life, yet such is the gentleness of time that the scars heal. Even so, certain moments haunt me. I think of that tragedy at Zandvoort during the Dutch Grand Prix when Roger Williamson became engulfed in flames from ruptured fuel lines after crashing into the Armco barrier. David Purley stopped, ignored the danger and tried to rescue the trapped driver. His courageous action, later recognized by the award of the George Medal, was in vain. A brilliant young driver had perished. The race continued, but for many all significance had been lost. Williamson's entrant and patron, Tom Wheatcroft, was distraught with grief. He asked if I would go with him to the mortuary for the identification as he was too upset to face the ordeal alone.

The road out of the circuit was jammed with spectators making their way home. Sand-dunes that minutes before had been natural grandstands for human ant-heaps had reverted to gentle un-dulations with flickering waves of marram grass. Soon the crowds were left behind and we drove along quiet side-lanes on a lovely summer evening that neither of us saw.

The mortuary was a simple building with a church-like atmosphere, except that instead of an altar, there was a coffin. The attendant gave me a key to unscrew one end and the lid was raised. If ever there was condemnation of motor-racing, it was there. Roger Williamson, in stained flame-resistant suit, had both hands raised before his face as if to fend off the approach of death. The instinctive urge was to take those outstretched hands and help him out. Formalities completed, the lid was screwed back. Roger Williamson was now only a name on the roll of racing victims.

Back at the Bouwes Hotel everyone was excited over a championship victory, but that night and ever since I can see again the horror on the face of the young man who lay alone as others celebrated.

Looking back over a quarter of a century of Grand Prix racing, I do not think so much of races won or lost, nor the skill and courage displayed. What I hold in mind and affection are those men, many close friends, who lived their lives wholly in the sport and died through it. In imagination they have become immortal characters in a sports epic. It will stay like that through the years ahead. They are no longer with us, but for those who knew them, our recollections of them are filled with sadness. But there is one consolation: memories never age.